MOSLEM ARCHITECTURE

MOSLEM ARCHITECTURE
ITS ORIGINS AND DEVELOPMENT

By

G.T. RIVOIRA

TRANSLATED FROM THE ITALIAN

BY

G. McN. RUSHFORTH

GYAN

Published by

GYAN

Gyan Publishing House
5, Ansari Road
Daryaganj, New Delhi-110002
Phone: 011-47034999, 9811692060
E-mail: books@gyanbooks.com

Distribution Network
gyanbooks.com
India, USA, Canada, UK, Australia, France

ISBN : 978-81-212-6218-7 (PB)
First Published, 1918

2nd Impression 2022

Printed at: Gyan Press, Delhi.

MOSLEM ARCHITECTURE
Author: G.T. Rivoira

MOSLEM ARCHITECTURE

ITS ORIGINS AND DEVELOPMENT

BY

G. T. RIVOIRA

TRANSLATED FROM THE ITALIAN

BY

G. McN. RUSHFORTH

1918

PREFACE

THIS book does not pretend to be a History of Moslem Architecture—the style which is sometimes described as Arabic, but wrongly, for the Arabs, like the Goths, the Langobardi, the Normans, and the other Barbarian Invaders, brought no architecture of their own with them into the countries which they conquered. What they carried was the scimitar and the Koran; and their energies were devoted to imposing the faith of the Prophet, and at the same time satisfying their insatiable lust for plunder and rapine.

Too many elements, whether of history, architecture, or art, are still wanting for the execution of such a colossal undertaking, and for carrying it out in the manner which I have in view: I mean the writing of a History based essentially on historical facts, on monuments of ascertained date, examined by the author in person, if not in every, at least in most cases, supposing that they are still in existence, and also founded on logical inferences.

My work, on the contrary, is devoted solely to an inquiry into the origins and the development of the elements which were destined to form one branch of that style. But it is the main branch, because religious architecture has always been the principal representative of the great building art: save only in the days of the Roman Empire, when architectural science found its highest expression in the Baths and Tombs.

The book is divided into two parts. In the first I describe, by the help of buildings selected from the most remarkable of their class, and erected in the most important centres, some of the chief stages in the development of the Mosque, from its birth down to the XII century. An appendix to this is formed by a short but searching examination of some of the most important ecclesiastical buildings of Armenia, which are so little known and yet so full of interest. The object of this investigation is to ascertain whether these buildings had any influence on the old Moslem or Christian architecture, and if so, what was its nature.

In the second part I discuss at length the new and attractive theory according to which the origin and development of the systematic use of the horse-shoe arch belongs to the Iberian peninsula. The scale of treatment is made necessary by the importance of some of the works which have been written in support of the theory. This section will, perhaps, arouse most controversy; but it is often from the contact of opposing views that a spark of light is struck.

This new book of mine is a sort of continuation, and at the same time the completion of my previous work: *Le Origini dell' Architettura Lombarda* (*Lombardic Architecture*). It is written, like its predecessor, from the standpoints of the archaeologist, the architect, and the historian—indispensable conditions for anyone who would undertake an investigation of this nature. It is my belief that the two works together will, sooner or later, be accepted as a safe guide for every competent and independent writer about the main types of religious architecture and the vaulting systems of the West, the Near East, and Northern Africa, in the period between the I and the XII centuries of the Christian Era.

TRANSLATOR'S PREFACE

In making this translation of Commendatore Rivoira's *Architettura Musulmana, sue origini e suo sviluppo* (Hoepli: Milan, March 1914) my chief object has been to produce a faithful version of the original, and I have endeavoured, so far as the idiom of the language allows, to preserve all the author's characteristic phrases and turns of expression. This fidelity, I may add, is guaranteed by the fact that Signor Rivoira's mastery of English has enabled him to control every word that I have written.

As in the author's *Lombardic Architecture*, we have employed a few architectural terms of Italian origin, not previously used in English, the principal ones being 'lesena' for pilaster-strip, 'pulvin' for impost-block, and 'raccord' for rudimentary pendentives and those of stalactitic and stalagmitic form. To these Signor Rivoira now adds names for two Oriental forms of the arch. The so-called 'ogee' he would describe as the 'cyma reversa arch' ('arco a due gole contrapposte'); and the form in which the curves at the base are continued by tangents or straight lines meeting in an angle at the top, as the 'mixtilinear arch' ('arco mistilineo').

For Oriental names I have generally followed the forms used in modern standard works, such as the *Encyclopaedia Britannica*, Prof. Bury's edition of Gibbon, and the Cambridge *Medieval History*. I have to thank Prof. J. B. Bury of Cambridge, and Prof. G. A. Cooke, and Mr. F. C. Conybeare of Oxford, for advice and assistance in these matters.

As the years of the Mohammedan era or Hijra (the Hegira of popular English), starting from July 16, 622, do not correspond to the years A.D., the author has indicated them by the number of the year A.D., followed by the last two or last three numerals of the next year. Thus 956-57 means the Mohammedan year running from July 956 to July 957; 1123-24 that from July 1123 to July 1124.

I have retained the measurements in metres given by the author, as they were made by himself on the spot; but I have added within brackets the approximate equivalents in English feet and inches.

In order to avoid repetition of the titles, references to Signor Rivoira's previous work in its three forms are given by the names of the publishers; and it will be sufficient to remind the reader once for all that these forms are:—

Le Origini dell' Architettura Lombarda. Loescher: Rome, vol. i, 1901; vol. ii, 1907.

Le Origini dell' Architettura Lombarda. Hoepli: Milan, 1 vol., 1908.

Lombardic Architecture. Heinemann: London, 2 vols., 1910.

G. McN. RUSHFORTH.

April 1918.

CONTENTS

PART I

PART II

LIST OF ILLUSTRATIONS

Moslem Architecture

PART I

It is an old and still accepted idea that the mosque of Mohammed (570-1-632) at Medina represents, in an elementary form, the prototype of the congregational mosques[1] of the first centuries of Islam.

According to Caetani,[2] the building erected by the Prophet was intended at the outset, in his own mind, for his personal and private use; but it assumed as time went on—owing to unforeseen circumstances, and by an unconscious process—first of all a public character, and later, after the Master's departure, a sacred character as well, becoming above everything else a real and genuine place of worship.

Lammens,[3] on the other hand, thinks that the mosque or 'masgid' came from the tribal 'maglis,' that is to say, the council-tent, the central point of social life for the individualist Arabs, with its sacred precinct, its far higher degree of inviolability than the ordinary tent, and the greater honour paid to it. This conception would, then, be applied to the Prophet's first abode at Medina, which would thus have become the earliest mosque of Islam and the meeting-place for the Companions. The idea would also be connected with the mosque founded by Sad ibn abi Waqqas at Kufa, which was designed for a place of meeting, and provided with shelter from extremes of weather.

[1] Lane, *Arabic-English Lexicon*, explains 'gâmi, the congregational mosque,' as 'the mosque in which the congregational prayers of Friday are performed.'

[2] *Annali dell' Islām*, vol. i, pp. 432-447.

[3] *Rivista degli Studi orientali*, vol. iv, pp. 240-250, Ziād ibn Abīhi.

However this may be, the fact remains that the plan of the principal mosques of the first centuries of the Moslem era, consisting of a central quadrangular court surrounded by colonnades, that on the south being deeper than the others and set apart as the place of prayer, has a real connection with the plan of the mosque at Medina. And this is what we shall see presently in dealing with some of them, either no longer in existence, but only described in books, or still standing either wholly or in part.

THE MOSQUE OF MOHAMMED AT MEDINA.—The following is its history, taken chiefly from Caetani.[1] When the Prophet entered Medina in the year 622 he determined to build his own house wherever the camel on which he was riding should stop of its own accord. This happened on a piece of private ground, which he forthwith purchased, started the work of laying out and building, and had everything finished by 623.[2] The result was a court about 100 cubits square, enclosed by walls nearly 7 cubits high, the lower part being built of stone and the upper of sun-baked clay bricks. No part was roofed. Connected with the structure, which had three entrances, were the dwellings of the founder and his wives. Not far off was a well. In one angle of the court was set, for the present, a bench under a tiled roof as a refuge for the most indigent of those who shared the Master's exile.

The 'qibla,' the point to which every Moslem turns when he prays, was placed in the north wall of the court looking towards Jerusalem, beneath a small roof supported by trunks of palm trees. Mohammed soon (624) ordered it to be moved to the south side, looking towards Mecca, where the holy place called the Kaaba was to be found. It now occupied the site where the principal entrance had been at first, the latter being moved to the original site of the qibla. The qibla consisted of a large stone.[3] The 'mihrab,' or niche pointing to Mecca, belongs to a later date.

As time went on the Master's companions complained of being exposed to the full force of the sun's rays, and a shelter was erected in the court, formed of interwoven palm branches smeared outside with clay, and supported by trunks

[1] *Annali*, vol. i, pp. 374-379, 432-468; vol. iii, 2, pp. 964-967; vol. iv, p. 197.

[2] CAETANI, *Chronographia Islamica*, pp. 4, 11.

[3] BURTON, *Personal Narrative of a Pilgrimage to Mecca and Medina*, vol. ii, p. 72.

of palm trees. The roof was so low that the faithful when they stood upright could touch it.

In the early days the Prophet used to address the faithful from a palm trunk fixed in the ground. Afterwards he had a pulpit made of tamarisk wood, with three steps, on the topmost of which he took his seat.[1] Burton says that later, in the time of the art-loving Caliph Walid I (705-715),[2] this took the form of the 'minbar' of to-day;[3] but Lammens holds that the minbar of early times is distinct from the pulpit of a modern mosque.[4] A minbar was provided for the congregational mosque at Fustat by Amr in 644-45.[5]

From the summit of the roof, Bilal, an old and faithful follower of the Master, endowed with a stentorian voice, summoned the faithful to prayer. This practice of calling the faithful to prayer by means of the human voice from some high place, such as the roof of the sacred building, was intended by the Moslems to avoid the use of the hammer, the rattle, the bell with its Christian associations, and the trumpets of Judaism.[6] It had this merit, that behind the physical utterance lay the far more persuasive and moving appeal of the spirit. The summoning of the faithful by a public crier is supposed to have had its origin in a custom in use in eastern Arabia.[7]

Mohammed's mosque was rebuilt in 638 by the Caliph Omar (634-644), as it had become too small. A considerable part was pulled down, and a new and larger structure erected, consisting of a walled enclosure with a cobble pavement and six entrances. The walls were built of sun-baked bricks, and the roofs formed of interwoven palm branches, coated with mud on the outside, and supported, according to some authorities, by palm-wood pillars, though others say that they were of bricks like those used in the walls. A restoration took place in 640.[8] Another renovation was carried out (646-47) under Caliph

[1] CAETANI, *Annali*, vol. ii, 1, pp. 213, 214.

[2] The dates of the Moslem sovereigns are taken from the chronological tables in LANE-POOLE's *The Mohammadan Dynasties*.

[3] BURTON, op. cit., vol. ii, p. 72.

[4] Université Saint-Joseph, Beyrouth, *Mélanges de la Faculté orientale*, 1907, pp. 96-100; LAMMENS, *Études sur le règne du calife omaiyade Mo'awia Ier*.

[5] CAETANI, *Chronographia*, p. 283. For the method of indicating the years of the Mohammedan era, see Translator's Preface, p. vii.

[6] MARGOLIOUTH, *Mohammed and the Rise of Islam*, p. 222.

[7] CAETANI, *Annali*, vol. i, p. 457.

[8] Ibid., *Chronographia*, pp. 202, 220.

Othman (644-656), and in 664-65 a 'maqsura' or fenced-off part of the mosque was constructed.[1] The walls were built of hewn stone, and the roof was of timber brought from India.[2]

In the days of Islam's power and splendour, Walid I (705-715), after laying the foundations of the mosque of Damascus (706-714), made Medina the object of his liberality, and set about a reconstruction, for which purpose he borrowed builders and mosaic-workers from the Greek emperor, as we are told by Ibn Khaldun,[3] who must have confused the caliph with his father, Abd al-Malik (685-705). The works were directed by Omar, son of Abd al-Aziz, who is said to have been the first to invent and adopt the mihrab,[4] though a niche of this kind seems to have been introduced at Damascus in the time of the famous Muawiya (661-680). The new mosque, which was finished in 709-10, had its roof supported by columns, and possessed four minarets, one at each corner. Its dimensions were 200 by 167 cubits.

Mahdi (775-785) enlarged it on the north side, the length of which was increased from 200 to 300 cubits. Additions were made by Mamun (813-833), and after a fire came another reconstruction, begun in 1256, and completed in 1289. The renewed structure was enlarged and embellished in the next period by the sultans of Egypt, but in 1483 it was struck by lightning and set on fire. It was rebuilt by Mohammed ibn Qait Bey (1495-1498), and embellished by Suliman I, 'the Magnificent' (1520-1566). Taken all together, this must have been the mosque seen by Burton in 1853,[5] and by Snouck Hurgronje in 1884-85,[6] and represented in the accompanying drawing (Fig. 1, p. 9), reproduced by Schefer[7] from a manuscript of 1574.

The mosque, as enlarged by Mamun, has been described by Ibn Jubair, who saw it in 1184. It was oblong in plan, the long axis running from south to north. A similar orientation was followed in the mosques of Samarra and Abudolaf, and elsewhere. The four sides were enclosed by cloisters.

[1] CAETANI, *Chronographia*, pp. 295, 493.

[2] BURTON, op. cit., vol. ii, pp. 73, 74.

[3] IBN KHALDOUN (Le Strange), *Prolégomènes historiques*, vol. ii, p. 268.

[4] IBN BATUTA (Defrémery, Sanguinetti), *Voyages d' Ibn Batoutah*, vol. i, p. 272.

[5] Op. cit., vol. ii, pp. 75-78.

[6] SNOUCK HURGRONJE, *Mekka*.

[7] Publication de l'École des Langues orientales vivantes, IIe série, vol. i, SEFER NAMEH, *Relation du voyage de Nassiri Khosrau en Syrie, en Palestine, en Égypte, en Arabie et en Perse* (Schefer), pp. lvii, lviii, 162, 163.

The north and south sides had five aisles apiece, running from east to west; the west side had four, and the east three. The length of the building was 196 paces, and the breadth 126. The roof was carried by columns built up of stone blocks morticed together, each drum being set on a bed of lead spread on the top of the one below it. There were no arches, and the roof rested immediately on the columns, which were coated with stucco, smoothed and polished, so that they presented the appearance of marble.

The walls of the place of prayer within, as well as the outside of its entrance wall, were faced, in the lower part, with marbles of various colours, and in the upper with mosaics representing plants of different kinds, with fruit hanging from their branches. In the case of the walls of the mihrab the decoration was more carefully executed than elsewhere. The inner face of the north wall of the court was treated in the same way, but the east and west walls (which had been through a restoration) were only coated with plaster painted with designs in colours, and the like. The walls contained nineteen entrances, fifteen of which were closed, and four were open.

The mosque was provided with three minarets, one at either end of the south side, of small dimensions, and tower-like appearance; the third one, at the south-east angle, having the form of an ordinary minaret.[1] There is every reason to think that the two plain tower-like minarets seen by Ibn Jubair were the work of Walid, showing as they did the primitive form of these structures.

Of a higher degree of sanctity than the mosque of the Prophet at Medina is:—

THE MOSQUE OF MECCA.—The following is a short account of this famous mosque, which consists of the Kaaba standing in the centre of a quadrangle enclosed by cloisters (Figs. 2, 3, pp. 9, 10).

The Kaaba, which means 'the square house,' has a mythical origin. Before its reconstruction, about the year 605, in the time of Mohammed, it consisted merely of four dry-stone walls, about the height of a man, without a roof. Later, the sacred structure, 18 cubits in length, was protected by two coverings, one of wool, the other of silk. Round the new shrine the Caliph Omar (634-644) in 638 had an enclosure formed, bounded by four

[1] IBN GUBAYR (Ibn Jubair) (Schiaparelli), *Viaggio in Ispagna, Sicilia, Siria e Palestina, Mesopotamia, Arabia, Egitto*, pp. 176-181, 254.

walls. Fresh alterations and enlargements were carried out (646-47, 649) by Othman (644-656), and after him by Abdallah ibn Zobeir, who rebelled against the Ummayyades, and was acclaimed caliph (683-84). Walid (705-715) rebuilt the quadrangle with a marble colonnade, and new additions were made by Mansur (754-775), and by Mahdi in 783-84. As he left it the mosque of Mecca—'masgid al-Haram'—remained till the time of Ibn Khaldun (1332-1406), and of Ibn Batuta who saw it in 1326.[1]

Ibn Jubair,[2] who came as a pilgrim in 1183, describes it as follows. The Kaaba was square, about 28 cubits high, barely 54 palms long, and about 48 broad. In metres these measurements would be respectively, 15 m. (50 ft.) in height, 12 (40 ft.) in length, and 10 (33 ft.) in breadth.[3] The walls were 5 palms thick, and constructed of stone courses accurately laid. The Black Stone, which was believed to have been dropped on the earth by God for Adam to sit on, was to be seen built up in the outside angle on the east. When Ibn Jubair saw it, it was split into four pieces, and this act of sacrilege he lays to the charge of the Carmathians of the Bahrayn, who had carried it off in 930. Within, the walls were lined half-way up with parti-coloured marbles, while the upper half was covered with plates of silver gilt. Marble was also used for the pavement. Three pillars of some Indian wood standing on the axis of the building supported the ceiling, which had a covering of coloured silk stuff. The exterior was draped with veils of green silk mixed with cotton warp, showing at the top a band of red silk bearing inscriptions. On the veils were worked arches, legends, and invocations. Light came through five windows of stained glass, and there were two entrances. One, that leading to the chapel, looked towards the east, and was at a height of over 11 palms from the ground. It was reached by a wide flight of steps, and its silver gilt doors of marvellous workmanship had been given by Caliph Muktafi (1136-1160). The other entrance was at the north angle, and led to the terrace roof of the building and also to the 'Station of Abraham,' a room containing a stone bearing the impression of a pair of feet, supposed to be those of the patriarch.

The building stood in the middle of a quadrangle, 400 cubits in length

[1] CAETANI, *Annali*, vol. i, pp. 90-99, 174-179; vol. iii, 2, pp. 961-964. CAETANI, *Chronographia*, pp. 201, 202, 295, 316. AMARI, *Storia dei Musulmani di Sicilia*, vol. i, pp. 45-47. IBN KHALDUN, *Prolégomènes historiques*, vol. ii, pp. 254-261. IBN BATUTA, op. cit., vol. i, pp. 305-327.

[2] Op. cit., pp. 54-83.

[3] SNOUCK HURGRONJE, op. cit., vol. i, p. 2.

and 300 in breadth, enclosed by a continuous three-aisled cloister having three rows of marble columns. Above was a battlemented terrace roof. Inscriptions were displayed referring to the works carried out in the mosque by order of Caliph Mahdi in 783. The Haram or sacred precinct had nineteen entrances, and there were seven minarets, four of which stood at the four corners. Ibn Jubair thought them singular in form. Six were square for half their height, built of stone with artistic carving, and surrounded by lattice work of wood carved with great skill: which means that it was encircled by a balcony protected by a parapet. In the upper half, the minaret had the form of a column—in other words, became cylindrical—with a facing of fire-baked bricks arranged in patterns. The summit was crowned by the ball, encircled by a balcony similar to the one below.

These six minarets, though they all had the same form, presented in every case differences of appearance. The seventh was unlike the rest, and among its stucco ornaments the eye was caught by the 'lattices with oblong openings, looking like mihrabs,' in other words, formed like an arcade. The ball at the top 'was carried on piers of masonry with openings between them,' i.e. a kiosk.

If we can trust a drawing reproduced by Schefer from a manuscript of 1574[1] (Fig. 4, p. 9), the minarets of the XVI century were not those seen by Ibn Jubair. His references to the minarets at Mecca are interesting, and we can only regret that the geographer did not mention their date. In any case we cannot suppose that they belonged to the work of Mahdi, for there is no trace of minarets of this form in the VIII century, nor, for the matter of that, in the two following ones. Perhaps they were due to Muktafi, who, in 1155, had given the Kaaba the beautiful doors of its main entrance.

In conclusion, we may notice that, out of regard for its sanctity, the plan of the al-Haram mosque at Mecca was never repeated.[2]

THE PRINCIPAL MOSQUE AT KUFA was erected in 639, by order of Sad ibn abi Waqqas, the traditional founder of Kufa (638-39), the houses of which were rebuilt of sun-baked clay bricks under the direction of Abu-l-Hayyag ibn Malik. It was square in plan, the base being the length of a bow-

[1] NASIRI KUSRU (Schefer), op. cit., pp. lvii, lviii, and frontispiece.

[2] CAETANI, *Annali*, iii, 2, p. 858.

shot. Above the front was a gallery open on all sides, which commanded a view of the country round. This gallery had marble columns of alien origin, carried off from buildings erected by the Persian kings, which supported the roof with its ceiling decorated in the style of a Byzantine church. The court was enclosed, not, in the first instance, by walls, but merely by a ditch. To the south of the mosque was erected the residence of the governor, which included the State Treasury. It was built of fire-baked bricks taken from Persian royal edifices at Hira, and the architect was Ruzbih of Hamdan (Ecbatana), who had previously been the Persian governor of the place.

During the caliphate of Muawiya I (661-680) the mosque of Kufa was rebuilt on a larger and more splendid scale under the direction of his lieutenant, Ziyad, who employed Persian workmen who were not Moslems. One of these, who in the past had worked for the Sassanid monarchs, and to whom Ziyad had imparted the idea that was in his mind, though he was unable to put it into form, made a design for him on the model of the structures raised by the Sassanid kings, that is to say, an immense colonnade with columns 30 cubits high, formed of stone drums from Ahwaz, held together by iron clamps and beddings of lead. The ends and the back side were closed by walls. The design was accepted.[1]

The new structure was, we may believe, the one seen by Ibn Jubair in 1184.[2] Its dimensions were very large. The place of prayer, on the south side, had five aisles, while the remaining three sides of the court had two apiece. These aisles were divided by columns built up of solid stone drums bedded on molten lead. The roof rested immediately upon them, and in height they far surpassed those of any other mosque.

To judge from still existing buildings, or from others which have disappeared, but of which we have descriptions, and until fresh discoveries are made, the second mosque of Kufa was, in the first place, the earliest embodiment of the type unintentionally formulated by Mohammed in the case of his own dwelling at Medina, that is to say, a court enclosed by a wall, and

[1] CAETANI, *Annali*, vol. iii, 2, pp. 857-860. *Rivista degli Studi orientali*, vol. iv, pp. 247-249; LAMMENS, *Ziād ibn Abīhi*. AMARI, op. cit., vol. iii, 2, pp. 826-828. CAETANI, *Chronographia*, pp. 199, 207.

[2] Op. cit., pp. 198-200.

FIG. 1.—Medina. Mosque of Mohammed.
(From a drawing of the XVI cent.)

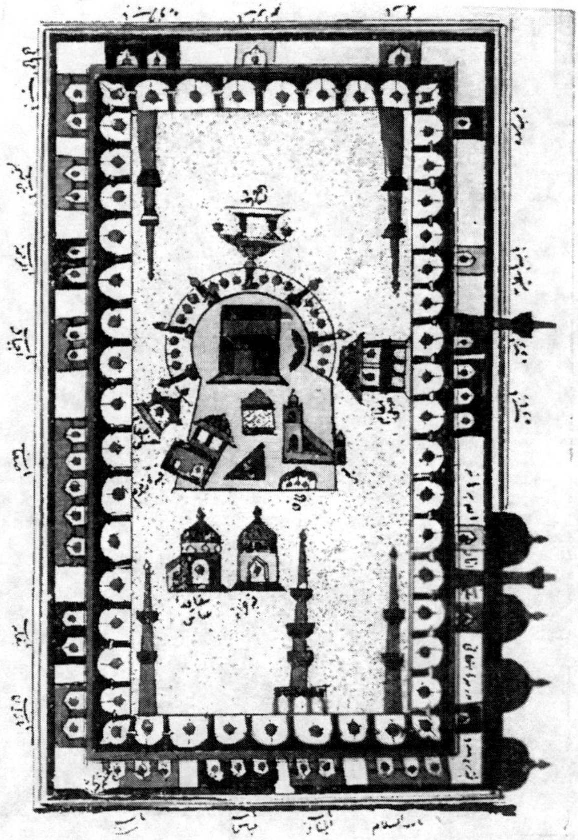

FIG. 4.—Mosque of Mecca. (From a drawing of the XVI cent.)

FIG. 3.—Mosque of Mecca, with the Kaaba, during a pilgrimage.

FIG. 2.—Mosque of Mecca, with the Kaaba.

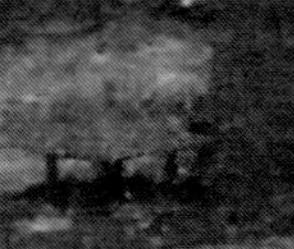

FIG. 6.—Coin of Marcus Aemilius Lepidus representing the Basilica Fulvia Aemilia in the Forum Romanum (Capitoline Collection.) (I cent. B.C.).

provided with a covered place having a flat roof supported by pillars,[1] a regulation which was the origin of the colonnaded mosque plans of the first Moslem centuries. And, secondly, it is the earliest instance of the court surrounded by cloisters. In the previous cases, the Kaaba of Mecca had a mere enclosure wall, and the court of the mosque of the Prophet at Medina was confined in a similar manner.

THE MOSQUE AL-AQSA AT JERUSALEM was thought by De Vogüé[2] to have been built on the site of Justinian I's (527-565) great basilica of the Virgin, which he pictured as having an aisled nave with timber roofs supported by two tiers of columns, and also by wall-shafts carried on corbels. Of this church he would have us see portions of the façade with its doors. When Chosroes II sacked the city in 614, the Christian sanctuary was probably burned, but it seems to have been restored at once, at any rate, so far as the church proper was concerned, for when the Caliph Omar (634-644) came to receive the submission of Jerusalem, he made his devotions in the building.

Later, Abd al-Malik (685-705) erected the mosque al-Aqsa on the site of the restored basilica of Justinian, and we may believe that he gave it the form of a court surrounded by porticoes of varying depth. The year 692 saw the completion of the work. The structure was barely finished before it suffered from earthquakes. In the caliphate of Mansur (754-775) the east and west sides collapsed and were rebuilt. Soon after, in the time of Caliph Mahdi (775-785), the building was once more ruinous and almost abandoned. The plan was then changed, the length being diminished and the breadth increased; and, apparently, the mosque received the form which, in spite of numerous modifications in detail which it has undergone, it preserves to-day. The changes made by Mahdi are supposed to have consisted in the construction of the domed transept, at the expense of the nave and aisles, and the addition of four aisles.

After the capture of Jerusalem by the Crusaders (1099) the Templars turned the mosque into a royal residence, built a church and living-rooms within it, and converted part of the substructures into stables. When Saladin recaptured the city and restored Moslem rule (1187), he had every trace of the Christian religion in the building obliterated, restored it to the form and uses of a mosque, and gave orders for its repair and embellishment. It was

[1] CAETANI, *Annali*, vol. i, pp. 446, 447. [2] *Le Temple de Jérusalem*, pp. 69-79, 99-104.

then that the transept was subjected to radical alterations, with the result that it has become an archaeological puzzle. In 1236 a nephew of Saladin erected the existing portal of the façade (Fig. 5, p. 19). In 1327 Nasir Mohammed repaired the back wall. Further restorations took place in 1345, 1347, 1509, 1817.

The story told by Le Strange[1] is different. Omar built a mosque at Jerusalem, in all probability of wood. Presumably about the year 691, Abd al-Malik rebuilt the mosque al-Aqsa. The greater part of it must have fallen in an earthquake which is put in the year 746, but is not mentioned by the ancient chronicles of Tabari (X century) and Ibn al-Athir (1160-1223). Mansur's restoration is placed about 771. A second earthquake is made responsible for another destruction, but it was rebuilt by Mahdi about 780, with increase of length and reduction in breadth. Between 828 and 844 Abdalla ibn Tahir, the independent governor of Khurasan, built a porch with marble columns in front of the northern façade.

The earliest description of this mosque, that of Muqaddasi (*c.* 985),[2] mentions Abd al-Malik's building, the walls of which were constructed of hewn stone, the blocks being dressed and adjusted with care, and crowned with battlements. He also refers to earthquakes which happened after the coming of the Abbasides (750), and involved the collapse of the whole building with the exception of the mihrab and its surroundings. Further, he notices the restoration carried out by a caliph, supposed to have been Mahdi, when the portions spared by the earthquakes were preserved.

The new mosque was more substantially constructed than its predecessor. It had twenty-six entrances, fifteen of which were in the front or north side, and eleven on the east. The doors of the façade were enclosed by the marble-columned porch of Abdalla ibn Tahir. The court, on the right or western side, had cloisters with marble columns and piers, and, on the further or northern side, rooms with vaulted ceilings decorated with mosaics. On the left or eastern side there were no cloisters.

The mosque proper had its central part covered by a lofty roof of great extent sloping outwards, above which rose a magnificent dome. The surfaces were covered with sheets of zinc. The structure was not in contact with the eastern wall of the court, but was separated from it by an interval, the reason being, either that Caliph Omar had ordered the erection of a place of prayer

[1] *Palestine under the Moslems*, pp. 83-171.

[2] MUQADDASI (Le Strange), *Description of Syria, including Palestine*, pp. 41-48.

in the said space, and the commands of the sovereign were regarded as binding; or because, if the building had been extended as far as the wall, the mihrab, which ought to come midway in that wall, would not have coincided with the axis of Abd al-Malik's rotunda, and this would have been a shock to Moslem sentiment.

The mosque suffered again from earthquakes in 1016 and 1034, when Abdalla ibn Tahir's porch fell, the walls enclosing the Haram were damaged, and the dome was shaken. Zahir (1020-1035) had the latter restored by the architect Abdalla from Cairo. In fact, Nasiri Kusru,[1] on his visit in 1047, found only five entrances on the north and ten on the east, which points to a reduction in the number of openings in order to increase the defensive value of the wall. The porch at the entrance had also disappeared. At this moment the dimensions of the mosque were 120 cubits from north to south, and 150 from east to west, which is equivalent to 300 by 240 ft. It contained two hundred and eighty marble columns supporting arches of stone. The central mihrab, flanked by four columns of cornelian colour, had decorations of enamelled work, like the massive dome out of which it opened. The ceilings were carved. The great central door in the entrance front was of metal covered with exquisite niello work, and had been given by Caliph Mamun (813-833).

In 1099 the building, which appears to have been damaged in the capture of the city, was handed over to the Templars, who rearranged it and reduced it to its present proportions. Ali of Herat, writing in 1173, recorded some of the measurements, which correspond fairly with the actual dimensions.

Saladin, on his recovery of Jerusalem, restored the edifice to its original use, re-dedicated the mihrab, executed various decorative schemes, and made the alterations still to be seen in the transept. Under Naṣir Mohammed, Sultan of Egypt (1293-94, 1298-1308, 1309-1340), the south wall of the mosque was rebuilt, with two windows piercing it, and marble ornamentation. A description of the mosque by the topographer Mujiraddin in 1496 shows that it was identical with what we see to-day. He gives the dimensions as 230 ft. from north to south, excluding the mihrab, and 170 ft. from east to west. On the north side were seven doors corresponding to as many aisles, on the west two, and on the east one.

[1] Op. cit., pp. 79-82.

Lastly, Caetani[1] believes that Omar, between 639-40 and 642-43, after restoring the Christian basilica erected on the ruins of the Temple of Jerusalem, raised, on the platform of Herod's Temple (B.C. 37-4), a mosque of very rough and primitive construction, consisting at best of timber, resting on the remains of the church of the Virgin, and covered with a roof of a temporary nature. This church was so notorious in the whole of Western Asia that it figures in Mohammed's famous dream, to be mentioned presently. As a proof of his view as to the poverty of Omar's building, he refers to the summary description given by Arculf,[2] who saw it about 670: 'Ceterum in illo famoso loco, ubi quondam templum magnifice constructum fuerat, in vicinia muri ab oriente locatum, nunc Sarraceni quadrangulam orationis domum, quam subrectis tabulis et magnis trabibus super quasdam ruinarum reliquias construentes, vili fabricati sunt opere, ipsi frequentant: que utique domus tria hominum millia simul, ut fertur, capere potest.'

I will now endeavour in my turn to give an approximate explanation of the facts.

(1) We know that Justinian's basilica, dedicated to the Mother of God, though begun by Archbishop Elias, was erected by that emperor at the instance of St. Sabbas, and with Theodoros for its architect, in the space of at least twelve years; and that it was called the 'New' church of the Virgin, apparently to distinguish it from two other churches of St. Mary, viz. the one known as 'in Probatica,' and the other in the Valley of Jehoshaphat,[3] both mentioned by Theodosius (*c.* 530).[4] Justinian's church must have been built after 530, as it is not referred to by Theodosius.

(2) The account in Procopius[5] brings out the difficulties which had to be overcome in the course of erection, as the church stood on a platform, part of which rested on the rock, while part was over a void, involving massive stone substructions. We learn from him that the church was called 'St. Mary's,' but distinguished in local usage as 'the New'; that its like was not to be seen elsewhere; that the exceptional width of the building created difficulties both as

[1] *Annali*, vol. iii, 2, pp. 950, 951; vol. iv, pp. 507-509. *Chronographia*, pp. 200, 239.

[2] TOBLER, *Itinera et descriptiones Terrae Sanctae*, vol. i, p. 145; *Arculfi Relatio de Locis Sanctis, scripta ab Adamnano.*

[3] CLERMONT-GANNEAU, *Recueil d'archéologie orientale*, vol. ii, pp. 137-160; *La prise de Jérusalem par les Perses en* 614.

[4] TOBLER, op. cit., vol. i, pp. 65, 66; THEODOSIUS, *De Terra Sancta.*

[5] *Corpus scriptorum historiae byzantinae;* PROCOPIUS, *De aedificiis*, vol. iii, pp. 321-324.

to the construction of the roof and the choice of a suitable material for it; that owing to the serious weight of the roof with its ceilings, columns of very great size had to be used; that the aisles (the number is not stated) were separated by colonnades in two tiers; and that the entrance was reached through a narthex, a square colonnaded fore-court, and a vestibule.

A hostel for pilgrims, and a hospital for the sick of the poorer classes, were attached to the church.

The design, in the matter of the colonnades, evidently followed that of Constantine's church of the Holy Sepulchre.[1] That design was of Roman origin, for we remember that the city of Rome afforded instances of two-storied basilicas with tiers of columns or piers, earlier in date than the Christian era and the age of Augustus. Thus there was the two-storied Basilica Fulvia Aemilia, so called from the censors of B.C. 179, Marcus Aemilius Lepidus and Marcus Fulvius Nobilior.[2] It is shown on a coin struck by Marcus Aemilius Lepidus (consul in B.C. 78) on the occasion of a restoration, which is reproduced by Babelon,[3] and shown in the accompanying illustration (Fig. 6, p. 10). Similar was the Basilica Julia, reconstructed by Augustus, and dedicated in A.D. 12,[4] as we are told by the younger Pliny.[5] It is hopeless to look for the design in the East before these dates, although, in the face of facts, it has been described as Oriental and Hellenistic.[6]

It should be made clear that this basilica of Constantine's at Jerusalem, which, we now know certainly, was distinct from and independent of the church called the 'Anastasis,' did not terminate in the extraordinary form which De Vogüé[7] imagined, though even nowadays there are people who shut their eyes and swallow it.[8] It ended simply in a semicircular apse of the same height as the rest of the building.[9] Equally devoid of foundation is

[1] EUSEBIUS (ed. Heikel), *Vita Constantini*, iii, 37.

[2] DE RUGGIERO, *Il Foro Romano*, pp. 396-399.

[3] *Description historique et chronologique des monnaies de la République Romaine*, vol. i, p. 129.

[4] DE RUGGIERO, op. cit., pp. 408-412.

[5] PLINIUS, *Epistolae*, v, 9; vi, 33.

[6] CATTANEO, *L'architettura in Italia dal secolo VI al Mille circa*, pp. 38, 39. *The Burlington Magazine*, Dec. 1911; STRZYGOWSKI, *The Origin of Christian Art*. LEROUX, *Les origines de l'édifice hypostyle en Grèce, en Orient et chez les Romains*, pp. 281-283.

[7] *Les églises de la Terre Sainte*, pp. 326-335, pl. vi.

[8] CABROL, *Dictionnaire d'archéologie chrétienne et de la Liturgie*, vol. i, 1, col. 186, 187; LECLERCQ, *Abside*.

[9] EUSEBIUS, *Vita Constantini*, iii, 38.

the three-lobed choir with which the imagination of others[1] has endowed the church of the Nativity at Bethlehem, as founded by the Empress Helena (327-333). A personal examination which I made of the outer walls, including testing of the different kinds of mortar employed, has confirmed me in the opinion, which I have stated elsewhere,[2] that this choir was really part of the works ordered by Justinian but not carried out according to his intentions. In fact he strongly disapproved of the attempt to fit a three-lobed sanctuary on to a basilican nave, and this is the inference to be drawn from the language which he used to his legate: 'The building which you have erected is badly put together.'[3] Fresh confirmation of my view has come from other sources.[4] Besides, in the time of Constantine, churches had semicircular endings, and not only in Palestine, but in Egypt as well, as the case of St. Menas at Kharb Abu Mina shows.[5]

(3) Antoninus of Placentia[6] saw the church about the year 570 as he descended from Sion, and it was evidently the same building, for he found that it possessed 'xenodochia.' He does not, however, indicate its topographical situation. Still, if we follow him in his pilgrim's round, we find him, after visiting the church of the Virgin, at prayer in the Praetorium, where stood the basilica of St. Sophia close to the platform which contained the remains of 'Solomon's Temple.'[7] We may infer from this, with some semblance of support, that Justinian's famous church stood in the neighbourhood of the Praetorium, and, more precisely, on what is known to-day as the Haram esh-Sherif; and this is the generally accepted view (Fig. 7, p. 19).

(4) There can be no doubt that St. Mary's was destroyed by fire in 614, sharing the fate of every other church in Jerusalem. It is equally clear that no attempt was made to save it from its state of desolation, for it is

[1] Harvey, Lethaby, Dalton, Cruso, Headlam, *The Church of the Nativity at Bethlehem*, pp. 1-30. Lethaby, *Mediaeval Art*, pp. 58, 59.

[2] G. T. Rivoira, *Le origini dell'Architettura Lombarda* (Loescher, Roma), vol. ii, pp. 24-27; (Hoepli, Milano), pp. 338-341; *Lombardic Architecture* (Heinemann, London), vol. ii, pp. 20-22.

[3] Migne, *Patr. gr.*, vol. cxi, col. 1070, 1071; Eutychius, *Annales*.

[4] *Palestine Exploration Fund*, 1908, p. 304; Dickie, *Masonry Remains around the Church of the Holy Sepulchre*.

[5] Kaufmann, *Die Menasstadt und das nationalheiligtum der altchristlichen Aegypter in der westalexandrinischen wüste*, vol. i, pp. 40-103.

[6] Tobler, op. cit., vol. i, p. 104; Antoninus Martyr, *Perambulatio Locorum Sanctorum*.

[7] P. Barnabé, d'Alsace, *Le Prêtoire de Pilate et la Forteresse Antonia*. P. Barnabé Meistermann, *Nueva Guia de Tierra Santa*, pp. 109-117.

not mentioned among the churches restored by the patriarch Modestus (616-626).[1]

(5) Arculf does not refer to it. The 'templum' mentioned in the passage quoted just above, means the Jewish Temple, not the church of the Virgin or any Christian building. Arculf always describes churches by the words 'basilica' and 'ecclesia.'[2]

Nor does he fix the exact situation of the mosque of Omar. The indication is vague: in the neighbourhood of the temple. He only fixes the site (or 'platea,' as Antoninus Martyr calls it) formerly occupied by Herod's Temple, which was 'in the neighbourhood of the eastern wall of the city.' This interpretation of Arculf's language is confirmed by Eucherius (*c.* 440), who wrote when neither Justinian's church nor the mosque of Omar were in existence. 'Templum vero, in inferiori parte urbis in vicinia muri ab oriente locatum magnificeque extructum, quondam miraculum fuit, ex quo parietis unius in ruinis quedam pinna superest, reliquis ad fundamenta usque destructis.'[3]

(6) Mohammed's famous and visionary journey by night to Jerusalem and the seventh heaven, which took place before his residence at Medina, and actually in the year 621, seems to me to be connected with the Temple of Jerusalem, assuming that the enigmatical language of a verse of the Koran (xvii, 1)—'Praise be unto Him who transported His servant by night from the sacred temple (al-Masgid al-Haram) to the farther temple (al-Masgid al-Aqsa)'—refers to Jerusalem; and always remembering that the story of the visionary journey rests almost entirely on tradition.[4] It was in that temple that the Prophet met Abraham, Moses, Jesus, and other prophets, and joined with them in prayer. In the centre, again, of that temple rose the Sacred Rock, the scene of Abraham's intended sacrifice of his son, the site of David's altar, the early 'qibla' of the Israelites, believed to be the centre of the world. On that rock had descended and been set up the ladder of fire which, with the help of the archangel Gabriel, Mohammed had climbed to visit the seven heavens, and by which he had returned to earth. That rock Abd al-Malik had tried to make the rival of the Black

[1] MIGNE, *Patr. gr.*, vol. lxxxix, col. 1427, 1428; *Epistola Antiochi monachi.* Vol. cxi, col. 1083; EUTYCHIUS, *Annales.*

[2] TOBLER, op. cit., vol. i, pp. 141-202; *Arculfi Relatio de Locis Sanctis.*

[3] TOBLER, op. cit., vol. i, p. 52; EUCHERIUS, *De Locis aliquibus Sanctis.*

[4] IRVING, *The Life of Mahomet*, pp. 82-95. NÖLDEKE, SCHWALLY, *Geschichte des Qorāns*, vol. i, p. 134. SPRENGER, *Das leben und die lehre des Mohammad*, vol. ii, p. 527.

Stone of the Kaaba. And to this day popular belief connects it with the Prophet's vision, and points in proof to the impression left by his turban and by the hand of the archangel Gabriel.

Of that temple nothing was left but the platform on which it stood, while it is possible that the rock was no longer exposed to view in the days of Mohammed, though it is still pointed out by the Bordeaux Pilgrim in 333.[1] But there can be little doubt that both survived in the vivid memory of the Jews, who were, in most cases, the source of the Prophet's inspiration when he came to lay down his rules of religious obligation.[2]

The Prophet's journey cannot have had any connection with Justinian's basilica of the Virgin. In this part of Asia the best known, the most sacred, and the most famous Christian monument was the Holy Sepulchre.

(7) The dimensions of the mosque of Omar cannot have been small, considering the number of the faithful which, according to Arculf, it could hold. The structure may have consisted of colonnades made up of shafts taken from other buildings, with wooden roofs. The employment of columns would explain the story of the collapse of the mosque,[3] which may have been due, not so much to the haste with which it was constructed, as to the width of the aisles. Arculf, in fact, mentions the use of great beams. The small account in which he held the edifice may be due to the absence of ornament, or to its very mean character. The mosque did not possess a mihrab, and the qibla was represented by a stone.[4]

It may be mentioned here that there was another mosque of Omar at Jerusalem, connected with the Holy Sepulchre, and built between 877 and 940.[5]

(8) It was Abd al-Malik who rebuilt Jerusalem's earliest mosque, and his object was to outdo in splendour the 'Martyrion' of the Holy Sepulchre. He achieved no small success, if we are to judge by the rotunda which he raised in front of the building, and by the elegance of the remains of the

[1] TOBLER, op. cit., vol. i, p. 17; *Itinerarium a Bordigala Hierusalem usque.*

[2] CAETANI, *Annali*, vol. i, pp. 457, 458.

[3] Ibid., vol. iii, 2, p. 942.

[4] MIGNE, *Patr. gr.*, vol. cxi, col. 1100; EUTYCHIUS, *Annales.*

[5] *Recueil d'archéologie orientale*, vol. ii, pp. 302-362; CLERMONT-GANNEAU, *La basilique de Constantin et la mosquée d'Omar à Jérusalem.*

FIG 5.—Jerusalem. Façade of the Mosque al-Aqsa (XIII cent.).

FIG. 7.—Jerusalem. View of the Haram esh-Sherif, or sacred enclosure.

FIG. 8.—Jerusalem. Mosque al-Aqsa. One of the colonnades of the central nave (VII and VIII cent.).

mosque which met the eyes of Muqaddasi,[1] and surpassed that of the great mosque of Damascus.

The language of the geographer[2] seems to imply that opposite to the mihrab seen by him, rose the dome of the central nave, carried on arches springing from isolated piers, and also on wall-piers. In that case the qibla of Abd al-Malik's mosque must have stood beneath a dome, and a transept must have existed, the plan being originally in the form of a **T**.

On the other hand, the account of Nasiri Kusru[3] shows that the central dome rested on sixteen marble columns, which might well suggest the idea of a reconstruction of the original dome between 985 and 1047, or, more precisely, in connection with the works ordered by Zahir. According to Ibn Khaldun[4] (who mistakenly ascribes to Walid what was done by his father), it was through the Greek emperor that the caliph obtained the builders and mosaic-workers required for the erection and decoration of the mosque al-Aqsa.

(9) De Vogüé[5] long ago called attention to the radical changes effected by Saladin at the end of the building. Now it seems to me that, if nothing else, the feature in this part which was constructionally of most importance, viz. the wooden dome, was on this occasion rebuilt from the ground. As a matter of fact, Ali of Herat in 1173 recorded the following dimensions of the dome itself: diameter, 40 ft., height from the pavement, 90 ft.[6] The dimensions of the existing dome, which is of ovoidal section and made of wood, are, on the contrary, hardly more than 24 m. (79 ft.) for the internal height, and 11 (36 ft.) for the diameter. Moreover, the niche-shaped pendentives, recalling those of the mosque of Hakim at Cairo, though lightened by hollow circles, suggest a later date than the second half of the XI century, and certainly could not belong to the ponderous dome seen by Nasiri Kusru.

(10) The central nave of the existing mosque, about 12 m. (39½ ft.) in width, is very probably in its main lines that of Abd al-Malik, remodelled by Mahdi (Fig. 8, p. 20). I say in its main lines, for the pointed arches are unquestionably later than the caliphate of Mahdi: in his time and in these countries pointed arches were not systematically used in buildings. The columns seem to belong to the work of Justinian, as is indicated by the

[1] Op. cit., p. 41.
[2] Muqaddasi, op. cit., pp. 41, 42.
[3] Op. cit., p. 80.
[4] *Prolégomènes*, vol. ii, pp. 268, 375.
[5] *Le Temple de Jérusalem*, p. 101.
[6] Le Strange, *Palestine under the Moslems*, pp. 108, 109.

uniformity of their bases and the flat moulding of these, just as in the case of the isolated columns in the so-called Golden Gate close by (Fig. 9, p. 20), which I regard as belonging to the same period. De Vogüé thought that it was later than the IV century, but not going beyond the end of the VI.[1] Moreover, some of the Corinthian capitals, especially the better specimens, such as the first and second seen in Fig. 8, which have been made for their places, belong to the time of Justinian, and, with their stiff and twisted leaves with their points sharply turned over, recall the capitals of the same class in the Golden Gate. The rest of the capitals betray a lifeless, stylistic imitation of those which we have described, and may be referred to the time of Mahdi, who, among other things, in a restoration of the nave, considerably increased its height so that it rose above the aisles, and gave it a gabled roof.[2] These also fit their columns, showing that they were made for their places. De Vogüé's failure to realize the nature of this imitative art led him into mistakes about the date of al-Aqsa. Byzantine Corinthian capitals may also be found in other parts of the mosque (Fig. 10, p. 29): some have the basket form (Fig. 11, p. 29), others are melon-shaped of the VI century. I have given elsewhere a brief account of the Byzantine capitals in Jerusalem.[3]

All this points to the conclusion that these columns, which are about 90 cm. (2 ft. 11 in.) in diameter, belonged to the basilica of the Virgin. Their squat proportions may be due, not to any diminution they have suffered, but to the intention from the outset of making them suitable for carrying a second range of columns, as well as supporting the great weight of the timber roof. Certainty as to their origin might be obtained by verification of the tint of the marble of which they are composed, for we know from Procopius that they were flame-coloured: 'which in colour resemble a flame of fire.' This, together with the inference drawn from the account of Antoninus of Placentia, is the only light which can be thrown on the existence of Justinian's basilica on the platform of Herod's temple. But about its orientation we may say something more, for whatever was its precise site in the locality, we may be sure that it was set east and west, as was usual in that period, and not north and south. There were no local conditions to make the latter course necessary. In any case, the words of Procopius

[1] *Le Temple de Jérusalem*, pp. 64-68.

[2] Muqaddasi, op. cit., pp. 41, 42.

[3] Rivoira, op. cit. (Loescher), vol. ii, pp. 22-26; (Hoepli), pp. 336-339; (Heinemann), vol. ii, pp. 19-21.

show that the sanctuary was at the east end: '. . . but a fourth part of the church was wanting towards the south and east, where the priests have to perform divine service.'

All the same, there is no reason to think that the present nave of the mosque al-Aqsa was originally the nave of the church of the Virgin. It has the Moslem and not the Christian orientation, and it is set in relation to the Dome of the Rock. I may add that the evidence of a marble slab with the print of one of the Saviour's feet in the transept of the mosque, which some have used to support the idea that the church originally stood here, is baseless. The footprint, supposing it to be the same, was noted by Antoninus Martyr in the church of St. Sophia.[1]

(11) It is not clear whether Abd al-Malik's mosque had minarets. The earliest accounts are silent about them, as is Muqaddasi, who lived at Jerusalem. The four minarets with which it has been provided appear only at a late period, and in narratives which are mostly of an apocryphal character.[2] Still it would not be surprising to find four towers for the call to prayer, in the form in which we do find them in 673, connected with the mosque of Amr at Fustat.

Abd al-Malik's mosque seems to have exhibited two noteworthy peculiarities. They are these: the dome rising above the mihrab, and the T-shaped plan. These features, apparently, did not belong to any earlier mosque.

THE CONGREGATIONAL MOSQUE OF AMR AT FUSTAT (OLD CAIRO) was erected in 642 by Amr, the invader of Egypt (639), during the caliphate of Omar (634-644), in the city of Fustat or 'Fossatum,' founded by him, and known by the double name of Fustat Misr.[3] Later, the city was enlarged by the suburbs of Askar (750) and Qattai (868),[4] and remained the capital of Egypt until the rise of Cairo.

At the outset its dimensions were not imposing. The roof was rude and low, and seems to have been supported by a few columns taken from other buildings. The floor was of pebbles set in concrete. It is very probable that the internal walls were built of unbaked bricks left rough. The lighting

[1] TOBLER, op. cit., vol. i, p. 104; ANTONINUS MARTYR, *Perambulatio Locorum Sanctorum.*

[2] LE STRANGE, *Palestine under the Moslems*, pp. 148-151, 170.

[3] BUTLER, *The Arab Conquest of Egypt*, pp. 339-341.

[4] HOUTSMA, BASSET, ARNOLD, HARTMANN, *Encyclopédie de l'Islām*, pp. 835-846, Caire.

presumably came from openings in the roof, just as it does in the great colonnade to-day. The orientation was inaccurate, and the whole building so uninviting that at the conclusion of the services the faithful preferred to adjourn for purposes of recreation to the surroundings of the Friday meeting-place in the open air.

Its dimensions were 50 by 30 cubits, that is to say, some 28 by 17 m. (about 92 by 56 ft.). There were six entrances, two on each of the north, east, and west sides respectively. It did not possess either an internal court, or a mihrab, or a minaret. It was bounded on every side by a street; and to the east, some 4 m. (13 ft.) distant, stood the house of the founder.

In 673, during the caliphate of Muawiya (661-680), Maslama ibn Mukhallad, the governor of Egypt, had it enlarged on the north and east, the floor covered with matting, an open court formed on the outside, the walls plastered, and four towers erected, one at each angle. The number of muezzins was increased, and they were ordered to chant the prayer at daybreak instead of using the hammer. All this took place in 672-73.[1]

Towards 696 the governor, Abd al-Aziz, pulled down the whole or a part, and rebuilt the mosque with additions on the west and north. But the roof still remained low, and ten years later it had to be raised. This implies that Abd al-Aziz demolished only part of the building, and was obliged to maintain throughout the low elevation of the original roof.

I may remark that the lowness and poverty of Amr's building are anything but calculated to prove the much-vaunted ability of the Coptic architects, or their love of lofty roofs; even supposing, as has been stated as a fact in some quarters, that, from the accession of Muawiya to the time of the Fatimids, the Moslem rulers employed their services for the works they carried out.[2]

In 711 the Caliph Walid I (705-715) gave orders to the governor, Qurra ibn Shiarik, to demolish it completely and rebuild it from the ground. The site was enlarged on the south and east, a mihrab constructed in the form of a niche, and four entrances made on the east, four on the west, and three on the north. The execution was entrusted to one Yahya ibn Hanzala, whom Amari suspects to have been of Persian origin; and the work was finished in the space of thirteen months.

[1] CAETANI, *Chronographia*, p. 588.

[2] WHISHAW, *Arabic Spain*, pp. 16, 123.

In 715-16 the treasury of the mosque was built. The fact that it was covered by a dome, and that afterwards a fountain was set beneath it, suggests that its form was similar to that of the treasury in the congregational mosque at Damascus: that is to say, it rested on isolated supports. In 750-51, when Salih ibn Ali was governor, four colonnades were added on the north. In 791 the governor Musa ibn Isa added an open space in front of the north wall. In 826 orders issued from the governor Abdalla ibn Tahir to enlarge the building on the west, preserving the original arrangements. The works were completed by Isa ibn Yazid (827-829). The mosque now covered an area of 190 by 150 cubits, or about 109 by 86 m. (358 by 283 ft.). The number of columns was reckoned at three hundred and seventy-eight. The walls were pierced by thirteen entrances, three on the north, five on the east, four on the west, one on the south; and there were five minarets.

We hear of other additions in 851-52 and 872, and also of a fire, the damage from which was repaired by Ibn Tulun. The earthquake of 885 did some injury, and in 886 another fire destroyed much of the work of Abdalla ibn Tahir, which was made good by Khumarawayh (883-895). In 936 nearly all the columns were embellished. In 968 a fresh addition was made. The mosque had mosaic decorations which Hakim (996-1020) in 997 concealed under whitewash. This caliph also carried out some works in the court. Under Mustansir (1035-1094) a minaret was added, and in the same caliphate Nasiri Kusru reckoned four hundred marble columns. In 1168-69, under the last Fatimite caliph, Adid (1160-1171), it was burned when Fustat was fired (the conflagration lasted fifty-four days) in order to prevent its occupation by Amalric, King of Jerusalem (1162-1173). Saladin, on becoming ruler of Egypt (1169-1171-1193), carried out a restoration in 1172-73, rebuilding the side which contained the qibla, that is the southern. Repairs were executed between 1250 and 1257, and between 1260 and 1277. On the last occasion the north wall was rebuilt. More repairs were done in 1288.

The mosque suffered severely in the memorable earthquake of 1303, when the colonnades on the north and east sides of the court collapsed. The Sultan Nasir Mohammed (1293-94, 1298-1308, 1309-1340) had it restored, the works being entrusted to the scribe Ibn Kattab. At the end of the XIV century it was on the verge of ruin, but the merchants had it restored, and the whole south side rebuilt. The work was finished in 1401. It seems that some repairs were executed under the Sultan Mohammed ibn Qait Bey (1495-1498). In 1798 the whole was restored, and the mosque assumed the general aspect which it presents to-day in spite of various minor repairs at different times.[1]

From the story of the vicissitudes of the structure here set forth, and mainly derived from the 'Kitab al-Mavaiz' of Maqrizi,[2] it will readily be seen how difficult, not to say impossible, it is to hit on the right solutions in a building which has undergone so many reconstructions and restorations. Difficulties of this kind are increased by the wretched condition of the sides of the court and their colonnades. Of those on the east and west only the bases survive; on the north only one row of columns is left. Under these circumstances I shall omit any detailed description, though the materials are ready to my hand, and confine myself to exhibiting the plan and two views of the building as it is to-day (Figs. 12, 13, 14, pp. 27, 29, 30), with the addition of a few pertinent observations.

(1) The mosque as founded by Amr, was simply a quadrangle composed of colonnades enclosed on every side by walls, and devoid of any trace of the plan which afterwards became distinctive of congregational mosques, and had been already applied in the second mosque of Kufa in the days of Muawiya. The internal divisions were, very probably, of equal breadth, for even now the central nave ending in the principal mihrab is no wider than the others.

Of Amr's structure no vestige whatever remains. Walid, with his demolition of the old mosque and enlargement of the new, erased it for ever from the list of Moslem monuments. The fact has been noticed before now.[3]

(2) The southern part of the present mosque, that is to say the place of prayer, though it may preserve fragments of the enclosing wall containing the qibla, as well as the plan of the aisles, with many of the marble columns of Roman or Byzantine origin, brought from other buildings, and belonging to Walid's reconstruction, Tahir's enlargement, and Khumarawayh's restoration, has nothing to show above ground older than Saladin's rebuilding or, perhaps, even the later one of 1401.

[1] CAETANI, *Annali*, vol. iv, pp. 563-570. BUTLER, *The Arab Conquest of Egypt*, pp. 343, 344. *The Journal of the Royal Asiatic Society*, 1890, pp. 759-800; CORBETT, *The history of the Mosque of Amr at Old Cairo*. LANE-POOLE, *A history of Egypt in the Middle Ages*, pp. 17, 73, 301, 302. AMARI, op. cit., vol. iii, 2, pp. 832, 833. NASIRI KUSRU, op. cit., p. 147.

[2] LANE, *The manners and customs of the modern Egyptians* (ed. E. Rhys), App. F., pp. 603-606.

[3] Ibid., App. F., p. 587.

The pointed arches larger than semicircles and raised on very tall imposts, which are used throughout, have certainly nothing to do either with Walid, to whose time belongs the earliest employment of the round arch with a slight suggestion of the horse-shoe form; or with Abdallah ibn Tahir, for the pointed arch larger than a semicircle, in its simple form, i.e. not elevated, was systematically used for the first time in the mosque of Ibn Tulun (872-73, 879); or with Khumarawayh, for it was only in 970 that the builders of the mosque al-Azhar decided to employ the pointed horse-shoe arch springing from a high base.

Consequently, all that has been asserted about the great antiquity of the mosque which bears the name of Amr, falls to the ground.

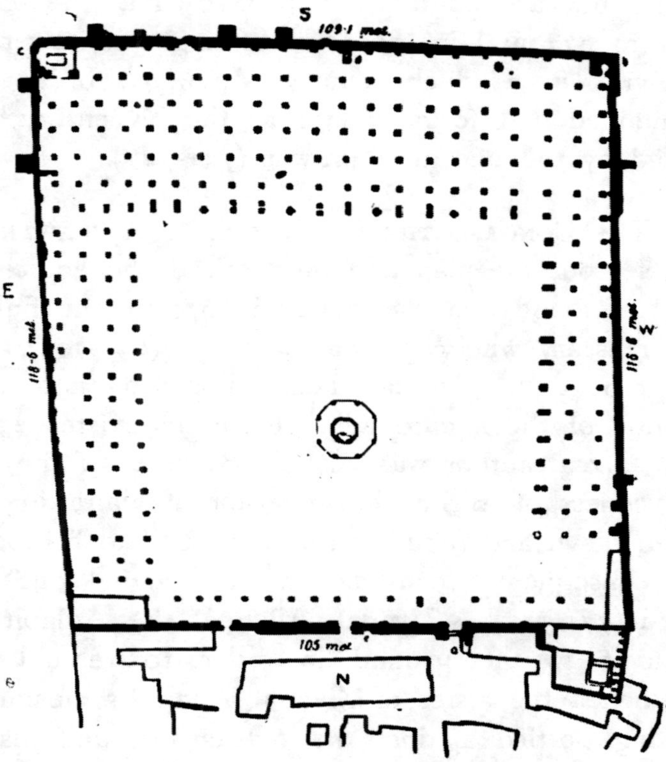

FIG. 12.—Fustat (Cairo). Plan of the existing Mosque of Amr.

(From *The Journal of the Royal Asiatic Society*, 1890.)

(3) We have no precise information as to the nature of the four towers erected in 673 by order of Muawiya. Maqrizi does not describe them as minarets. It has been supposed that they had the form of wooden sentry boxes set at the angles of the flat roof and reached by stairs outside the building, and were used for the call to prayer: that they were in fact the germ of the great tower minarets of the future. This idea receives some support from the fact that, as late as 1050-51, the traditional site of the muezzin's chamber was on the roof of the place of prayer.[1]

But Maqrizi does mention the erection of a minaret by order of

[1] *The Journal of the Royal Asiatic Society*, 1890, pp. 771-773; CORBETT, *The history of the Mosque of Amr at Old Cairo.*

Maslama ibn Mukhallad 'for the mosque which was in Fustat'—presumably the congregational mosque of Amr. If this is so, there must have been five structures used by the muezzins for the call to prayer. Butler speaks definitely of minarets inscribed with the name of Maslama.[1] Caetani[2] merely says that he built the first minaret. We will not attempt to solve the riddle, but are content to believe that the first minaret at Fustat was built in 673 and in the form of a simple tower, for we do not forget that in Syria, from which country Muawiya's order to Maslama came, minarets maintained that form as late as the X century,[3] while in Africa it is represented by the one at Kairawan (721-727).

THE CONGREGATIONAL MOSQUE OF KAIRAWAN.—Okba, governor of Africa, first set out the plan and then raised the edifice,[4] apparently of clay.[5] The work of foundation was begun in 670-71 and finished in 674-75.[6]

Hassan, who captured Carthage (696-705), found the structure standing and rebuilt it. It has been supposed that to this occasion belongs the erection of the square minaret still in existence; but we shall see presently that its real author was Bishr. By order of the Caliph Hisham (724-743), at the request of Bishr, the governor of Kairawan, the mosque was once more pulled down and rebuilt, as it was found to be too small. A third demolition and consequent reconstruction was carried out by the governor of Africa, Yazid (772-787). Ziyadat Allah I, the Aglabite emir of Africa (816-837), razed it to the ground in order to rebuild it. Ibrahim II (874-902) lengthened the aisles of Ziyadat Allah I's mosque, that is to say, he set the existing portico against the old façade, and also constructed the porticoes on the east and west of the court.[7] He made the gate al-Behu, or the

[1] BUTLER, *The Arab Conquest of Egypt*, p. 343.

[2] *Chronographia*, p. 588.

[3] MUQADDASI, op. cit., p. 75.

[4] ADZĀRI (Fagnan), *Histoire de l'Afrique et de l'Espagne intitulée Al-Bayano'l-Mogrib*, vol. i, pp. 15-17. IBN KHALDOUN (De Slane), *Histoire des Berbères et des dynasties musulmanes de l'Afrique septentrionale*, vol. i, p. 328. *Journal Asiatique*, 1841, vol. i, pp. 117-120; DE SLANE, *Histoire de la province d'Afrique et du Maghrib, traduite de l'arabe d'En-Noweiri.*

[5] AMARI, op. cit., vol. i, pp. 114, 115.

[6] CAETANI, *Chronographia*, pp. 548, 609.

[7] In order to simplify matters I always treat the side containing the qibla as the south (though this does not exactly coincide with the direction of Mecca), which also fixes the relative orientation of the other sides of mosques.

FIG. 10.—Jerusalem. Mosque al-Aqsa. Capital of the VI cent.

FIG. 11.—Jerusalem. Mosque al-Aqsa. Capital of the VI cent.

FIG. 13.—Fustat (Cairo). Mosque of Amr (VIII-XVIII cent.).

FIG. 14.—Fustat (Cairo). Mosque of Amr. One of the outer aisles with architraves of carved wood.

FIG. 16.—Kairawan. Congregational Mosque (IX cent.).

Pavilion, with the cupola belonging to it, and also the cupola in front of the mihrab. He embellished the wall above the mihrab, as well as the mihrab itself. Through all these changes the original mihrab and Bishr's minaret were left untouched. We hear of various later alterations, but they made no essential difference in the appearance of the building.[1] We will now examine it in detail.

The mosque forms an oblique parallelogram, with its principal axis directed towards Mecca. About a third of the space is occupied by the place of prayer, in front of which is a colonnaded quadrangle (Fig. 15, p. 32). The place of prayer, temple, or mosque proper (Fig. 16, p. 30), consists of sixteen parallel aisles bisected by a central wider aisle or nave, each of which contains seven bays formed by arches, the whole being bounded on the south by a broad aisle. These two main aisles, which strike the eye both in plan and elevation and form the letter **T**, recall, as has been remarked,[2] the plan of the early Christian basilicas, such as the Constantinian church of St. Peter on the Vatican at Rome, founded by Pope Silvester (314-335).[3]

Ziyadat's new building and Ibrahim II's additions are self-evident. We find confirmation, too, of the statement in Bakri (1068) that Ziyadat Allah completely demolished the pre-existing mosque, retaining nothing but the original mihrab, and that against his will.[4] This mihrab was not made by Okba, in whose days the qibla was designated by a stone. The earliest mihrab seems to have been the one erected in the congregational mosque of Damascus.

Ziyadat Allah's mosque is, as a whole, the one we see to-day, both in plan and elevation. It was based on the form of a **T**, with just the same number of parallel aisles and arched bays as still exist. The horse-shoe arch was used exclusively. In order to make the roof as high as possible, without an excessive weight of wall, the arches were set up on high imposts, which recall the similar elevation of the architraves in the pillared

[1] *Les monuments historiques de la Tunisie*, deuxième partie, *Les monuments arabes;* SALADIN, *La mosquée de Sidi Okba à Kairouan*, pp. 7-31. MERCIER, *Histoire de l'Afrique septentrionale* (*Berbérie*), vol. i, pp. 203-207, 254, 255, 280. AMARI, op. cit., vol. i, p. 154; vol. ii, p. 48. EL KAIRUANI (Pellissier et Rémusat), *Histoire de l'Afrique*, pp. 42, 43, 79, 83.

[2] SALADIN, *La mosquée de Sidi Okba à Kairouan*, p. 40.

[3] DUCHESNE, *Le liber pontificalis*, vol. i, pp. 176, 193, 194.

[4] *Journal Asiatique*, vol. xii, pp. 412-492; EL BEKRI (De Slane), *Description de l'Afrique septentrionale.*

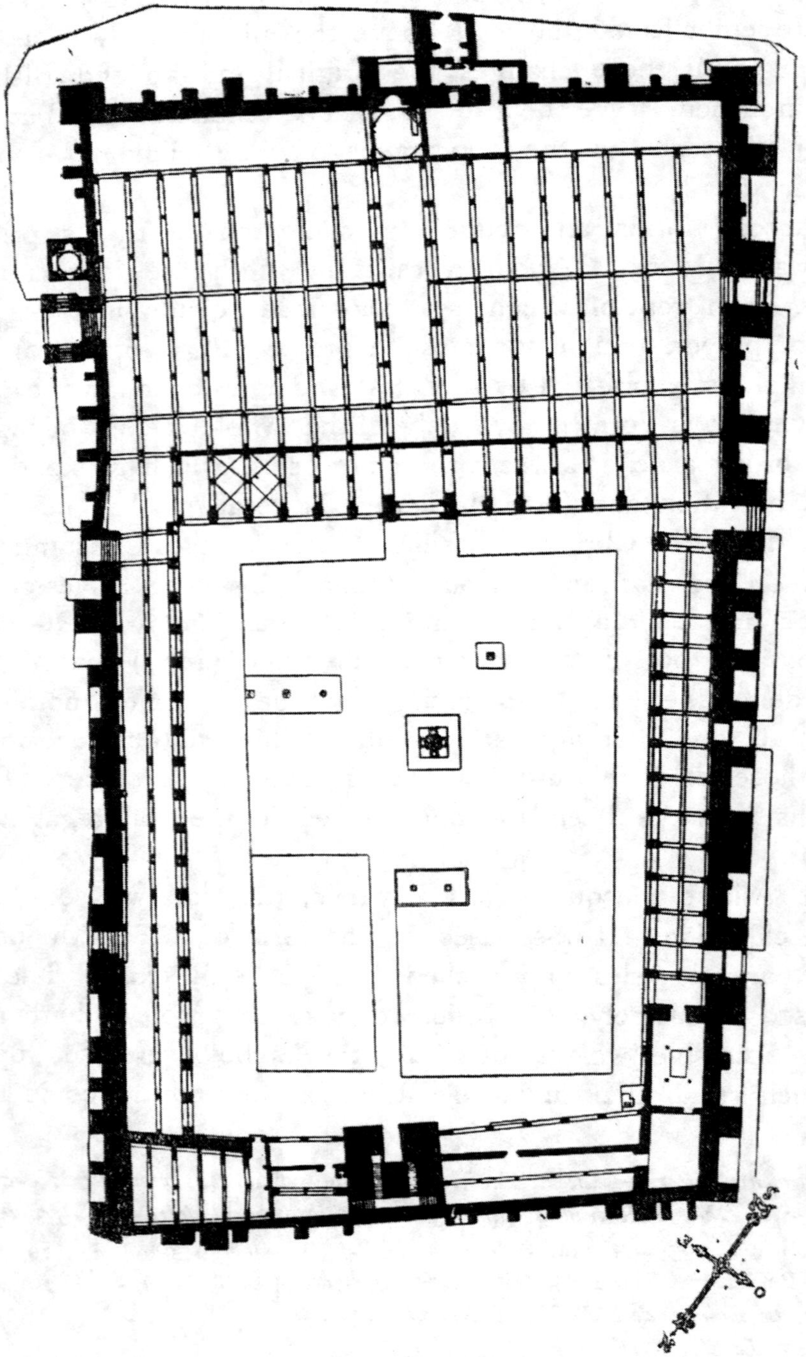

FIG. 15.—Plan of the Congregational Mosque of Kairawan (IX cent.).

(From SALADIN, *La mosquée de Sidi Okba à Kairouan.*)

hall of the temple of Hathor at Denderah (I century, A.D.) (Fig. 17, p. 39). This feature of boldly stilted arches was destined to become one of the characteristics of Moslem architecture.

In the colonnades which open on the court, as well as in those belonging to the great transverse nave, columns were used in pairs in order to provide starting points for both the longitudinal and the transverse arches. The same device appears in the central nave wherever a similar combination of arches occurs.

The arches were secured, after the Arabic practice, from the danger of parting asunder or of earthquakes, by fixing chains or wooden beams in the imposts, but there was nothing to counteract any pressure on the outer walls. Chains had already been used by the Byzantines, as for instance in St. Irene at Constantinople (VIII century). In order to give more cohesion to the building, two of the transverse arcades, the third and the sixth, were connected with the eastern and western walls by means of arches springing from wall-shafts.

Behind Ziyadat Allah's mihrab, as retouched by Ibrahim, the original mihrab still exists walled-up.

The only columns used were of alien origin. Very few of these are fluted, but they form a varied collection of marbles, sometimes of the greatest beauty, the like of which I have never seen equalled in any of the ancient mosques, erected as such, which I have examined. Some of these shafts have bases of every description, some have none at all. Some stand on the pavement, others are partly buried beneath it. Others are made to fit their place by the addition of a plinth.

The capitals, in the same way, were taken from ancient buildings. Every shape, every kind of technique may be seen; and their range includes the Christian as well as the Pagan centuries. There are Corinthian capitals with acanthus foliage, whether of Roman or Byzantine character; Composite with plain or carved leaves; cubical funnel-shaped capitals with lotus leaves framed by a band of reticulated carving, recalling specimens in San Vitale at Ravenna (526-547); in other cases covered with zigzag ribbons or tendrils. Nor is the melon-shaped type wanting.

The capitals are surmounted by shallow abaci of wood. A wooden abacus has the advantage of providing an elastic stratum above the capital, thus protecting it from fractures. It is also more economical, as wood is very easy to work.

Ibrahim II made no extension of Ziyadat Allah's mosque, but only some alterations. He constructed the dome over the mihrab, embellished the building, and added to its front a two-aisled portico crowned by a cupola. In my opinion Ziyadat's mosque was reached through the enclosure formed by the present outer wall without its surrounding colonnades, which were added by Ibrahim II. What Ibrahim did may be summed up as follows:—

(1) Two new colonnades were constructed inside the central nave leading to the mihrab, thus diminishing its width, while at the same time it was strengthened against the thrust of the dome which rose in front of the mihrab. This dome was erected at the same time. From the columns sprang horse-shoe arches of slightly pointed form, decorated with bands twisted into a knot at the apex, like those of the external arcades.

The dome (Figs. 18, 19, pp. 35, 39) rests on three open arches, and a fourth which is built up. They spring from clusters of isolated columns and from wall-columns. The blind arch is decorated with a triplet of arches framing rectangular windows, and a couple of niches, the whole enclosed in a single arch, as was the fashion at Ravenna.[1] The spandrel spaces are filled by niches and roses.

The transition from the square base to the octagon inside is formed by four hood-shaped pendentives at the angles in the form of shells. Round the octagon run eight blank arches springing from colonnettes supported by brackets. Four of them act as relieving arches to the pendentives, the others surmount cusped arches, each of which is pierced by a sexfoil opening. This internal octagon is represented on the exterior by a square mass relieved by arcading.

In its turn the octagon inside passes into the circular drum of the dome by means of spherical pendentives.[2] The drum itself is relieved by arches, some blank and others pierced by windows. The way in which the transition is effected recalls that in the baptistery of Neon at Ravenna (449 or 458-477). Externally the drum has a polygonal form. The cupola itself is composed of concave segments, the ribs starting from corbels.

When the dome was built, the wall in which the mihrab is set was decorated with metallic lustre tiles brought from Baghdad, and at the same time the mihrab itself must have been altered, as is shown by its slightly pointed main arch. The arches in Ziyadat's work are invariably round.

[1] Rivoira, op. cit. (Hoepli) p. 40; (Heinemann), vol. i, p. 39.

[2] Ibid. (Heinemann), vol. i, pp. 29-35, 39, 63.

But it is just possible that the alteration was made when the Fatimid Muizz tried to change the position of the qibla (656-57).[1]

(2) The eastern and western walls were strengthened on the inside by means of wall-arches carried on columns.

(3) A two-aisled portico (Fig. 20, p. 40) was constructed along the front of the place of prayer, slightly pointed arches of horse-shoe form being used, and alterations made in Ziyadat's façade, the arches of which (less carefully built than those of Ibrahim II) are larger than semicircles, and have decorative bands which are continuous instead of forming a knot at the top like those of the outer portico.

FIG. 19.—Kairawan. Congregational Mosque. Details in the dome of the mihrab (IX cent.).

In front of the central entrance was a dome called the 'Qobba bab al-Behu,' or dome of the gate of the pavilion. Bakri[2] writes of it in glowing terms. It was rebuilt in the first half of the XIX century. In its present form the square base passes into the octagon by means of niches in the angles filled in with two spherical segments. The octagon has on each face an arch, four of which frame the pendentives, and is lighted by windows. It passes into the circle of the drum by the aid of shafts supported on corbels, which are designed to carry those parts of the drum which hang in the air. The interior of the drum is encircled by an arcade pierced with windows. The cupola is divided into concave sections, the ribs being supported by brackets.

With regard to this dome we may remark that the device of using colonnettes for angle raccords is of considerable antiquity. The internal

[1] BAKRI, *Journal Asiatique*, vol. xii, pp. 412-492; EL BEKRI (De Slane), *Description de l'Afrique septentrionale.*

[2] Ibid.

octagon of the Tower of the Winds, or Horologium of Andronicus at Athens, dating from the II century B.C., or the early years of the first,[1] passes into the circle of the roof by means of dwarf shafts at the angles (Fig. 21, p. 40).

(4) The lateral colonnades of the court were constructed. These must be 'the aisles added to the mosque' by Ibrahim II,[2] unless by these 'aisles' are meant all the cloistered sides of the court. As Ziyadat's outer walls were preserved, they were strengthened by the addition of wall-arches, just as in the place of prayer. All these colonnades, viz. that in front of the sanctuary, and the two on the east and west sides of the court, evidently belong to the same age, except where they have been retouched or rebuilt. The masonry of the walls of the façade, where they have not been repaired, is uniform; and the slightly pointed arches have been decorated with a band framing the arch and forming a knot at the summit, the centre of the knot being marked by a disc of green enamel. A number of these discs are still in place.

With very few exceptions the marble columns used are of alien origin, and various means have been taken to fit them to their places. In some cases marble carvings of the Roman epoch have been used for the purpose. The capitals (Figs. 22, 23, 24, 25, p. 41) are also antiques, and illustrate every possible form and date, as do those in the mosque proper. By way of exception there are a few made expressly for their places, with clumsy plain leaves. The finest specimens were reserved for the colonnade through which the sanctuary is approached. Here, among others, are a couple of funnel shape, with leaves of the wild thistle completely undercut, and pine cones at the angles, exactly like those on the breccia colonnettes of the mihrab. In the eastern cloister may be seen three of the funnel type exhibiting discs, leaves, and crosses, the latter being either erased or mutilated: the whole without undercutting.

The western side has original wall-arches. The eastern side in the last century underwent a considerable amount of restoration and reconstruction.

In addition to the important works which we have described, Ibrahim must also have erected the two-aisled portico on the north side of the

[1] E. A. Gardner, *Ancient Athens*, pp. 488-491.

[2] Ibn Khaldoun, *Histoire des Berbères et des dynasties musulmanes de l'Afrique septentrionale*, vol. i, pp. 420, 421.

court, thus completing the quadrangular cloister in front of the mosque. As a matter of fact this part, in spite of the alterations and renewals which it has undergone, does betray, where the masonry is ancient, its identity in date with Ibrahim's work.

The minaret which bisects the northern arcade is placed to the left of the main axis of the mosque (Fig. 26, p. 42). It is in the form of a massive tower about 26 m. (85 ft.) high, the side in front being not less than 10.70 m. (35 ft.), and is constructed of materials taken from older buildings, including carved and inscribed stones of the Roman period. The walls are 3.30 m. (10 ft. 10 in.) thick at the base.

The door which opens on the court exhibits another fragment of Roman origin in its lintel, above which is a relieving arch of horse-shoe form. In the XI century a second entrance was made, as is mentioned by Bakri.[1] It has similar rectangular windows with relieving arches of the same form.

At the point where the tower is set back a second stage begins, the faces of which are relieved by blank arches of horse-shoe form. The materials, so far as can be judged from the very little which is visible inside, are different from those of the lower stage of the tower. The form of the external arches would suggest the time of Ziyadat Allah; but as things are, it would be hazardous to give any definite opinion about it, for we do not know whether the earliest minarets terminated in a simple roof to cover the tower and shelter the muezzin, or in some construction of masonry. The earliest example of a minaret with an additional structure on the top that is known to me is the one erected by the Caliph Mutawakkil (847-861) at Samarra, where the shaft was designed to carry a kiosk crowned by a cupola.

Above the second stage rises a third, with open arches supporting a cupola resting on angle niches. It is the result of a reconstruction carried out in the first half of the XIX century.

The lowest stage is the minaret built by Bishr, acting under the orders of Hisham, and not by Hassan as Bakri says.[2] It was precisely in the time of Hisham that the site was secured, for the foundations were laid in water,

[1] *Journal Asiatique*, vol. xii, pp. 412-492; El Bekri (De Slane), *Description de l'Afrique septentrionale.*

[2] Ibid.

as we are told by the same writer.[1] The confusion in Bakri must be due to the mention of Hassan's name in place of that of Hisham.

The exterior faces of the walls, both of the mosque and of the court, including the buttresses of various form and size with which they are strengthened, are so uniformly covered with coats of whitewash that any sort of examination of them is impossible. I will confine myself to noting that the very few pieces of wall surface which are visible, viz. those in the tower buttresses at the outer angles of the mosque proper, have every appearance of belonging to the work of Ibrahim II.

Of the ten entrances which existed in the time of Bakri in the XI century, the two now walled up, which opened into the frontal portico, must be the oldest. They were designed to give access to Ziyadat's court, and were closed in the course of the works of Ibrahim II. What the age of the others may be I cannot say. I only note that the cupola of the portico in front of the 'Bab Lella Regiana' gate, erected in 1284 (Fig. 27, p. 51), has the same form as the one belonging to the corresponding western gate, as well as the one which crowns the minaret, and was rebuilt in the last century. In all three the square base has, besides the angle niches, a small niche in each side.

Apart from its state of preservation and the great variety of ancient columns and capitals which it contains, the most remarkable features of the congregational mosque of Kairawan are: the T plan of the two main aisles, the wooden ties for the arches, the hood-shaped pendentives in the dome over the mihrab, and the minaret, so far as it is original.

The plan may possibly have been used previously in the mosque al-Aqsa at Jerusalem; but we have no certain information. As far as I can see, the mosque of Kairawan was the first example. In Walid's mosque at Damascus (706-714) the architect merely led up to the qibla by a wide transverse aisle.

As to the wooden ties, apparently a device of the Moslem age, though, as we saw before, they were found in St. Irene at Constantinople as early as the VIII century, it has been said that they were employed as far back as the time of Abd al-Malik in the Dome of the Rock at Jerusalem (687-691).[2] Doubts, however, have been thrown on the date of the arches to which they belong. And therefore those in the mosque of Kairawan may be regarded as the oldest specimens. It seems to me that these ties

[1] *Journal Asiatique*, vol. xii, pp. 412-492; El Bekri, *Description de l'Afrique septentrionale.*

[2] De Vogüé, *Le Temple de Jérusalem*, p. 83.

FIG. 17.—Denderah. Temple of Hathor. Portico (I cent.).

FIG. 18.—Kairawan. Congregational Mosque. Dome of the mihrab (IX cent.).

FIG. 20.—Kairawan. Façade of the Congregational Mosque (IX cent.).

FIG. 21.—Athens. Tower of the Winds or Horologium of Andronicus. Interior of the cupola (II or I cent. B.C.).

FIG. 22.—Kairawan. Congregational Mosque. Capitals of the colonnades.

FIG. 24.—Kairawan. Congregational Mosque. Capitals of the colonnades.

FIG. 23.—Kairawan. Congregational Mosque. Capitals of the colonnades.

FIG. 25.—Kairawan. Congregational Mosque. Capitals of the colonnades.

Fig. 26.—Kairawan. Congregational Mosque. Minaret (VIII, IX?, and XIX cents.).

Fig. 28.—Seville. The Giralda (1184-1196).

are connected with the great elevation given to the arches, demanding some counteracting force.

With regard to the conical pendentives, I have not succeeded so far in discovering along the northern coasts of Africa any examples earlier than those in Italy. It was probably by way of Sicily, evacuated by the Byzantines in 882, and finally conquered by the Moslem armies of Ibrahim in 895, that this Romano-Campanian invention reached Kairawan. Nor have I come across any older examples shaped like shells and framed within arches, and recalling the decorative treatment of the upper stage in the interior of the baptistery of Saint Jean at Poitiers (possibly belonging to the years 682-696).[1]

The minaret is the oldest now in existence, and its long life has by no means reached its close. The thickness of the walls, the character of the materials used, the kind of mortar employed, may well assure it some other thousand years of existence, provided that it does not succumb to some natural catastrophe, or to the still more dangerous effects of man's destructive impulses.

The square form, with occasionally a cylindrical upper part, is the prevailing one in early Moslem times, and is illustrated by the minarets of Mutawakkil (847-861) at Samarra, and of Ibn Tulun (872-73-879), and Hakim (990-1003) at Cairo. Abd al-Rahman III's (912-961) rebuilt minaret at Cordova is another example. All the Syrian minarets of the X century belong to the same class.[2]

In addition to its early date the minaret at Kairawan, in the plainness of its exterior, presents one feature which throws some light on the development of structures of this kind. The earliest minarets were plain square towers. The four belonging to the great mosque of Walid at Damascus were, in this respect, just like that at Kairawan. Such at least is the impression given by Ibn Jubair, who in 1184 saw two of them still there (viz. the one on the east and the one on the west) in the form of towers.[3] If they had exhibited any kind of ornament he would have said so, for he mentions various things in the mosque less worthy of notice. The minarets of the mosque at Medina, probably the work of the same caliph, were, as we saw, of a similar fashion.

[1] Rivoira, op. cit. (Loescher), vol. ii, pp. 84-88; (Hoepli), pp. 385-389; (Heinemann), vol. ii, pp. 52-54.

[2] Muqaddasi, op. cit., p. 75.

[3] Ibn Jubair, op. cit., p. 257.

It is not till we reach the IX century and the minaret of the great mosque of Samarra (847-861), or that of the mosque at Abudolaf (which, from its analogies with the former, may also be ascribed to the IX century), that we meet with architectural decoration in the form of niches at the summit or at the base. For though Muqaddasi[1] seems at first sight to say that the minaret erected by Hisham (724-743) for the magnificent White Mosque at Ramleh in Palestine (reduced by the earthquake of 1033 to a heap of ruins[2]) was embellished with columns, his real meaning is that these columns of great size were used in the mosque itself. Not till the caliphate of Abd al-Rahman III (912-961) do we meet with any free use of architectural and artistic ornament: and what there is, is worthy of that distinguished ruler. Thus Edrisi,[3] describing the minaret of the congregational mosque of Cordova, mentions that the four sides were ornamented with two tiers of arches springing from marble columns of great beauty, and that the front was further embellished 'with the products of the various arts of gilding, lettering, and painting.' This elaborate decorative treatment of minarets must have created a tradition in the Spanish provinces if it lasted till the gradual decay of the Moslem dominion, as is evidenced by the Giralda at Seville (1184-1196) (Fig. 28, p. 42), originally the minaret of the principal mosque of the city, which fell into Christian hands in 1248. It seems to have been inspired by the now curtailed minaret of Hassan at Rabat in Morocco (1178-1184).

This gradual growth of the artistic treatment of the minaret may be compared with the similar evolution in the case of the bell-tower or campanile. At Ravenna the bell-tower of Sant' Apollinare Nuovo was, between 850 and 878, embellished by the insertion of two- and three-light openings with marble shafts, and sometimes terra-cotta bowls ('ciotole') fixed in the spandrels of the arches; and also by the use of the saw-tooth stringcourse.[4] At Milan, again, the tower of San Satiro, of 876, exhibited for the first time the architectural scheme which was to be characteristic of the Lombardic campanile and its derivatives.[5] I would note here that the date

[1] Op. cit., pp. 33, 34.

[2] Nasiri Kusru, op. cit., p. 64, note.

[3] Edrisi (Jaubert), *Géographie*, vol. ii, pp. 62, 63.

[4] Rivoira, op. cit. (Loescher), vol. i, pp. 48-54; (Hoepli), pp. 45-58; (Heinemann), vol. i, pp. 44-53.

[5] Ibid. (Loescher), vol. i, pp. 273-275; (Hoepli), pp. 203, 204; (Heinemann), vol. i, p. 169.

1045, which there has been an attempt to attach to its oldest part, is wrong. Both masonry and artistic features are opposed to it.

Before leaving the congregational mosque of Kairawan, I may say a few words about the origin of the Composite capital—a digression suggested by the very frequent occurrence of that form among the alien capitals there to be found.

I have dealt elsewhere [1] with its invention, which I place in the reign of the first two Flavian emperors (69-81); and I have pointed out that it appears in its developed form on the Arch of Titus (79-81), erected after his death (Fig. 29, p. 52). It was still unknown in the time of Augustus (29 B.C.-14 A.D.), as we learn from Vitruvius, who lived under the great emperor to whom he dedicated his book,[2] or else, as has been thought, in the last quarter of the century preceding the Christian era.[3] In that work there is no mention of the Composite among either the principal or the derived forms of capitals.[4]

THE DOME OF THE ROCK, OR QUBBAT AS-SAKRAH AT JERUSALEM, COMMONLY CALLED THE MOSQUE OF OMAR, stands over the Sacred Rock in the centre of Herod's temple. Its founder was Abd al-Malik, and his object was to restore the ancient Jewish qibla and make it a rival to the Black Stone of Mecca, so as to divert the streams of pilgrims from the latter city. His real motives were dynastic and political; and in the structure he raised he aimed at dazzling the eyes and the minds of the followers of Mohammed, and making them forget the grandeur and magnificence of the rotunda of the Holy Sepulchre. Such is the account of Muqaddasi.[5]

The fact of the foundation is still attested by the well-known inscription in Cufic characters, running above the cornice of the colonnade which supports the dome. Caliph Mamun's (813-833) fraudulent substitution of his own name for that of the real founder is easily detected. As a matter of fact, the Arabic writers unanimously ascribe the building to its true author.

The foundation was accompanied by the erection of the mosque al-Aqsa, in imitation of Constantine's idea of the 'Martyrion' and the 'Anastasis' at Jerusalem, orientated on the same axis.

[1] *Nuova Antologia*, 1904, fasc. 790; RIVOIRA, *Della scoltura ornamentale dai tempi di Roma imperiale al Mille.*

[2] *De Architectura*, lib. i.

[3] CHOISY, *Vitruve*, vol. i, pp. 365-369.

[4] *De Architectura*, iii, 5; iv, 1; iv, 3; iv, 7.

[5] Op. cit., p. 23.

The works and expenses were put in charge of the learned Rija ibn Hayah of the Kinda tribe, and Yazid ibn Sallam, a native of Jerusalem, with his two sons as assistants. Later, Suliman (715-717) fetched another inhabitant of Jerusalem to superintend the erection of his magnificent mosque at Lydda; and the man was a Christian called Bakah.[1] The rotunda was begun in 687, and the works were completed in 691. It is said that they swallowed up the revenues of Egypt for seven years. On the eastern side a building was erected intended for a treasury.

The workmen were drawn from every part of the Moslem provinces. Ibn Khaldun,[2] who, as we saw, substituted the name of Walid for that of Abd al-Malik, would make out that the workmen were sent by the Emperor of Constantinople. What is certain is that when, some years later, in 700, the same Abd al-Malik wanted to repair the damage which Mecca and his temple had suffered from an inundation, he entrusted the works to a Christian architect.[3]

Under Caliph Mamun the building underwent some restoration, but what its nature was we do not know. One view is that it was confined to some repair of details,[4] while another is that the outer wall was rebuilt.[5] The latter appears to be based on the bronze tablet with Cufic inscription attached to the outer face of the lintel over each of the four entrances, bearing the date 831, and referring to works carried out by order of Mamun, who entrusted them to an emancipated slave, Salih ibn Yahya. If this theory be correct—and the earthquake shocks which shattered the mosque al-Aqsa suggest that the Dome of the Rock must have felt their effects to some extent—it would explain up to a certain point the falsification of Abd al-Malik's inscription.

The earliest description is that of Ibn al-Fakih (903). We learn that it had four entrances, each with its marble porch; and each entrance had four doors. The number of windows was fifty-six. The dome had an inner and an outer cupola, the latter being gilded. Twelve piers and thirty columns supported the structure. The aisles were covered with sheets of lead, and the whole was faced with marble. Here the number

[1] Le Strange, *Palestine under the Moslems*, p. 304.

[2] *Prolégomènes historiques*, vol. ii, pp. 268, 375.

[3] Amari, op. cit., vol. iii, 2, p. 837.

[4] De Vogüé, *Le Temple de Jérusalem*, p. 86.

[5] *The Survey of Eastern Palestine*, 1889; Conder, *The Adwan Country*, pp. 60-63.

of columns is inexplicable, as there cannot have been more than twenty-eight combined with the twelve piers. A similar difficulty is caused by the forty-eight or more columns recorded by Ibn abd Rabbih (about 913).

Some repairs were executed in 913. We have another description by Muqaddasi about the year 985. The octagon had four porches, with four doors apiece, that is to say, three which opened between the columns of the portico, and one in the outer wall. The interior contained three concentric colonnades with low ceilings. The central part was circular, with marble columns and round arches carrying a high drum pierced with large windows, and the dome. The dome was double. The internal dome was divided into ornamental compartments; the external dome was simply constructed of timber covered with sheets of gilt metal. There was a free space between the two domes, which were kept in place by iron rods crossing one another. The rest of the structure, including the drum, was decorated, both internally and externally, with marbles and mosaics, after the fashion of Walid's mosque at Damascus.

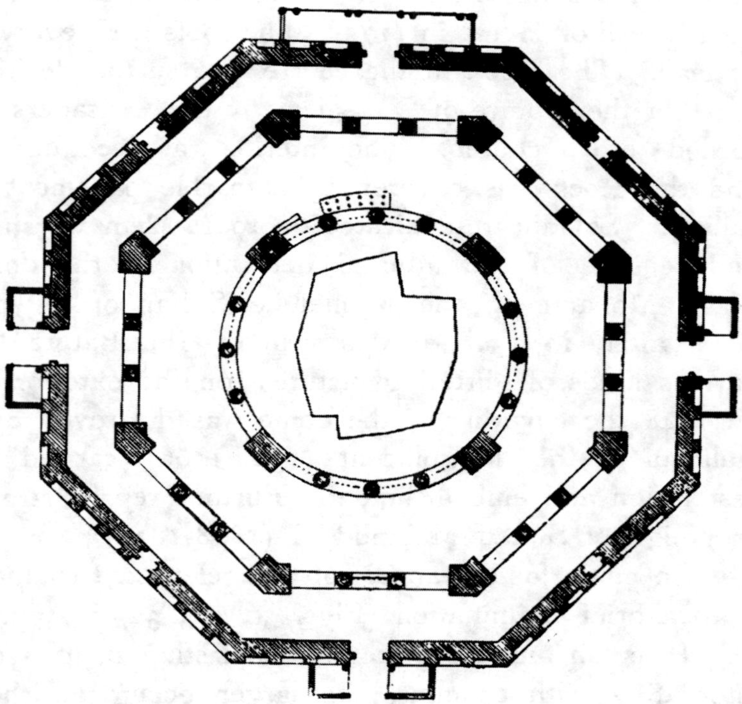

FIG. 30.—Jerusalem. Plan of the Dome of the Rock (VII, IX, XI, and XII cents.).

In 1016 the dome collapsed in an earthquake, and the outer walls at the south-east angle were damaged. Zahir, the Caliph of Egypt (1020-1035), ordered the restorations recorded for the years 1022, 1027, and 1033. Among the works executed on this occasion were the mosaics of the drum. The restored building was not long after (in 1047) visited and described by

Nasiri Kusru.[1] His measurements agree with the actual ones, but the same cannot be said of the distribution and number of the supports. The smaller colonnade in those days contained four piers alternating with pairs of columns (eight in all); the larger had eight piers with twenty-four columns interposed in threes. In the present building it is in the smaller colonnade that the alternation of piers and three columns occurs, while that of piers and pairs of columns is in the larger. The existing arrangement is the same as that seen by Ali of Herat in 1173. The roofs were everywhere covered with sheets of lead. The Rock in the centre was surrounded by a marble balustrade.

On the capture of Jerusalem by the Crusaders in 1099 the building was turned into a church. The interior was decorated with Christian paintings, and the Rock was covered by a marble pavement and enclosed by an iron railing. Saladin re-dedicated it to Moslem worship, with some restoration and renewal of the internal decoration of the dome. In 1318 and 1319 Nasir Mohammed, the Mameluke Sultan of Egypt, effected some repairs. Soon after, in 1326, it was seen by Ibn Batuta,[2] who found it rich 'with various kinds of glittering pictures' on the exterior as well as in the interior. In 1448 the covering of the dome was destroyed by a fire, but was replaced. Suliman I the Magnificent (1520-1566) carried out important works of restoration and embellishment. Further repairs are attested in 1776, and in the reign of Sultan Mahmud II (1808-1839).[3]

So much for the annals of this celebrated rotunda. We will next subject it to a brief examination (Figs. 30, 31, 32, 33, pp. 47, 51, 52, 53).

It is an annular structure, consisting of two concentric circles of piers alternating with columns, the larger octagonal, the smaller circular. The outer wall forms a regular octagon, each side measuring about 21 m. (69 ft.) on the outer face which contains seven lofty blank arches, five of which are pierced by as many large windows, round-headed in construction, or in other cases by four windows and a door. The four entrances are placed at the cardinal points, and each is protected by a porch.

In the outer range the round arches spring from Ravennate pulvins of varying height so as to fit the columns, and are kept in place by substantial wooden ties, each of which consists of a pair of rafters fitted together, con-

[1] Op. cit., pp. 89-93. [2] Op. cit., vol. i, p. 122.

[3] De Vogüé, *Le Temple de Jérusalem*, pp. 73-98. Le Strange, *Palestine under the Moslems*, pp. 83-171.

cealed under an embossed and painted stucco decoration or a skin of marble facing of the XVI century. In the inner range, on the other hand, the arches spring immediately from the capitals, and here again they have wooden ties, but left plain and bare.

The eight trapezoidal piers at the angles of the larger or outer range are extended so as to carry the beams of the aisle roofs. On the other hand, the four belonging to the inner range, which are rectangular, but on their longer sides follow the curve of the dome, are carried up so as to form the external buttresses designed to strengthen the drum. The inner face of the drum is decorated with mosaics.

The capitals are of two kinds: (1) Corinthian, slightly bell-shaped, with two rows of acanthus leaves, the points of which arch over, in style intermediate between Roman and Byzantine. One of them has a cross on the abacus. (2) Composite (Fig. 34, p. 52) with vase-shaped outline like the former, and acanthus leaves which are either free or bend over at the tips as before. They are all of alien origin, as are the shafts which they surmount, and the bases of the latter, now concealed within XVI-century pedestals, but known to be of the same character. They are obviously later in date than the capitals of the church of the Nativity at Bethlehem (327-333) (Fig. 35, p. 54), which are still Roman in style; but they are earlier than the birth of the Byzantine capital with crisply raffled leaves of the *Acanthus spinosus*, which was invented by the School of Salonica in the V century.

The dome, slightly curved inwards at the base, where the internal diameter measures 20.60 m. (about 68 ft.), is of wood and double, the outer dome being covered with lead. The inner surface has stucco decoration, painted and gilded. At the spring of the dome runs a wooden gallery, following its curve and opening into the interior. It is reached by an iron staircase fixed against the outer face of the drum. The internal height of the dome is 30.60 m. (about 100 ft.) above the floor of the aisles.

When the outer face of the external wall on the west and south-west was stripped during the restoration of 1873 and 1874, the nature of the masonry was laid bare. It consisted of courses of stone blocks of various heights. At the top of the wall an unsuspected decorative feature was discovered in the shape of a range of decorative niches crowning the octagon and forming a sort of external gallery, not for use, but to serve as an ornamental finish to the building. It belongs, in fact, to the class of galleries the earliest specimen of which is to be seen in the apse of Sant' Ambrogio at Milan (789-824) (Fig. 36, p. 53). The illustrations published by Clermont-Ganneau[1] show these niches (of which there were thirteen on each face) as round arches springing from dwarf piers, with angle shafts carved out of the piers, and surmounted by Lombardic cubical capitals formed by the interpenetration of a sphere and a cube. Observations made before the niches were once more hidden by the replacing of the facing showed that originally they were open arches, which were afterwards turned into niches decorated with mosaics, and were finally filled in with stone. Clermont-Ganneau considered that they were of the same date as the foundation of the rotunda, and originally intended for windows which, later, were blocked by the lowering of the roof of the aisles.

As it is impossible to be sure whether the construction of the outer wall was really all of a piece, or even to compare it with other walls in the building with the object of establishing their identity in date, I confine myself to the following observations.

(1) The outer wall near the top is set back to the extent of a metre, the original intention being, no doubt, to provide a support for the timbers of the roof; and accordingly the existence of windows in that part of the wall would be inexplicable. From another point of view it is incredible that the beams rested on the top of the wall, thus giving room for the supposed windows to light the aisles, for in that case the slope of the roof would have interfered, at the point where it touched the drum, with the plane of light of the drum itself, or else would not have had a sufficient gradient to throw off the rain water. Therefore we must dismiss the idea of a range of windows at the top of the wall.

(2) Ibn al-Fakih, who counted the windows in 903, found only the fifty-six which are there to-day. And though he records the number of piers, of columns, and even of the steps leading to the platform on which the octagon stands, he makes no mention of the niches which crowned it.[2]

(3) In 1047 Nasiri Kusru[3] measured the height of the perimetral walls, and found it to be 20 cubits, that is to say, nearly the same as the present height of 11 m. (about 36 ft.). He also gives an account of the way in

[1] *Palestine Exploration Fund; Archaeological Researches in Palestine during the years 1873-1874; The Kubbet es Sakhra*, 1899, vol. i, pp. 179-227.

[2] Le Strange, *Palestine under the Moslems*, pp. 120, 121.

[3] Op. cit., p. 91.

FIG. 27.—Kairawan. Congregational Mosque.
Lella Regiana Bab (XIII cent.).

FIG. 31.—Jerusalem. The Dome of the Rock (VII, IX, XI, and XII cents.).

FIG. 32.—Jerusalem. The Dome of the Rock. Interior (VII, IX, XI, and XII cents.).

FIG. 29.—Rome. Arch of Titus. Capital.

FIG. 34.—Jerusalem. The Dome of the Rock. Capital of the VI cent.

Fig. 33.—Jerusalem. The Dome of the Rock. Interior, with the Sacred Rock (VII, IX. XI, and XII cents.).

Fig. 36.—Milan. Basilica of Sant' Ambrogio. View of the end of the church, with the apse of 789-824.

FIG. 35.—Bethlehem. Church of the Nativity. One of the colonnades of the nave (327-333).

which they were built; but he makes no allusion to the range of niches: yet we know that his architectural description of the rotunda is both minute and accurate. Not one geographer, or topographer, or pilgrim mentions these niches, up to the day when Suliman covered them up with his new facing.

(4) The cubico-spherical Lombardic capital, the history of which I have traced elsewhere,[1] is never found—at least I have never been able to find it—in the East before the time of the Crusades. Hence it is unlikely that such a conspicuous use of it should have been made in the days of Abd al-Malik, and that afterwards it should have been forgotten for so many centuries both in Palestine and in Syria.

If I may hazard what is merely an opinion, and always assuming that the walls are all of one date, I think that when the outer wall was built, or rebuilt under Mamun, it was intended to finish it off with battlements, as had been done in the congregational mosque of Damascus;[2] but later, after the walls had been constructed, the design was changed; arches were turned at the top of the walls, and then converted into niches. This work is the more likely to have been done in the time of Mamun, considering that, a little later, the minaret of the mosque of Mutawakkil at Samarra (847-861) was ornamented with niches at the summit, a feature which, on the other hand, did not appear in the congregational mosque of Damascus (706-714), in the construction of which, possibly, some of Abd al-Malik's workmen from Jerusalem were engaged. At a later date, during the Crusaders' occupation of Jerusalem, or, perhaps, in the course of Saladin's restoration, the angle shafts, with their cubical capitals, were carved, while the mosaics, with which the outer face of the wall was covered in its upper half, were either renewed or restored. Finally, when Suliman had the whole wall refaced, the niches were built up.

Constructively, the windows in the Dome of the Rock are round-headed like the arches of the colonnades. It was the new facing which altered their appearance. The doors, placed at the cardinal points of the compass, are rectangular, and have lintels with recessed relieving arches. The porches which protect them have been either altered or rebuilt.

The arrangement of the interior does not appear to be original, as has been always supposed. The only part which can be regarded as original is the

[1] RIVOIRA, op. cit. (Loescher), vol. ii, pp. 563-566; (Hoepli), pp. 254-257; (Heinemann), vol. i, pp. 207-209.

[2] MUQADDASI, op. cit., p. 17.

disposition of the piers. Nasiri Kusru says distinctly that only two columns alternated with the piers in the smaller circle, while there were three in the larger; whereas Ali of Herat saw them distributed as they are to-day. The inference would be that between 1047 and 1173 the annular arcades were rebuilt, with an increase of the number of columns in the one which carried the drum and the dome—the object being to augment its capacity for bearing the superimposed weight—and a diminution of the number in the outer circle. The band with Abd al-Malik's inscription would not be touched, though the decoration below it would be renewed.

My own examination of the building does not confirm De Vogüé's view that the problems which it involves are of easy solution. On the contrary, it presents me with a whole series of questions demanding answers. To satisfy them would require the testing of the masonry in the different parts of the building, as well as a fresh examination of its artistic features. These problems have been increased by the instructive information which Clermont-Ganneau has furnished about the buttresses at the base of the dome, which differ in structure from that of the lower part of the drum on its outer face, and also about the stringcourse breaking the inner surface of the drum, and evidently belonging to the age of the Crusades. A third point is the construction of the piers in the inner circle, which are composed of rough blocks of stone and even of rubble, and are quite unlike the masonry of the outer wall.

Round about the great rotunda stand various smaller ones, records of which exist from the year 903 onwards. At that date, according to Ibn al-Fakih, they consisted of the Dome of the Chain, situated in front of the eastern entrance of the Dome of the Rock, which was supported by twenty marble columns and covered with lead; the Dome of the Prophet, to the north of the Rock; and the Dome of the Ascension. They are also mentioned by Muqaddasi in 985, who describes them as of small dimensions, covered with lead, supported by marble shafts, and open on all sides.[1]

We will confine ourselves to the Dome of the Chain (Fig. 37, p. 63), as Arabic writers[2] have stated that it was founded by Abd al-Malik to serve as a treasury; nor have there been wanting those who, in our own days, have believed that it is contemporary with the Dome of the Rock.[3]

[1] LE STRANGE, *Palestine under the Moslems*, pp. 121, 123.

[2] Ibid., pp. 145, 153.

[3] DE VOGÜÉ, *Le Temple de Jérusalem*, p. 104.

This structure is a kiosk, consisting of an internal range of six columns supporting a hexagonal drum covered by a cupola, and an external concentric one of eleven columns (two being included in the mihrab) which form the outer open hendecagonal arcade. The arches are semicircular, with wooden ties. The marble shafts with their bases have been brought from elsewhere. The capitals are of various types and dates, from the funnel or melon-shaped ones of Byzantine origin, down to others betraying the artistic decadence which we shall see in the capitals made expressly for the galleries in the congregational mosque of Damascus, and to be ascribed to the time either of Abd al-Malik or of Mahdi. Lastly, there are some of Arabic style and still later date.

It is obvious that the building has undergone frequent alterations. Thus we know that Ibn al-Fakih (903) found it possessing twenty marble columns, whereas Nasiri Kursu (1047) saw eight marble columns and six stone piers. At the present time only seventeen columns are to be seen. Mujiraddin (1496) states distinctly that it was rebuilt by Baybars I (1260-1277), Sultan of Egypt.[1]

Such being the state of the case, and the facings preventing an examination of the masonry, it is impossible to speak definitely about the building. I will only mention the following points:—

(1) Two features, the round arches and the wooden ties which some of them have, may bring it into relation with the Dome of the Rock, and suggest that it belongs to the same date. But do not the walls of the mosque al-Aqsa, the date of which is quite uncertain, also contain round-headed windows? And as for the wooden ties, is there not a serious doubt whether those in Abd al-Malik's building may not be later than 1047?

(2) It would be astonishing to find a building of such light construction, and yet strong enough to survive the series of earthquakes which have passed over the Haram, and shattered or damaged the structures upon it.

(3) Lastly, if it is true that its original purpose was a treasury, it cannot have had its present form, but rather must have resembled the treasury belonging to the mosque of Walid at Damascus (which we shall deal with presently), viz. a group of columns supporting an enclosed structure covered by a dome.

The Dome of the Rock, the most beautiful of the earlier Moslem religious

[1] Le Strange, *Palestine under the Moslems*, pp. 121, 152, 153.

buildings, judging by those which survive and I have seen, conveys two important lessons.

The persistent use of the round arch all through the works carried out in the building before the time of Suliman—the service-gallery in the dome, with its three-lobed arches, is an exception—indicates the form of arch to which Abd al-Malik's workmen were accustomed, which was still in use after his time, and is recorded by Muqaddasi.

The adoption of a wooden dome illustrates the traditional practice in Palestine of using timber for cupolas of large size, a practice perhaps due to the frequency and severity of earthquakes in those regions. Thus the 'Anastasis' of the Holy Sepulchre at Jerusalem had a wooden roof, as I have shown elsewhere.[1] And my opinion has the following evidence behind it.

The very brief account of Eusebius[2] leaves us without information as to the nature of the roof of the rotunda of the Resurrection. But the monk Antiochus[3] tells us that at the capture of Jerusalem (614) by Chosroes II it was burned, a fact which betrays the material of which it was composed. He also informs us that it was restored by the patriarch Modestus (616-626). An Armenian pilgrim tells us that the dome of the restored building was raised on two tiers of columns, twelve in each range; and that its height of 100 cubits was equal to the diameter of the whole building.[4] We learn from Arculf[5] that it consisted of two concentric ranges of isolated supports enclosed within an outer wall.

Modestus afterwards reconstructed the dome as it was before, that is to say, in wood. The fact is confirmed by the statement of Eutychius[6] that, between 813 and 833, the patriarch Thomas imported fifty cedar and pine trunks from Cyprus, and set to work to rebuild it. 'Gradually removing the roof he reconstructed it by the insertion of these new beams.' But his reconstruction took the form of a double dome: 'Above this roof he erected another one of wood leaving a space between the two in which a man could

[1] RIVOIRA, op. cit. (Loescher), vol. ii, pp. 14-36; (Hoepli), pp. 327-348; (Heinemann), vol. ii, pp. 12-26.

[2] EUSEBIUS, *Vita Constantini*, iii, 34.

[3] MIGNE, *Patr. gr.*, vol. lxxxix, col. 1427, 1428; *Epistola Antiochi Monachi.*

[4] *Palestine Exploration Fund*, 1896, pp. 346-349; (Nisbet Bain), *Armenian Description of the Holy Places in the Seventh Century;* MOSES KAGANKATWATSI, *History of Agvan.*

[5] TOBLER, op. cit., vol. i, pp. 146-150; *Arculfi Relatio de Locis Sanctis.*

[6] MIGNE, *Patr. gr.*, vol. cxi, col. 1130, 1131; EUTYCHIUS, *Annales.*

walk'—just like the Dome of the Rock. This explains why he was accused of having rebuilt it on a larger scale than the old one, and in consequence, put in prison.

But in Jerusalem the 'Resurrection' was not the only round church with a wooden roof, for the same material was used in that of the Ascension on the Mount of Olives, which was rebuilt from the foundations by the patriarch Modestus [1] to replace Constantine's church on the same site.[2] It is described by Arculf,[3] who states that its plan imitated that of the Resurrection, and that it had a wooden roof, except in the central part, where it was open to the air.

The plan of Abd al-Malik's great building has been invariably regarded as Byzantine or Hellenistic in origin, from the idea that it was derived from Constantine's round churches at the Holy Places, and that these were earlier than the annular rotundas of the West. Choisy [4] connects it with the cathedral of Bosra (511-12), the plan of which he describes as Eastern. I have demonstrated elsewhere,[5] by the evidence of facts, the incorrectness of so unfounded yet widely accepted a theory, revived of late by Strzygowski [6] with fresh additions; and I have shown how, on the contrary, it was in Pagan Rome that the conception of the annular rotunda, with columns or piers, vaulted, and crowned with a true and proper dome, was created and developed; for in architecture new ideas appear first in germ, and only later reach development and perfection. The demonstration was perfectly natural, for the circular plan was a characteristic product of Roman architecture, and its origin may be traced back to the primitive Italian hut-dwelling.[7] When the new discoveries of Boni on the Palatine at Rome have been fully investigated, they will be found to shed fresh light on the subject.

All that the East did was occasionally to produce circular buildings of unbroken outline, with an internal colonnade designed as an additional support for the roof, which was usually conical in form. Such was the Tholos of

[1] MIGNE, *Patr. gr.*, vol. lxxxix, col. 1427, 1428; *Epistola Antiochi Monachi.*

[2] EUSEBIUS, *Vita Constantini*, iii, 43.

[3] TOBLER, op. cit., vol. i, pp. 162-165; *Arculfi Relatio de Locis Sanctis.*

[4] *Histoire de l'architecture*, vol. ii, p. 97.

[5] RIVOIRA, op. cit. (Loescher), vol. ii, pp. 31-36; (Hoepli), pp. 343-348; (Heinemann), vol. ii, pp. 23-26.

[6] *The Burlington Magazine*, Dec. 1911; *The Origin of Christian Art.*

[7] STUART JONES, *Companion to Roman History*, pp. 89, 190.

Epidaurus,[1] the plan of which I reproduce from Marquand[2] (Fig. 38). But whenever an Eastern architect wanted to cover the central space of such buildings with a vault, he had to turn to Roman models for the design.

On the present occasion, without discussing the grander circular structures still standing, such as the Pantheon (120-124), and the Imperial Mausoleum known as Santa Costanza (326-329), I confine myself to reproducing a series of plans of enclosed buildings of circular plan, vaulted, and of either simple or annular form, taken from Montano[3] (Figs. 39, 40, 41, 42, 43, 44, pp. 61, 62, 65) and Bramantino[4] (Figs. 45, 46, 47, 48, 49, p. 66). The fact that these buildings were designed for tombs or temples, as well as their structural importance, show that they cannot be later than either the year 313, or the transfer of the seat of empire to Constantinople. In one case I also reproduce the elevation (Fig. 42) as it shows an unlighted gallery round the upper stage—a sort of anticipation of the service passages round mediaeval apses. Some of these structures were of very great size: one, for instance, on the road to Marino, was more than 19 m. (62 ft.) in diameter.

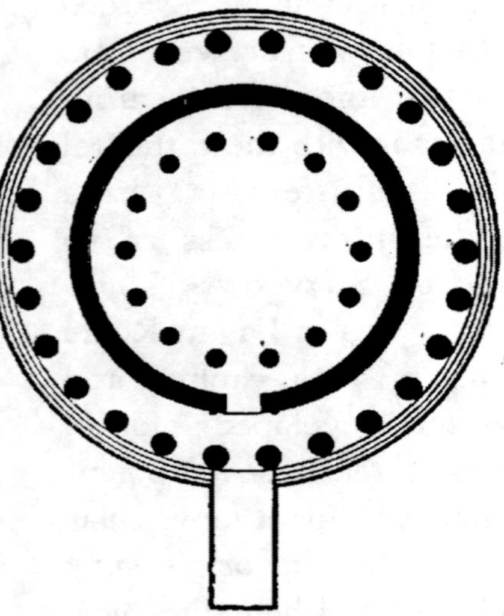

FIG. 38.—Epidaurus. Tholos.

The plan of the annular rotunda was not the only creation of the Roman as against Eastern builders. The fact is equally true of polygonal structures with recessed rectangular or semicircular niches. Constantine's octagonal church at Antioch has indeed

[1] CAVVADIAS, Τὸ ἱερὸν τοῦ 'Ασκληπιοῦ ἐν 'Επιδαύρῳ, pp. 48-71.

[2] *Greek Architecture*, pp. 306, 307.

[3] *Scielta de varii tempietti antichi*, tavv. 2, 30; *Raccolta de tempii e sepolcri disegnati dall' antico*, tavv. 5, 22, 23, 40.

With regard to the illustrations of Montano it may be noted: that the plans are correct; that the elevations have the missing parts restored from what survived; and that the decorative and artistic details are on the whole imaginary. There is no foundation for Soria's statement (in the Preface to Montano's work) that the buildings which he describes 'could not possibly have existed in elevation'; for some of them are standing at the present day, such as the Nymphaeum of the Horti Liciniani and the round church of Santa Costanza.

[4] MONGERI (Studi del Bramantino), *Le rovine di Roma al principio del sec. XVI*, tavv. 47, 53, 54, 55, 69.

been alleged as the prototype of this design; and, as a matter of fact, its interior did display an alternation of such recesses: 'Within, the house of prayer was raised to an immense height, having the form of an octagon, surrounded on every side by chambers (or compartments) both on the upper and on the ground floor.'[1] And it seems to have had a flat roof.[2] But a building of this kind, the appearance of which cannot be satisfactorily reconstructed from such a slight and vague description, has no predecessors

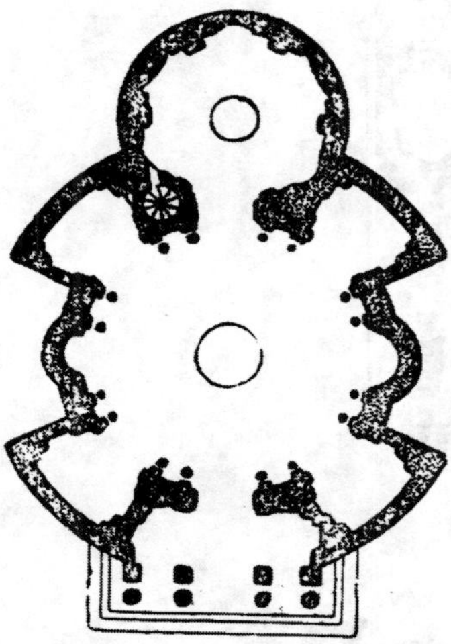

FIG. 39.

FIG. 40.

FIGS. 39 and 40.—Plans of ancient Roman circular buildings.
(From MONTANO, *Scielta de varii tempietti antichi*, tavv. 2, 30.)

in the Eastern world. Rome, on the other hand, at one time displayed innumerable structures of this type, mostly of the Pagan epoch and sepulchral in character, exhibiting the most extraordinary, ingenious, complicated outlines imaginable. The plans of some of these are here reproduced, borrowed from Bramantino[3] (Figs. 50, 51, p. 67) and Montano[4] (Figs. 52, 53, 54, pp. 67, 68). Another may still be seen in the great Nymphaeum of the Licinian Gardens (253-268).

[1] EUSEBIUS, *Vita Constantini*, iii, 50.

[2] DE VOGÜÉ, *Syrie centrale. Architecture civile et religieuse du Ier au VIIe Siècle*, vol. i, p. 15.

[3] MONGERI, op cit., tavv. 29, 33.

[4] *Scielta de varii tempietti antichi*, tavv. 42, 43; *Raccolta de tempii e sepolcri disegnati dall' antico*, tav. 21.

The complicated internal outline of buildings with the circular plan had been developed at Rome in the early Imperial age, starting with

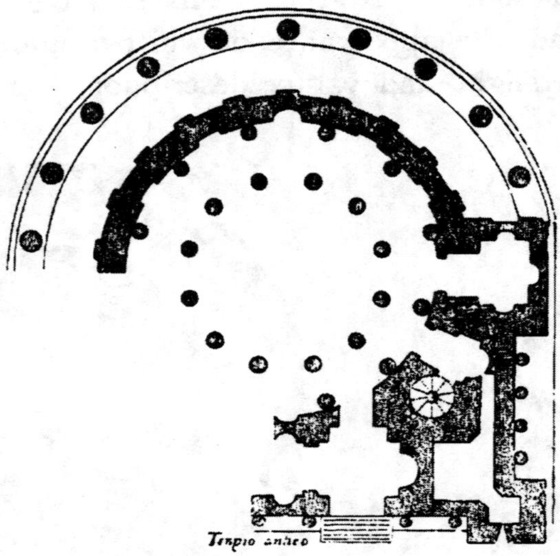

FIG. 41.

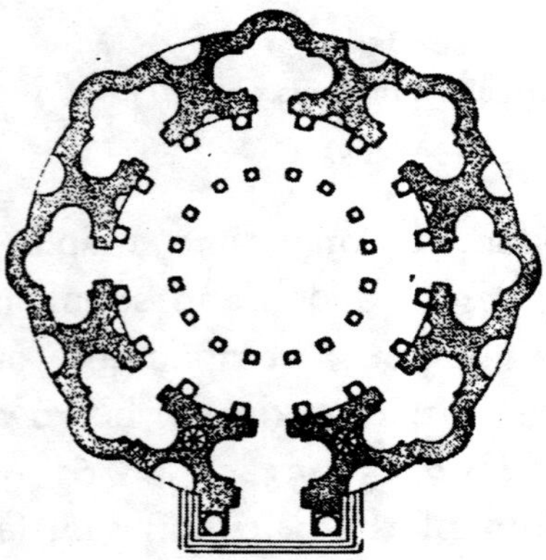

FIG. 43.

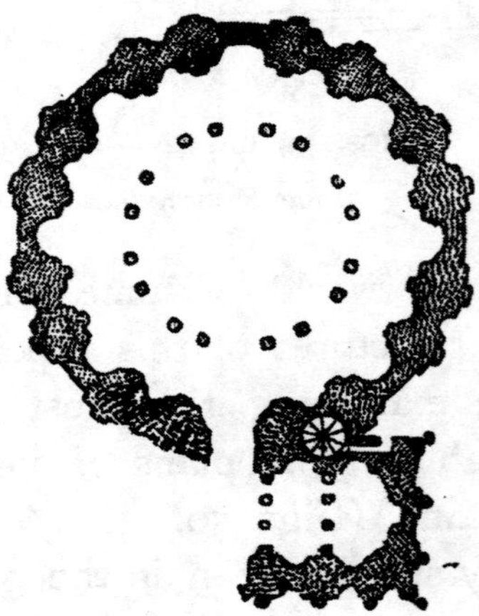

FIG. 44.

FIGS. 41, 43, and 44.—Plans of ancient Roman circular buildings.

(From MONTANO, *Raccolta ae tempii e sepolcri disegnati dall' antico*, tavv. 5, 23, 40.)

the Frigidarium in the Stabian Baths at Pompeii, which were of Oscan origin in the II century B.C., but had been remodelled some time after the establishment of a Roman colony there (80 B.C.) in the time of

FIG. 37.—Jerusalem. The Dome of the Chain, or 'Judgment-seat of David.'

FIG. 56.—Tivoli. Villa of Hadrian. Vestibule of the 'Piazza d'Oro' (125-135).

FIG. 57.—Rome. Building in the Campus Martius, called the 'Tempio di Siepe' (117-138).

(From GIOVANNOLI, *Vedute degli antichi vestigj di Roma*, fogl. 39.)

FIG. 60.—Spalato. The Imperial Mausoleum, now the Cathedral (300-305).

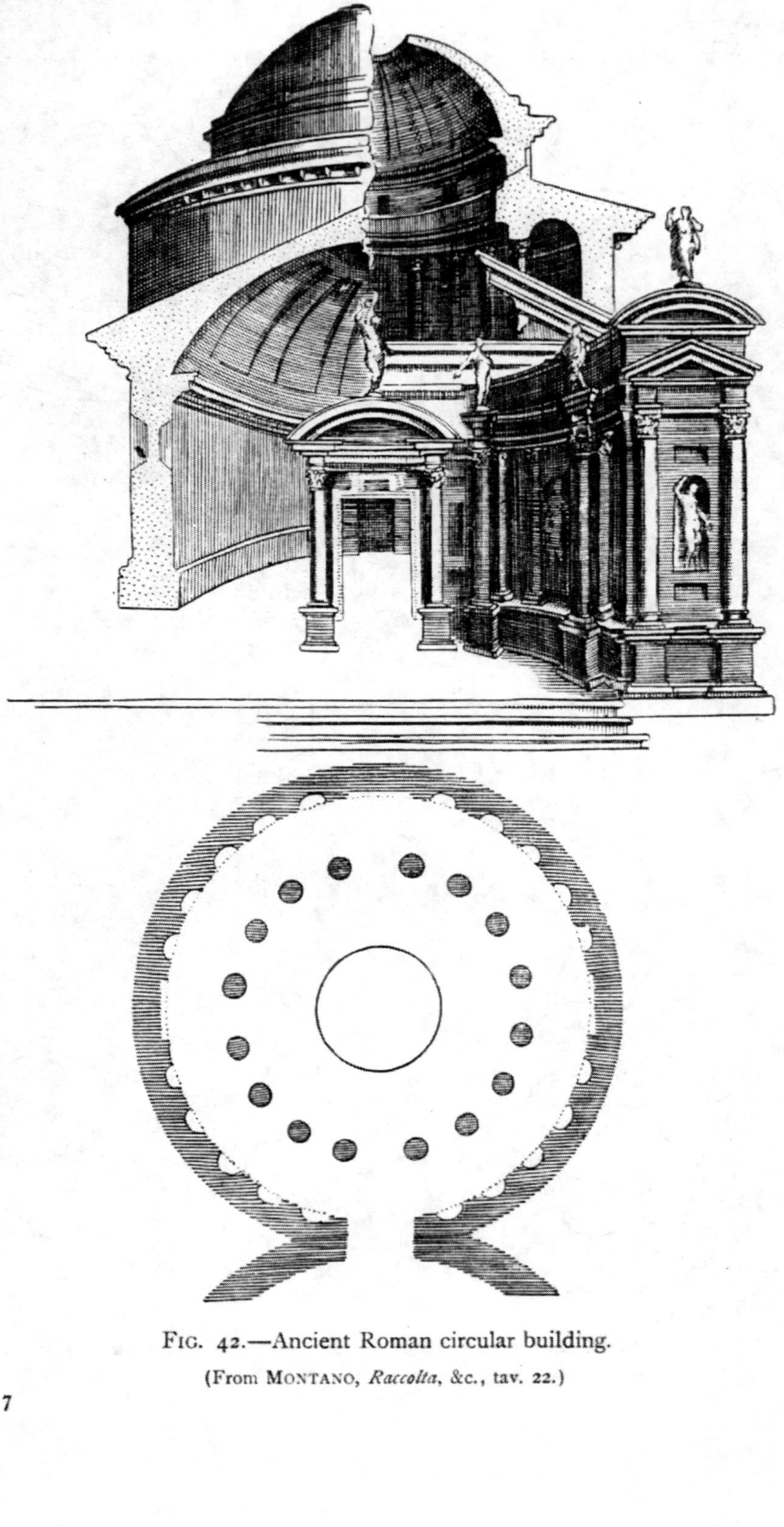

FIG. 42.—Ancient Roman circular building.

(From MONTANO, *Raccolta*, &c., tav. 22.)

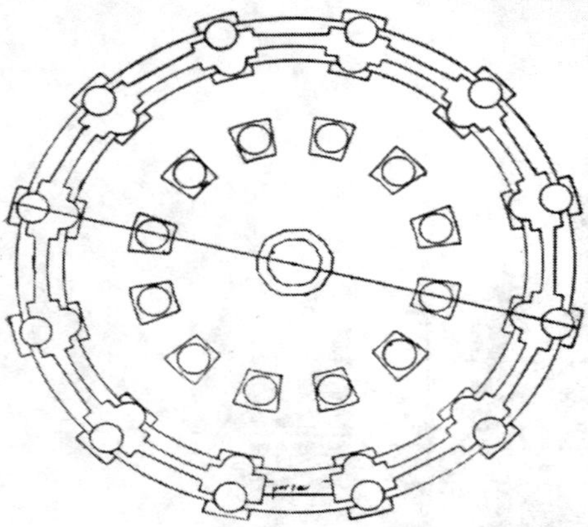

FIG. 45.

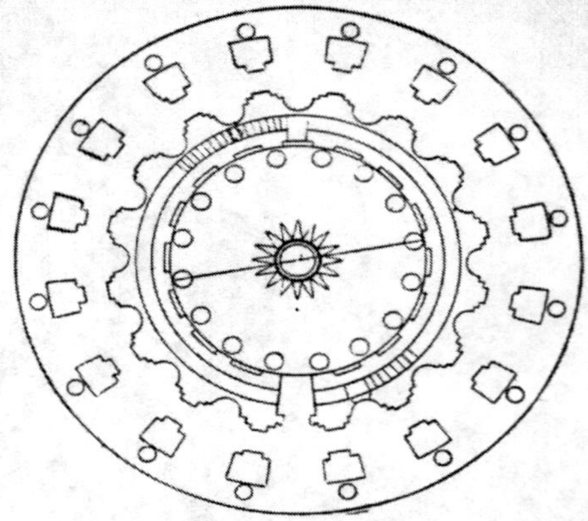

FIG. 46.

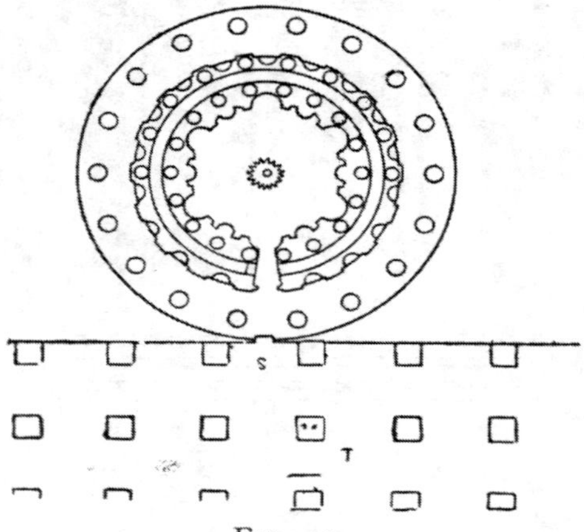

FIG. 47.

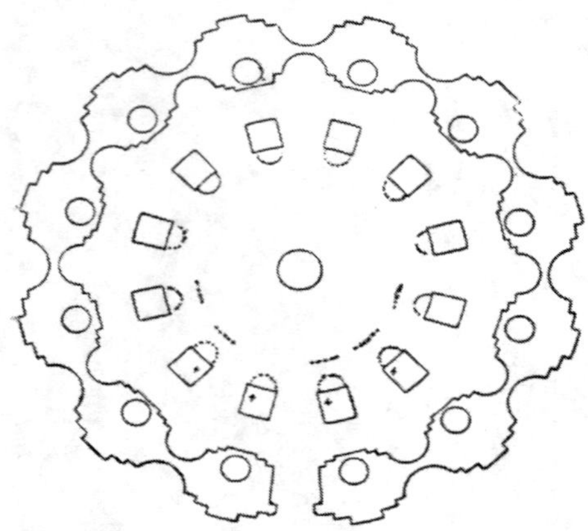

FIG. 48.

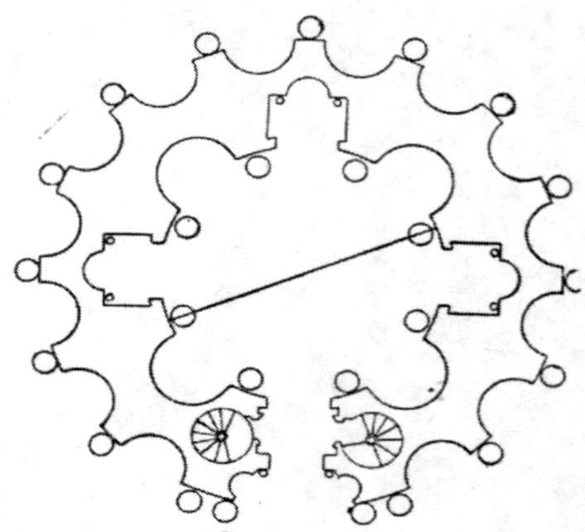

FIG. 49.

FIGS. 45, 46, 47, 48, and 49.—Plans of ancient Roman circular buildings.
(From MONGERI, *Le rovine*, &c., tavv. 47, 53, 54, 55, 69.)

Sulla.[1] Another instance is the Domus Augustana as rebuilt (about 85) by Domitian. But it was the Emperor Hadrian, with all his architectural genius,[2]

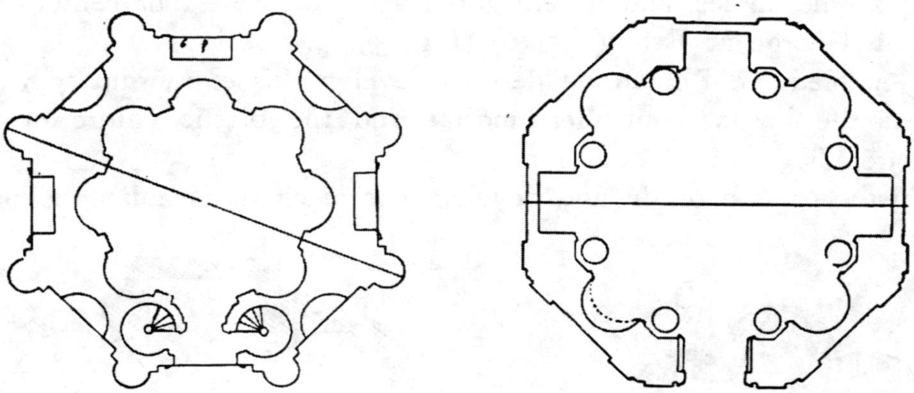

FIG. 50. FIG. 51.

FIGS. 50 and 51.—Plans of ancient Roman polygonal buildings.
(From MONGERI, *Le rovine*, &c., tavv. 29, 33.)

who gave the chief impulse to the creation of structures with elaborate outlines, not merely in plan, whether of the interior or exterior, but also in elevation, and in the cupola. Among such works of his may be mentioned the vestibule of the 'Piazza d'Oro' in the Villa at Tivoli (125-135) (Figs. 55, 56, pp. 63, 68), and the so-called 'Tempio di Siepe' (Fig. 57, p. 63), the appearance of which has been preserved by

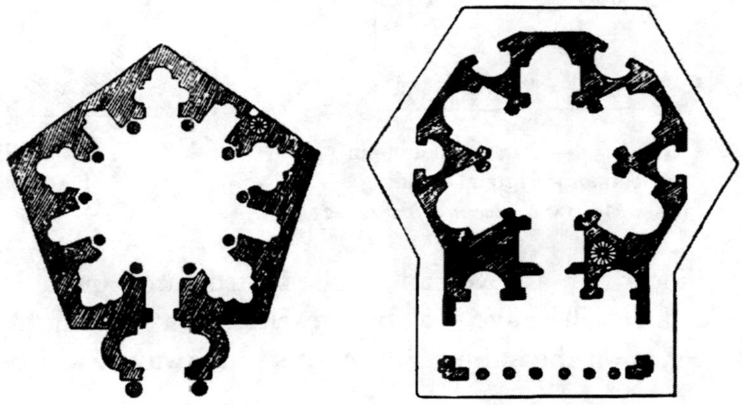

FIG. 52. FIG. 53.

FIGS. 52 and 53.—Plans of ancient Roman polygonal buildings.
(From MONTANO, *Scielta*, &c., tavv. 42, 43.)

[1] *British and American Archaeological Society of Rome*, Feb. 15th, 1910; RIVOIRA, *The Roman Thermae, The Baths of Diocletian. Rivista di Roma*, 1910, pp. 378, 379, 411-415; RIVOIRA, *Origine delle terme dei Romani.*

[2] R. ACCADEMIA DEI LINCEI, *Rendiconti*, vol. xviii, fasc. 3; RIVOIRA, *Di Adriano architetto e dei monumenti adrianei. Nuova Antologia*, 16 Aprile 1910; RIVOIRA, *Adriano architetto e i monumenti adrianei.*

Alò Giovannoli,[1] while Hülsen has discovered its plan among the Uffizi drawings at Florence.[2] This very interesting design is here reproduced (Fig. 58, p. 69), preceding as it does, with its square block hollowed out into four niches at the angles, and its elongated apse, by some four centuries the church of St. George at Ezra (515-16) (Fig. 59, p. 70).

What enabled the Roman builders to develop this extraordinary variety of plan was the hardness of their mortar and the plastic nature of their building materials.

The history of the origin and development of circular vaulted buildings,

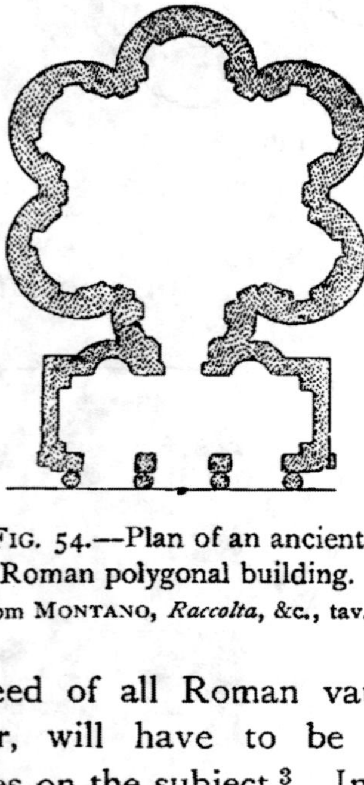

FIG. 54.—Plan of an ancient Roman polygonal building. (From MONTANO, *Raccolta*, &c., tav. 21.)

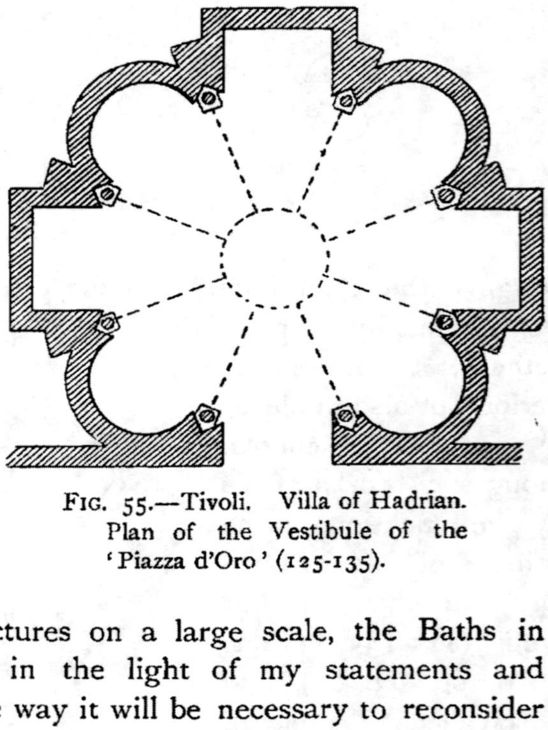

FIG. 55.—Tivoli. Villa of Hadrian. Plan of the Vestibule of the 'Piazza d'Oro' (125-135).

and indeed of all Roman vaulted structures on a large scale, the Baths in particular, will have to be rewritten in the light of my statements and researches on the subject.[3] In the same way it will be necessary to reconsider

[1] *Vedute degli antichi vestigj di Roma*, foglio 39.

[2] *Sonderabdruck aus den jahresheften des Österreichischen Archäologischen Instituts*, xv, 1912, pp. 124-142; *Trajanische und Hadrianische bauten im Marsfelde in Rom.*

[3] *Le origini dell' architettura lombarda. Lombardic architecture.* R. ACCADEMIA DEI LINCEI, *Rendiconti*, vol. xviii, fasc. 3; RIVOIRA, *Di Adriano architetto e i monumenti adrianei. Nuova Antologia*, 16 Aprile 1910; RIVOIRA, *Adriano architetto e i monumenti adrianei. Rivista di Roma*, 1910, pp. 378, 379, 411-415; RIVOIRA, *L'origine delle Terme. Journal of the British and American Archaeological Society of Rome*, vol. iv, pp. 353-360; RIVOIRA, *The Roman Thermae, The Baths of Diocletian.*

the question of the diffusion of this type of building from Rome as a centre, and the nationality of those by whom that diffusion was carried out. And it must not be forgotten that, just when the Roman science of construction and statics reached its zenith, and immediately after the transfer of the seat of empire to Constantinople (330), the East was found to be so poor in architects and builders, that first Constantine the Great (334 and 337), and then Constantius II (344), were obliged to grant exemption from public burdens in order to attract them.[1] Such a state of things was unheard of in Imperial Rome before she lost the source of her vitality.

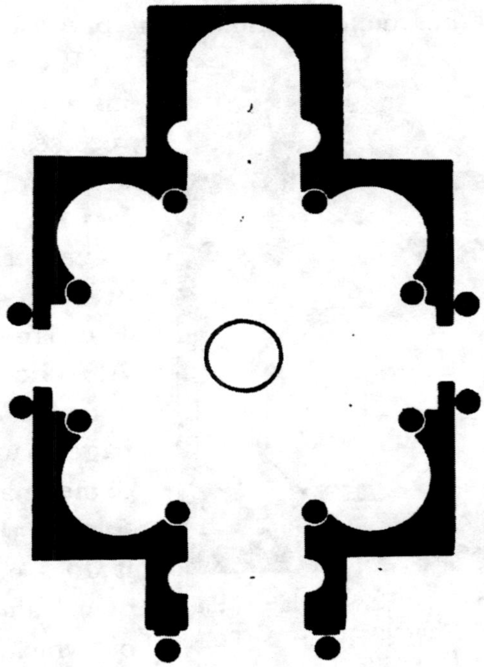

FIG. 58.—Rome. Plan of the building in the Campus Martius called the 'Tempio di Siepe' (117-138).
(From the drawing, No. 2976, in the Uffizi at Florence.)

In these days when Schools of Art are being discovered all over the East, and theories run riot on the evidence of little else than jewellery, enamels, ivories, textiles, painting, and carving—as if it were to sources like these that architects went for the solution of constructive and statical problems, or for the suggestion of new types of plan and elevation—this history which has to be written, and these studies which have to be made, will be found to be full of instruction, for they will bring to light three facts.

The first is that the grandest Imperial vaulted buildings, showing the greatest variety and complexity of form, are of Roman origin.

The second is that the ideas embodied in the plans and construction of such buildings were spread abroad by means of Latin architects educated in the Roman school.

The third is that the share of Greek or Hellenized architects in creating this type is either small or negligible. Let it be remembered that Apollodorus, summoned to Rome by Trajan, left his mark on the emperor's new Forum

[1] HAENEL, *Codices Gregorianus Hermogenianus Theodosianus*, lib. xiii, tit. iv, 1-3.

in the shape of buildings which were elegant in appearance, but had flat ceilings; and not in the form of vaulted structures on a grand scale and of original plan. And when he built the Baths of Trajan, he merely imitated the existing Baths of Titus, without leaving any impress of originality upon them. In fact, who has ever thought of the architect from Damascus as specially distinguished for his thermal buildings?

Thus, for example, in Diocletian's palace at Spalato (300-305),[1] the general plan of which goes back to the Roman stationary camp,[2] evidence will be found in more than one feature, from the architectural point of view, of Roman design and Roman workmanship. For instance, the Imperial Mausoleum with its internal recesses (now the cathedral) belongs to a Latin sepulchral type of building (Fig. 60, p. 64); and no less Roman is the heavy, overloaded, internal architrave, recalling the one in the same emperor's Baths at Rome—a fashion which began in the time of Hadrian (117-138), as is shown by the drawing of Alò Giovannoli which I used as an illustration in a former work, and reproduced here again a few pages back (Fig. 57, p. 63).[3] The remarkable brick dome, made up of tiers of fan-shaped arches (Fig. 61, p. 73), has no analogy in any Eastern work, but it does connect itself with the very singular cupola of an ancient Roman annular rotunda, a drawing of which, by some unknown hand of the XVI century, I found in the Uffizi Collection at Florence. It is developed from spherical pendentives, and is supported by compound piers (Fig. 62, p. 73). Again, the corbelled arcade of the Golden Gate (Fig. 63, p. 74) recalls, on a smaller scale, those, either horizontal or stepped, on the principal front of Diocletian's Baths at Rome, which were opened in 306 (Fig. 64, p. 74).

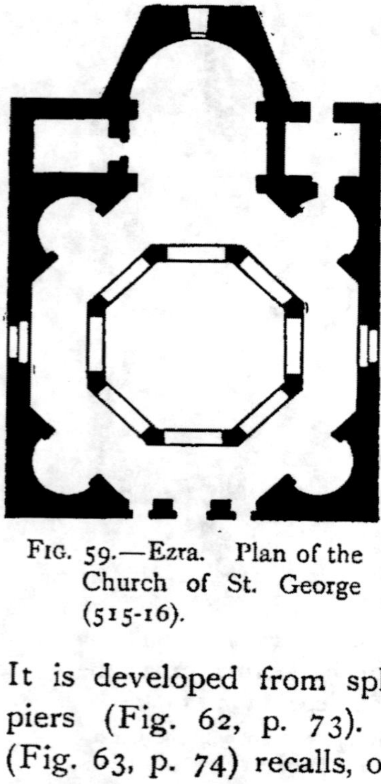

FIG. 59.—Ezra. Plan of the Church of St. George (515-16).

Another point which I would note about Diocletian's palace is that the feature of arches springing directly from columns is not of Oriental origin, as

[1] BULIĆ, RUTAR, *Guida di Spalato e Salona*, p. 67.

[2] FROTHINGHAM, *Roman Cities in Northern Italy and Dalmatia*, pp. 311, 312.

[3] RIVOIRA, op. cit. (Heinemann), vol. ii, p. 40, Fig. 401.

is universally believed.[1] It really comes from Campania. The earliest authentic instances of open colonnades carrying arches are to be found in

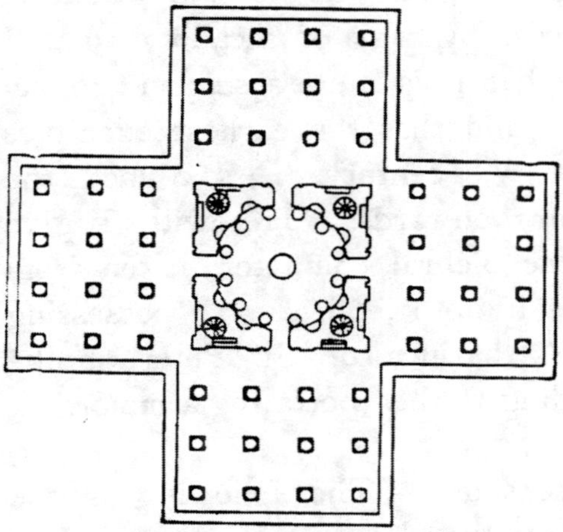

FIG. 66.—Plan of an ancient Roman building with four porticoes.
(From MONGERI, *Le rovine*, &c., tav. 58.)

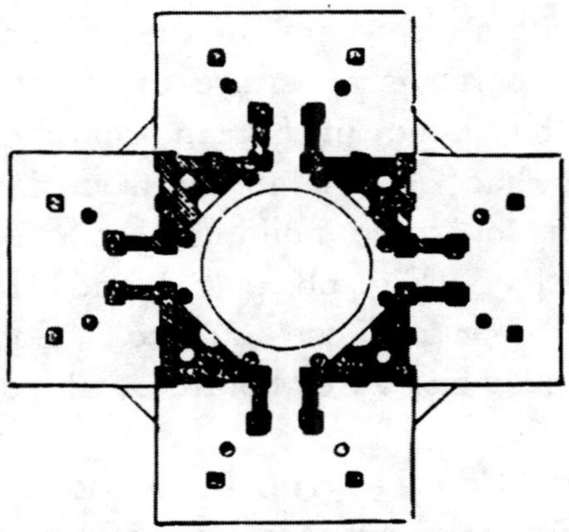

FIG. 67.—Plan of an ancient Roman building with four porticoes.
(From MONTANO, *Scielta*, &c., tav. 25.)

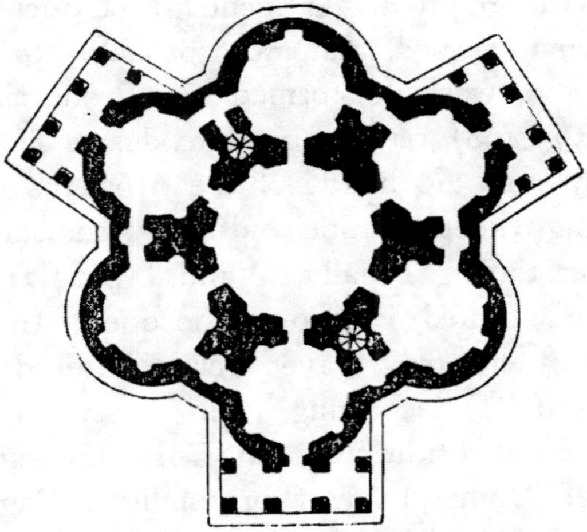

FIG. 68.—Plan of an ancient Roman building with three porticoes.
(From MONTANO, *Raccolta*, &c., tav. 3.)

the 'oecus' of the House of Meleager (Fig. 65, p. 74), and the peristyle of the House of Fortune at Pompeii. Other writers have already called

[1] *Bullettino di Archeologia e Storia dalmata*, 1908, Supplemento, pp. 1-17; STRZYGOWSKI, *Spalato, una tappa dell' arte romanica nel suo passaggio dall' Oriente nell' Occidente.*

attention to the fact that it was the Romans who developed the arcade as an important architectural feature.[1]

Before leaving the Dome of the Rock I should like to call attention to the four porches which cover the entrances, by way of recalling what I have written elsewhere on the subject;[2] viz. that it is mere assertion[3] to say that the porch is a feature of Eastern origin, and that the earliest examples are to be found in Syrian churches of the VI century. As a fact, the Romans had used it freely from Pagan times onwards. Herewith I give the plans of three buildings, apparently of sepulchral character, taken from Bramantino[4] (Fig. 66, p. 71) and Montano[5] (Figs. 67, 68, p. 71), possessing three or four porticoes apiece. Constantine's basilica of St. Peter at the Vatican also had an elaborate porch corresponding to the 'porta regia maior.'

THE CONGREGATIONAL MOSQUE OF DAMASCUS. — The following is the commonly received account of the origin of the Ummayyad mosque at Damascus.

A temple of the Sun or of Jupiter, going back to the pre-Roman epoch, and probably to the reign of Antiochus of Cyzicus (112-95 B.C.), or else belonging to the Roman period, and most probably to the first or second century of the Christian era, was transformed into a church by Theodosius I (378-395), or Arcadius (395-408), or else by Theodosius II (408-450). When Damascus fell irrevocably into the hands of the Moslems in 636, they made a division of the building, keeping one half for themselves and assigning the other half to the Christians. Finally, Walid I (705-715) took possession of the whole building and turned it into a mosque. In so doing he may have entirely rebuilt it, or he may have merely altered it, or, again, he may have confined himself to decorating it in a style of great splendour and magnificence. The local tradition, both Christian and Moslem, agrees that the great mosque of Damascus was originally a Pagan temple, which afterwards became a Christian church, and was finally transformed into a mosque.

[1] MARQUAND, op. cit., p. 255.

[2] RIVOIRA, op. cit. (Loescher), vol. ii, pp. 237-239; (Hoepli), pp. 271-273; (Heinemann), vol. i, pp. 220-221.

[3] CATTANEO, op. cit., pp. 75, 76.

[4] MONGERI, op. cit., tav. 58.

[5] *Scielta de varii tempietti antichi*, tav. 25; *Raccolta de tempii, e sepolcri disegnati dall'antico*, tav. 3.

Fig. 61.—Spalato. Dome of the Imperial Mausoleum, now the Cathedral (300-305).

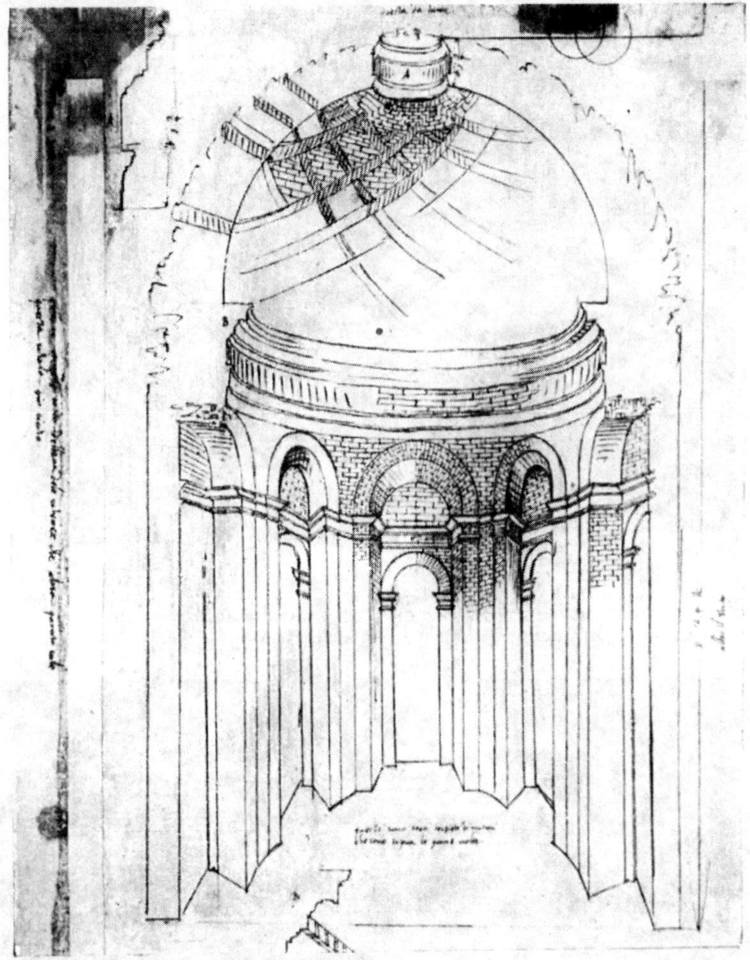

Fig. 62.—Ancient Roman circular building.

(From a drawing in the Uffizi at Florence, No. 1330 *verso*, Indice Ferri, p. 217.)

Fig. 63.—Spalato. The Golden Gate (300-305).

Fig. 64.—Rome. The Baths of Diocletian. Main façade. Remains of architectural decoration.

Fig. 65.—Pompeii. House of Meleager. Remains of open colonnade with arches.

Let us now examine the building and see what account it can give of itself in its present condition.

The site is a rectangle of some 163 by 98 m. (about 530 by 320 ft.), enclosed by four walls which have square towers at the angles. Rather less than half of the enclosure is occupied by the part devoted to worship. The rest of the area consists of a court surrounded on three of its

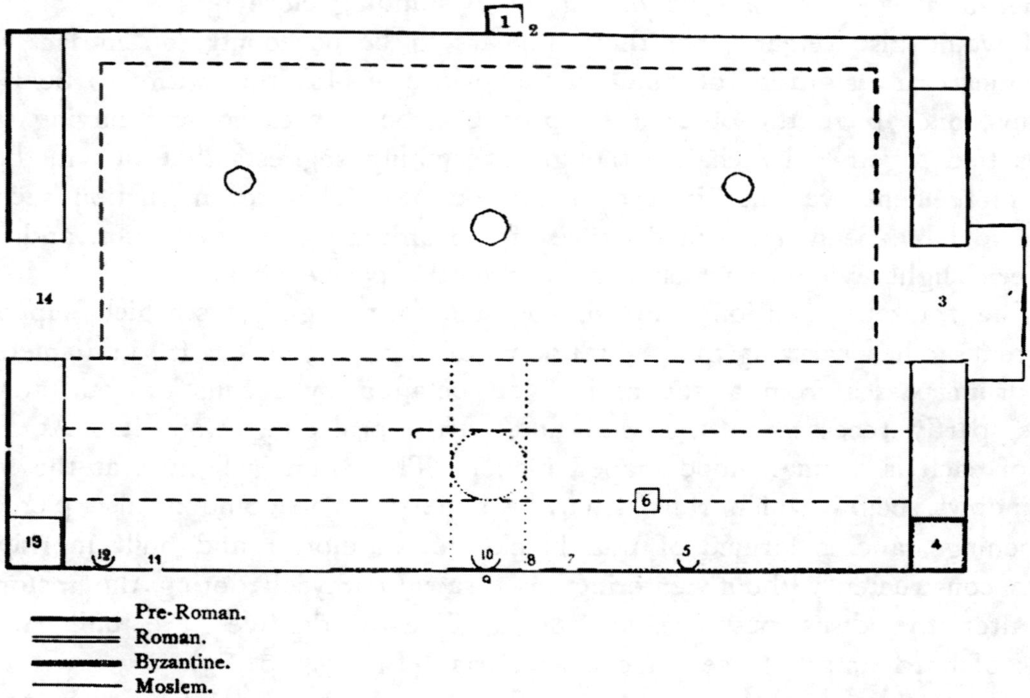

FIG. 69.—Damascus. – Sketch plan of the Mosque of Walid (VIII cent.).

1. Minaret al-Arus.
2. Bab al-Amara.
3. Bab Gayrun.
4. Minaret of Isa.
5. Mihrab al-Sahabah.
6. Tomb of John the Baptist.
7, 8, 9. Entrances to the temple of the Roman period.
10. Mihrab al-Maqsura.
11. Bab Ziyadah.
12. Mihrab al-Hanbali.
13. Minaret al-Gharbiya.
14. Bab al-Barid.

inner sides by covered walks intended to shelter the faithful (Fig. 69). The interior of the place of prayer (Figs. 70, 71, pp. 77, 78), measuring about 139 by 38 m. (452 by 125 ft.), is divided into three aisles of equal breadth, running east and west. A cross-aisle cuts it into two equal halves. Each half is divided by eleven arches, which spring from columns standing on pedestals and carry a second tier of smaller arches springing from squat columns which support the beams of the roof.

I may remark at this point that the oldest example of a sacred building containing a nave with two tiers of columns designed to carry the roof, is to be found in the so-called temple of Neptune at Paestum (perhaps of the V century B.C.) (Figs. 72, 73, pp. 83, 84), a title which Spinazzola regards as erroneous, it having been recently discovered that the name belonged to another and older temple (VI century B.C.) standing close by.

I would also remark that there appears to be no foundation in fact for the conjectural restoration of a hall in the palace of Mshatta[1] with two tiers of columns, one above the other, the upper one being arcaded and having the arches tied together by chains, though everything suggests that this method of reinforcement was not in use at the period. This reconstruction seems to me to have been made in defiance of the ordinary rules of statics, and on the very slight evidence which the ruins of the palace afford.

The transept mentioned above contains four large piers which support the great arches carrying the central dome of about 13 m. (43 ft.) in diameter. The drum passes from a square into an octagon by means of four angle niches, partly recessed in the wall and partly projecting from it. At the base of each is a small hood-shaped niche. The drum is lighted at the top by windows, below which runs a narrow gallery. The dome is also pierced by openings, and is formed of tufa blocks set in mortar and built in rings. It was constructed without centering, as I saw for myself during the restoration after the disastrous fire of 1893. The pendentives are built with blocks of hard limestone set in coarse mortar (Fig. 74, p. 83).

The portions of the transept on either side of the dome have flat roofs, and in that to the south is placed the central mihrab. This plan of a building with longitudinal aisles, bisected by a transept, was no novelty. The Basilica Aemilia in the Forum at Rome, in the shape in which it was rebuilt by Aemilius Paullus in 55 B.C., the work being finished in 34 B.C.,[2] had its nave and three aisles divided by a cross-aisle in the middle. This has been made clear by the recent excavations. It was, no doubt, through this transept, which must have had a door at either end, that the armed horse and foot soldiers passed when they came down from the Esquiline and burst into the Forum on the occasion of Galba's murder.[3]

[1] *Jahrbuch der Königlich Preuszischen Kunstsammlungen*, 1904, pp. 205-373, taf. v. and vi. SCHULZ, STRZYGOWSKI, *Mschatta*.

[2] DE RUGGIERO, op. cit., pp. 399, 400.

[3] Bibliotheca Teubneriana, *Plutarchi vitae parallelae*, vol. v, Γάλβας, cap. xxvi.

FIG. 70.—Damascus. Mosque of Walid before the fire of 1893. One of the colonnades of the central nave (VIII cent.).

Fig. 71.—Damascus. Mosque of Walid under restoration. Central nave (VIII cent.).

The sanctuary is enclosed on three sides by walls, and lighted by numerous round-headed unsplayed windows. The fourth or northern side is open to the court by an arcade with piers, above which rises the lofty wall which contains the windows.

After the fire of 1893 the interior was restored on the old lines. The transept, however, was in part rebuilt, the other part being merely restored; and the drum of the dome was increased in height by nearly a metre. Before that date the upper of the two arcades had square dwarf piers and semicircular arches. In the lower tier the columns, which stood on pedestals, were surmounted by capitals, the majority of which were Corinthian, of various dates and styles, in some cases not fitting their columns. They carried pulvins forming imposts for the arches, which were of slightly horse-shoe form. Moreover, the dome was elliptical in shape, with two centres; and was entirely built of tufa blocks set in mortar of unsuitable character. Its form was due to the fact that the piers were set so as to form a slightly oblong plan.

The four piers of the drum of the dome consist in each case of two separate piers set back to back, of different heights and measuring in section 3.20 by 1.80 m., and 3.20 by 2.40 m. (about 10½ by 6 ft. and 10½ by 8 ft.). We cannot be sure when this strengthening took place. We do know, however, that Walid's dome had to be built twice over; for the first one fell owing to the want of experience of the builders who, in view of the saturated nature of the subsoil, ought to have raised the angle piers on piles, and not merely on vine wood faggots. The result was that the dome had to be built over again.[1]

Moreover, one of the Cufic inscriptions on these piers tells us that the original dome was rebuilt in 1082,[2] under the direction of Malik Shah when Muktadi was caliph (1075-1094), in consequence of the fire of 1069,[3] or else after another mentioned by Ibn Jubair,[4] which may be identified by the occasion of the siege and capture of Damascus about the year 1077. Accordingly, the duplication of the piers must have taken place either under Walid, or in 1082. I incline to the latter date, as it is inconceivable that after the collapse of the first dome, involving as it did the reconstruction of

[1] MAQRIZI (Quatremère), *Histoire des Sultans Mamelouks de l'Égypte*, vol. ii, 1; App., p. 266. CAETANI, *Annali*, vol. iii, 1, p. 388.

[2] *Journal Asiatique*, 1891, i, pp. 420-423; VAN BERCHEM, *Notes d'archéologie arabe.*

[3] MAQRIZI, *Histoire des Sultans Mamelouks de l'Égypte*, vol. ii, 1, App., p. 285.

[4] Op. cit., p. 259.

the foundations of the supporting piers, the latter should be erected in a duplicated form, and not as single solid piers.

I find no description of Walid's dome. Muqaddasi[1] only says that it was of great size, and was crowned by an orange supporting a pomegranate, both of gold. It is not improbable that it was modelled on the Dome of the Rock at Jerusalem (687-691), and may have had a double cupola of wood, rising out of a high circular drum. We do not know how the drum was connected with the arches of the square base. It may have been by squinches, but it was certainly not by means of niches like the present ones, copied from their predecessors, as Choisy[2] believed, thereby misleading students of architectural origins. If we go back to the history as told us by the monuments themselves, in the days of Walid the Moslem world as yet knew nothing of the pendentive in the form of a tall niche, still less of the kind employed at Damascus. What it did know was a squinch or raccord serving the same purpose. One has recently been discovered in Persia, in the ruins of the palaces of Chosroes II (591-628) at Qasr es-Sherin.[3] So far as we can judge, the ordinary niche-shaped pendentive did not make its appearance among the Moslems before the caliphate of Aziz (975-996), as we shall see when we come to the mosque of Hakim at Cairo. The other form, which also consists of a niche, but with its sides standing free as at Damascus, is of later origin, and we shall discuss it when we deal with the mosque al-Azhar (970-972) at Cairo.

In reality, the dome, as it existed before 1893, must be ascribed to the XV century.

I note here that an idea of the appearance of Walid's cupola might be obtained, if we possessed it, from the description of the green dome of the residence of the Emir Muawiya, afterwards caliph (661-680), which stood to the south of the precinct of the mosque,[4] and gave its name (al-Hadra) to the whole building.

Of Malik Shah's dome, on the other hand, we have a vivid and detailed description by Ibn Jubair.[5] It was a double cupola, hemispherical in form, and recalled the Dome of the Rock at Jerusalem. The two cupolas, one

[1] Op. cit., pp. 17, 18.

[2] *L'art de bâtir chez les Byzantins*, pp. 85, 166, pl. xxi.

[3] De Morgan, *Mission scientifique en Perse. Recherches archéologiques*, vol. iv, 2, pp. 341-357.

[4] Maqrizi, *Histoire des Sultans Mamelouks de l'Égypte*, vol. ii, 1, App., p. 263.

[5] Op. cit., pp. 254, 255, 286-289.

above the other, separated by a wooden flooring, were formed of timber strengthened by radiating ribs, also of wood, converging at a crowning wooden ring, and were tied together half-way by iron rods. The outer cupola was covered with sheets of lead like the other roofs of the mosque. The interior one was richly ornamented on its inner surface with rosettes carved in wood and other artistic and original carvings, as well as with exquisite polychrome decorations. The whole was a blaze of gold. The dome was reached by a staircase on the outside, and through one of the windows at the bottom of the outer cupola. There was another set of windows in the inner cupola. The base rested on four piers. It was circular in form, built of large blocks of stone, and lighted by windows which had dwarf piers in the jambs.

Anyone who has studied on the spot the Dome of the Rock at Jerusalem will at once be struck by the numerous analogies between its cupola and the one at Damascus as described by Ibn Jubair. Note especially that it was reached from the roof, that it was surrounded by a gallery, that one could enter it, go round it, and examine the interior of the mosque. We also see how the writer has exaggerated the soaring height of the Damascus dome. The Dome of the Rock, imposing as it is, has no excessive elevation; and the one at Damascus, as we are told by Ibn Jubair himself, was reputed to be lower.

At the time when Malik Shah's dome was built, its base also must have been constructed. His dome was probably destroyed, as has been suggested by others,[1] in the catastrophe caused by order of Tamerlane in 1400, when everything in the mosque which was not of stone was destroyed by fire. The consequent restoration was carried out by order of the Sultan of Egypt, Malik Muayyad (1412-1421).[2] It was then that the previous wooden cupola was replaced by one of masonry, which has been rebuilt since the fire of 1893. In the reconstruction of the XV century must be included the drum, which then assumed a polygonal form. The one which Ibn Jubair saw in 1184 was circular.[3]

The very incomplete study of the structure of the outer walls of the mosque, which is all that the existing conditions allowed me to make, has enabled me to arrive at results which agree, on the whole, with Mr Dickie's

[1] Saladin, *Manuel d'art musulman*, vol. i, p. 81.

[2] Maqrizi, *Histoire des Sultans Mamelouks de l'Égypte*, vol. ii, 1, App., pp. 286, 287.

[3] Op. cit., p. 288.

account.[1] The eastern wall, with the adjuncts at the angles on the north and south sides, is built of blocks of stone, and is strengthened on its outer face by wall-piers carrying an architrave with a dentilled cornice, part of which survives. This is the oldest work in the building, and is regarded as pre-Roman (Fig. 75, p. 84).

In the southern wall, partly rebuilt in its western half in 1318-19,[2] are remains of a structure slightly projecting from the line of the wall, and with masonry of a different type from that which we have seen before. It contains three doors, viz. a larger one in the centre with a smaller one on either side; each of the latter being surmounted by an 'aedicula,' and separated from the larger one by a pair of niches. This work is believed to be of the Roman period, and its carving recalls specimens in the temples at Baalbec (II and III centuries). The Biblical Greek inscriptions on the two doors which can be seen on the outside (Fig. 76, p. 87), viz. the central one and the one to the left, seem to have been added when the Pagan temple gave place to the church of St. John the Baptist. This transformation appears to have taken place in the reign of the Emperor Arcadius, who, according to a lost Greek inscription, restored the building.[3] But, even if he were not its founder, its construction and completion may be to a large extent due to him.

The other parts of the southern wall which were not rebuilt in the XIV century (including the angle adjunct on the eastern side and the quadrangular bases of the two minarets at the south-east and south-west corners), and are strengthened by buttresses, reveal, in their lowest part, the fact that they were not built in either the Roman or the pre-Roman period, or again at the same time as the upper part of that wall, which belongs to the work of Walid. They must be ascribed to the Christian epoch previous to the Moslem conquest. The north and east sides may, with the exception of the angle adjuncts mentioned above, be regarded on the whole as belonging to the VIII century. The three Roman doors were blocked up in the time of Walid, and the central one was partly filled by one of the transept wall-piers, while the western one gave place to the principal mihrab. The

[1] *Palestine Exploration Fund*, 1897, pp. 268-282; *The Great Mosque of the Omeiyades, Damascus.*

[2] MAQRIZI, *Histoire des Sultans Mamelouks de l'Égypte*, vol. ii, 1, App., p. 282.

[3] PORTER, *Five Years in Damascus*, vol. i, pp. 61-77.

FIG. 73.—Paestum. Temple with colonnades in two tiers (V cent. B.C.?). Interior.

FIG. 74.—Damascus. Mosque of Walid under restoration. Central dome (VIII, XI, XV, and XIX-XX cents.).

FIG. 72.—Paestum. Temple with colonnades in two tiers (V cent. B.C. ?).

FIG. 75.—Damascus. Mosque of Walid. Wall of the pre-Roman period.

wealth of precious stones described by the Arabic writers earlier than the XI century,[1] as lavished on the decoration of the latter, is quite in keeping with Walid's standard of magnificence. Moreover, the 'garib' or central aisle with its imposing entrance, set at right angles to the mosque, was intended to confer all the dignity possible on the sacred recess, and to bring it better within the view of the throngs of the faithful in the court.

It has been stated that this mihrab was the first to be made in the form of a niche, the second being that in the mosque at Medina as restored by Walid.[2] But in fact the earliest niche pointing in the direction of the qibla seems to have been made at Damascus before the time of Walid, and this would be the subordinate mihrab seen, at the same time as the principal one, by Muqaddasi,[3] who says that it was intended for the private use of the sultan, and that, having fallen into a bad state, it was restored in his time to its original condition at the said sultan's expense.

Ibn Jubair[4] calls it the mihrab of the Companions of Mohammed, incorrectly according to Caetani,[5] and adds that it was the first built in Islam. From a statement by Ibn Khaldun[6] it may be gathered that this niche was the work of Muawiya. What he says is this: the 'maqsura' is the isolated enclosure, containing the mihrab and everything in and near to it, reserved for the sultan at the time of public prayer; the use of such an enclosure is said to have been introduced by the founder of the Ummayyad dynasty in consequence of the assassination of the Caliph Ali (656-661), of the attempt on Amr, the governor of Egypt, and of the serious wound inflicted on Muawiya himself in 661 by the Kharijite sectaries.

This inference is opposed to the view of Lammens,[7] as the maqsura (one of the secular creations ascribed to Muawiya) was originally a kind of private closet set apart for the sovereign in the mosque, to which he retired for the purpose of deliberation. The Abbasides transformed it into a private enclosure from which they assisted at the services in the mosque. Moreover, the attempt on Muawiya must have happened more than two years before the murder of Ali, or at least in 659.

[1] Le Strange, *Palestine under the Moslems*, pp. 227, 228, 236.

[2] Maqrizi, *Histoire des Sultans Mamelouks de l'Égypte*, vol. ii, 1, App., p. 283.

[3] Op. cit., p. 18.

[4] Op. cit., pp. 255, 256.

[5] Caetani, *Annali*, vol. iii, 1, p. 389.

[6] *Prolégomènes historiques*, vol. ii, p. 72.

[7] Université Saint-Joseph, Beyrouth, *Mélanges de la Faculté Orientale*, 1907. *Études sur le règne du calife Omaiyade Mo'awia Ier*, pp. 32, 33, 94, 95.

The fact, nevertheless, remains that Muawiya had the first maqsura made at Damascus, in 664-65 according to Caetani;[1] and Asakir's (†1175)[2] statement that the congregational mosque at Damascus did not originally possess a prayer niche, does not exclude the possibility that it was provided with one under that caliph. However that may be, before the construction of Walid's great niche, another of smaller size had already been erected by Moslems;[3] and this was clearly the one which was restored in the time of Muqaddasi and left untouched by Walid. Hence the necessity for its repair about the year 985.

Besides these two mihrabs Ibn Jubair noticed a third, known as that of the Hanifites, placed, for reasons of symmetry, in the western half of the south wall. It was, perhaps, made in the course of the works of 1082, for it is not mentioned by Muqaddasi.

I observe here that the mihrab is derived from the apse of the church, and not from the shrine of the principal image of Buddha.[4]

Near the western angle of the south wall is a door with a relieving arch above it, but not ancient. The original main entrance on this side of the mosque was the Bab as-Saat (the Gate of the Hours), which was towards the south-east angle.[5] It is interesting to read the description by Ibn Jubair[6] of the remarkable water-clock which was the origin of the name of the gate.

The front of the mosque (Figs. 77, 78, pp. 87, 88) was from the first designed with arcades having arches of slightly horse-shoe form, supported by piers measuring 1.50 by 1.20 m. (about 5 by 4 ft.), as I was able to ascertain during the recent works of restoration, my view being confirmed by the architect (Apery) in charge of them, and not by columns, as has been so often stated. These arches had doors, and were not left open, as has been stated.[7] As late as the X century all the Syrian mosques, with the exception of the one at Jericho, were closed in the same way on the side of the court.[8] Later, the arches in question seem to have been thrown open, though they were provided with curtains.[9]

The end wall of the transept, which is strengthened by buttresses corresponding to the arcades inside and the buttresses of the south wall,

[1] *Chronographia*, p. 493.

[2] CAETANI, *Annali*, vol. iii, 1, p. 384.

[3] Ibid., vol. iii, 1, pp. 388, 389.

[4] HAVELL, *Indian Architecture*, pp. 5, 6.

[5] MUQADDASI, op. cit., p. 20.

[6] Op. cit., pp. 261, 262.

[7] SPIERS, *Architecture East and West*, p. 222.

[8] MUQADDASI, op. cit., p. 75.

[9] MAQRIZI, *Histoire des Sultans Mamelouks de l'Égypte*, vol. ii, 1, App., p. 273.

FIG. 76.—Damascus. Mosque of Walid. Architrave of door of the Roman period.

FIG. 77.—Damascus. Mosque of Walid before the fire of 1893. Façade (VIII cent.).

Fig 78.—Damascus. Mosque of Walid under restoration. Façade (VIII cent.).

Fig. 79.—Damascus. Mosque of Walid under restoration. North and west sides of the court (VIII and XV ? cents.).

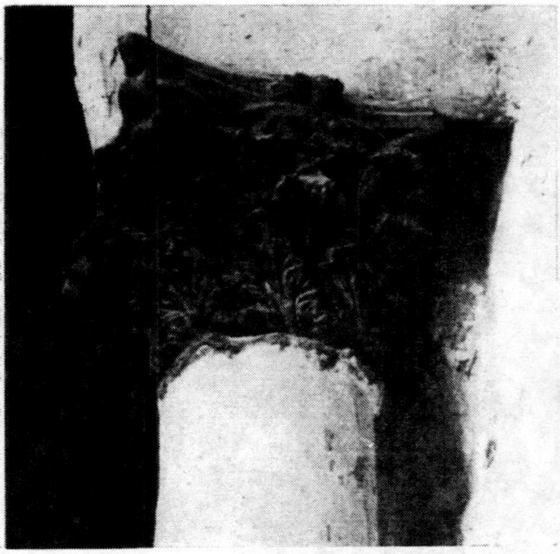

FIG. 80.—Damascus. Mosque of Walid. Capital of the Graeco-Roman period.

FIG. 81.—Damascus. Mosque of Walid. Capital of the Moslem period.

FIG. 82.—Damascus. Mosque of Walid under restoration. North side of the court (VIII and XV? cents.) with the minaret al-Arus (X and XII cents.).

FIG. 83.—Damascus. Tomb of Saladin.

FIG. 84.—Damascus. Mosque of Walid after the fire of 1893. Façade (VIII cent.) and minaret al-Gharbiya (1483).

is pierced by a triplet of arches (the supports have been rebuilt with abaci surmounting the capitals, instead of pulvins as at first), above which is a triplet window. Both are enclosed in a single large arch. The gable contains a window flanked by two round openings.

The quadrangle on to which the front looks is surrounded by a two-storied cloister (Fig. 79, p. 88). The upper gallery on the east and west sides retains the original alternation of piers and columns. That on the north, with piers only, is due to a reconstruction later than the XIV century, for Ibn Batuta [1] († 1377) found the old arrangement of columns and piers still there.

The arches on the ground floor are rather larger than semicircles; those of the upper story are round. These arches were designed with polychrome voussoirs, like those in the vestibules.

The columns have been brought from other buildings, and are sometimes made to fit by the aid of pedestals. They are surmounted by alien Corinthian capitals of the Graeco-Roman period (Fig. 80, p. 89), but also in some cases by capitals of various kinds made for their places. Some of these are cubical funnel-shaped with the angles cut off, the surfaces thus obtained being sometimes occupied by leaves. Others are surrounded by smooth leaves, the tips of which are alternately pointed and rounded. Others are of rude Corinthianesque type, with acanthus or even palm leaves, almost devoid of undercutting, and sometimes having, instead of cauliculi, crocket leaves at the angles. There must also have been some of Composite type. The specimen of poor workmanship here illustrated (Fig. 81, p. 89) may have come from the upper gallery on the north side. The capitals in the galleries are surmounted by pulvins.

In the northern side of the quadrangle a door opens: the Bab al-Faradis (Gate of Paradise or of the Gardens) of Muqaddasi,[2] the Bab an-Natifiyyin (Gate of the Sweetmeat Sellers) of Ibn Jubair,[3] known to-day as the Bab Amara. Doubts exist [4] as to where the gate so named by Muqaddasi stood, in view, for one thing, of his statement about the age of the minaret close by, known as the Madinet al-Arus (Minaret of the Wife), and supposed to have been built by Walid,[5] and therefore to be the oldest in existence,[6] which is not the case (Fig. 82, p. 89).

[1] Ibn Batuta, op. cit., vol. i, p. 200. [2] Op. cit., p. 20. [3] Op. cit., p. 260.

[4] Muqaddasi, op. cit., p. 20, note 2. Le Strange, *Palestine under the Moslems*, p. 230.

[5] Maqrizi, *Histoire des Sultans Mamelouks de l'Égypte*, vol. ii, 1, App., p. 273.

[6] Porter, op. cit., vol. i, pp. 61-77.

The oldest part of this minaret, that is to say, the large square tower, shows two different kinds of masonry. Near the ground it consists of big blocks; the upper part is built of dressed stone. Neither resembles the work of Walid's time in the mosque and quadrangle.

The view which I take of its history is as follows. It was built a little before Muqaddasi's coming to Damascus (about 985), was seriously damaged by the fire of 1174,[1] and was rebuilt, except the lowest part, by Saladin the Great, whose tomb is close by (Fig. 83, p. 90). To this rebuilding belongs the square tower with its roof: the slight structure above it is a later addition. Western influence of the XII century is betrayed by the two-light openings in the main tower, with pointed or horse-shoe arches and cubical capitals cut out of the same piece as the shaft and base, enclosed in the sunk face of a single arch, and also by the small arched corbel course below them.

The minaret seen by Muqaddasi was a simple tower, and in the X century the Syrian minarets were of that form.[2] It was also decorated with mosaics, and as I do not find that minarets were so embellished before the erection of that built by Abd al-Rahman III at Cordova in 945-46, we have here the proof of Muqaddasi's statement that the minaret al-Arus at Damascus was of recent origin in 985.

Walid's mosque had four minarets placed at the angles of the outer wall. Two of them are the south-east and south-west corner towers of the original Christian building, the lowest parts of which still survive, and upon which Walid built. The other two stand at the interior north-east and north-west angles, and were built by him. This arrangement was derived from the four corner turrets erected in 673 under Muawiya's orders in the mosque of Amr at Fustat. It was also applied to the mosque at Medina on the occasion of Walid's restoration.[3] The fact that the towers at Damascus are older than the mosque is confirmed by the very early belief that the minarets were originally watch-towers or astronomical observatories of the Greek period, and that they had belonged to the church of St. John.[4]

The minarets on the north side fell,[5] and were not rebuilt. They were no longer there in Ibn Jubair's time, as we learn from him.[6] The other two

[1] MAQRIZI, *Histoire des Sultans Mamelouks de l'Égypte*, vol. ii, 1, App., p. 287.

[2] MUQADDASI, op. cit., p. 75.

[3] BURTON, op. cit., vol. ii, p. 75.

[4] LE STRANGE, *Palestine under the Moslems*, p. 234. MAQRIZI, *Histoire des Sultans Mamelouks de l'Égypte*, vol. ii, 1, App., p. 273.

[5] MAQRIZI, op. cit., vol. ii, 1, App., p. 273.

[6] IBN JUBAIR, op. cit., p. 257.

on the south side are not original. The eastern one, the Madinet Isa (Minaret of Jesus), having been damaged by the fire of 1271-72, was rebuilt in a more artistic form at the cost of the Christians, who were believed to have been responsible for the fire.[1] It is not, therefore, of the XI century as Saladin suggests.[2] The western one, the Madinet al-Gharbiya, was restored in 1483[3] by Qait Bey, Sultan of Egypt (1468-1495) (Fig. 84, p. 90).

From the east and west sides of the outer wall of the mosque project two vestibules, which also have upper galleries. They are known as the Bab Gayrun or Gate of Gayrun, and the Bab al-Barid or Gate of the Post. Here, too, the capitals of the columns are in some cases of alien origin, while others have been made for their places (Figs. 85, 86, p. 99). The western vestibule has a double colonnade in front of it, with funnel-shaped capitals carrying pulvins, possibly of the VIII century, and with piers at intervals, forming a covered gallery leading to a great monumental arch, known as the Bab al-Barid (Fig. 87, p. 99), the pediment of which was originally supported by two cruciform piers at the ends and four columns between them. The carving is clearly of the same date as that on the triple southern entrance to the mosque. Its Corinthian capitals, too, recall many of the same order in the lower galleries round the court.

The three domed structures standing in the court of the mosque are none of them original, or even as old as the time of Ibn Jubair, as may be seen from his description of their predecessors.[4] The one of octagonal form, however, on the west, with its alien columns standing on the modern pavement of the court and surmounted by Graeco-Roman capitals (Fig. 88, p. 100), is interesting from our point of view, as it shows us a reproduction on a small scale of the one mentioned by Muqaddasi,[5] which was evidently the same as that seen two centuries later by Ibn Jubair, and was the ancient treasury of the mosque. It was an octagon consisting of eight lofty columns decorated with polychrome mosaics, and supporting a large domed structure.

I may remark here that as late as the X century in Syria the public treasury of the principal cities of each province was to be found in the chief mosque of the place, where it occupied a chamber raised upon piers or columns.[6] A structure of this kind must have been derived from the typical

[1] MAQRIZI, *Histoire des Sultans Mamelouks de l'Égypte*, vol. ii, 1, App., p. 273.

[2] *Manuel d'art musulman*, vol. i, p. 81.

[3] PORTER, op. cit., vol. i, pp. 61-77.

[4] IBN JUBAIR, op. cit., pp. 257, 258.

[5] Op. cit., p. 18.

[6] MUQADDASI, op. cit., p. 75.

'horrea' of Roman times, standing on four isolated supports. An instance of the traditional survival of its form is to be seen in the interesting and sometimes elaborately carved 'hórreos' of the province of Oviedo in Asturias.

The great Ummayyad mosque of Damascus, placed fourth in order of dignity by the Moslem world, those of Mecca, Medina, and Jerusalem taking precedence, was from the first regarded as one of the wonders of architecture. It is described as the most magnificent in Islam by Yaqubi[1] in 891, by Istakri (951), whose work was republished by Ibn Haukal[2] in 978, and by Muqaddasi about the year 985.[3] Others called it one of the palaces of paradise.[4] The caliphs Mahdi (775-785) and Mamun (about 813-833) after seeing it declared that it was unrivalled and the most wonderful building in the world,[5] an encomium which was not interested, coming as it did from two of the Abbasides.

Its fame was probably due to the excessive splendour and wealth of its decorations. We know that the work carried out by Walid, begun in 706 according to Masudi's (953)[6] account, took eight years to finish, as we are told by Ibn al-Fakih (about 903).[7] And the cost was so great that, according to the last authority, it absorbed the land tax of the empire for seven years. With a building where such a free use was made of alien material, and in which portions of the pre-existing structure were preserved, such enormous expense must have been largely due to the decorations and embellishments, the beauty of which baffled description. Moreover, gold and precious stones were used in lavish profusion.

The walls of the place of prayer, both without and within, were completely faced with parti-coloured marbles, enamelled tiles, and mosaics glittering with gold, depicting vegetable forms and famous cities. The battlements crowning the building, which have all disappeared, were also embellished with mosaics. Below the gilded ceilings with their stucco ornaments ran a band of inscriptions on a gold ground. The capitals were gilded. The piers and arches with their gilt keystones were decorated with mosaics. The interior of the dome, as we have already seen, was radiant with gold, while

[1] Le Strange, *Palestine under the Moslems*, p. 232.

[2] Ibid., p. 236.

[3] Op. cit., p. 17.

[4] Maqrizi; *Histoire des Sultans Mamelouks de l'Égypte*, vol. ii, 3, App., pp. 275, 276.

[5] Ibid., p. 276.

[6] Société Asiatique; Maçoudi, *Les Prairies d'Or*, p. 87 (Barbier de Meynard).

[7] Le Strange, op. cit., p. 233.

its exterior was crowned by a golden orange surmounted by a pomegranate of the same metal. The principal mihrab was a blaze of gilding, and around it were inlaid great cut pieces of agate and turquoise. Above was a golden vine. The pavement was of mosaic. The windows and the arches of the arcade in the northern wall were filled with gilded lattices and glass of many colours. The pavement of the court was of marble. In the galleries and vestibules, walls, arches, and windows had mosaic decoration. The ceilings and vaults were finely painted, and had stucco ornaments. The doors were of gilt metal. All the openings were protected by strips of lead.[1]

Important specimens of the original decorations of the building are to be seen in the two vestibules in the shape of: marble facings; marble intarsia work with geometrical designs; stucco ornaments; window lattices of cement with remains of coloured glass; mosaics with trees, whorls, vases containing foliage; doors with metal-plated leaves; painted arabesques. Then on the north front of the transept are some very interesting remains of mosaics with architectural designs, representing, no doubt, some of the cities mentioned by Muqaddasi.[2] Two examples of Walid's decorations are here illustrated (Figs. 89, 90, pp. 100, 101).

I may observe that Walid's principal mihrab was not the one seen by Ibn Jubair in 1184. The works of 1082 included, not only the rebuilding of the central dome of the mosque, but also the reconstruction of the private enclosure, the roof, and other parts.[3] The distinctive feature of the mihrab was no longer the inlaid precious stones and the golden vine, but arcading. 'Within the niche are small niches on the face of the wall, flanked by colonnettes of spiral form resembling bracelets, which look as if they were turned on the lathe.'[4] The same type of decoration must have been repeated, though in a simpler form, in the XV century restoration, for it was still to be seen there in 1893. The decoration of mihrabs with arcading reaches its full development in the mosque of Sultan Qalaun at Cairo (1279-1290) (Fig. 91, p. 102).

The object of Walid in lavishing all this magnificence and splendour on

[1] MUQADDASI, op. cit., pp. 17-19. IBN JUBAIR, op. cit., pp. 252-265, 286-289. LE STRANGE, *Palestine under the Moslems*, pp. 233-240. MAQRIZI, *Histoire des Sultans Mamelouks de l'Égypte*, vol. ii, 1, App., pp. 262-288.

[2] Op. cit., pp. 17, 18.

[3] *Journal Asiatique*, 1891, i, pp. 420-423; VAN BERCHEM, *Notes d'archéologie arabe*.

[4] IBN JUBAIR, op. cit., p. 259.

the mosque of Damascus was not so much to exalt himself and his house, as to eclipse the finest churches of Syria and Palestine which he had seen, especially that of the Holy Sepulchre at Jerusalem, and the churches of Lydda and Edessa,[1] and at the same time to glorify Allah.[2] Ideas which were worthy of a great Imperial ruler: of a caliph whose contemporaries said that at Damascus, in his time, the talk was all of palaces and public buildings,[3] forgetting that it was also the reign under which the crescent was planted on the walls of Samarcand, India was conquered up to the foot of the Himalayas, North Africa was finally subdued, and the Iberian peninsula annexed.

We have no definite information about the artists employed in this famous mosque. Muqaddasi[4] says that for the mosaics workmen were brought from Persia, India, Western Africa (i.e. Libya, Tunis, and Algeria), and Constantinople. The fact that he omits Egypt from the list is very interesting, discountenancing as it does the legend about the great importance of the Copts in the art and architecture of this century. As bearing on this it may be noticed that when Muawiya I (661-680) made an architectural innovation at Mecca by the use of bricks and mortar, he had recourse to workmen from distant Persia, and not to the Copts who lived close by.[5] It is also clear that no Egyptians were employed by Abd al-Malik for his great buildings at Jerusalem.

As to Persia, I may remark that builders of experience were scarce, not only in the time of Sapor II (310-379),[6] but equally so under Chosroes I, as we shall see presently; nor was there any change in the days of Chosroes II, who, on the capture of Jerusalem in 614, spared the lives of skilled craftsmen in order to carry them off as prisoners to his own dominions.[7] Later, Persia was able to supply other countries with workmen.

Ibn Jubair,[8] again, says that for the building Walid 'ordered the king of the Romans (Rum) at Constantinople to send him twelve thousand workmen

[1] Muqaddasi, op. cit., pp. 22, 23. [2] Le Strange, *Palestine under the Moslems*, p. 261.

[3] Pizzi, *L'Islamismo*, p. 200. [4] Op. cit., pp. 18, 19.

[5] Université Saint-Joseph, Beyrouth, *Mélanges de la Faculté orientale*, 1907, p. 137; Lammens, *Études sur le règne du calife Omaiyade Mo'awia Ier*.

[6] Faustus of Byzantium, Vatican MS. 9545, lib. v, cap. iv.

[7] *The English Historical Review*, 1910, pp. 507, 508; Conybeare, *Antiochus Strategos' Account of the Sack of Jerusalem* in A.D. 614.

[8] Op. cit., p. 252.

from his country.' Ibn Khaldun, in his turn, writes that 'the king of the Greeks' was compelled to provide the architects and builders for the construction of the mosque, and artists for its mosaic decorations.[1] It seems that Walid obtained his craftsmen from the Greek emperor by the threat, in case of refusal, of marching his armies into the Imperial territories, and also of destroying the churches existing in the Moslem dominions, including those of Jerusalem and Edessa, as well as the other structures left by the Romans.[2] Ibn Batuta[3] says that the workmen were twelve thousand in number.

My belief is that Muqaddasi's account is to be preferred, and that it refers not only to mosaic workers but to all kinds of craftsmen and builders (those provided by the Emperor of Constantinople coming, as they would, not only from Greece but also from his Italian dominions), and includes Syria and Palestine among the countries from which they came. The existence of a large dome of wood points to the form used in the past in the latter countries for domes of considerable span, beginning with the churches of the Resurrection and the Ascension at Jerusalem, and going down to the cathedral of Bosra (511-12), and the church of St. George at Ezra (515-16).[4]

We have still to decide what work was really executed by Walid's architects and builders, acting under the superintendence of Zaid ibn Wakid.[5] This is a problem of much greater difficulty than that of roughly dating the different parts of the outer walls of the mosque, as it is not possible to make the necessary excavations in the floors. Hence, whatever is stated here will be rather in the nature of conjecture, combined with a weighing of opinions, than of a definite conclusion. Still it will have the merit of setting the subject as a whole in a clearer light than has hitherto been shed upon it, for the benefit of those who make a study of this celebrated building.

The architect of the congregational mosque of Damascus preserved of the plan of the previous structures merely the outer lines of the enclosure, and of these he retained only those parts which seemed to him solid enough to bear the weight of new buildings. He was obliged to do this

[1] IBN KHALDUN, *Prolégomènes historiques*, vol. ii, pp. 268, 375.

[2] MAQRIZI, *Histoire des Sultans Mamelouks de l'Égypte*, vol. ii, 1, p. 265.

[3] Op. cit., vol. i, p. 198.

[4] RIVOIRA, op. cit. (Hoepli), p. 331; (Heinemann), vol. ii, p. 15.

[5] LE STRANGE, *Palestine under the Moslems*, p. 233.

owing to the considerable elevation which he proposed to give to the place of prayer; and it was also demanded by the two-storied cloister round the court. Having completed the new outer wall—in parts merely raised in height; in others built new from the foundations — adding the two towers at the extremities of the north side, and increasing the height of the other two on the south as bases for the minarets, he erected, parallel to the south wall, three colonnades, equidistant from one another, with two tiers of arches, the columns in the lower tier being antiques. The three aisles thus formed were terminated by the new arcaded façades on the north. The transept was also erected with its great central dome. The two smaller cupolas which flanked it on the north and south in the time of Ibn Jubair [1] were added later than the X century. There is no trace of them in Muqaddasi.[2] The sanctuary proper having been thus formed, the two-storied galleries and vestibules were next erected, with the four entrances.

We know only in an incomplete and confused way what was contained within the enclosure wall previous to the time of Walid. It is clear, indeed, that a large church dedicated to the Baptist was in existence at the same time as the mosque; but we know nothing about the exact site, form, and orientation of these buildings, and we can only make conjectures about them. For instance, we do not know precisely to what part of the church the noble triple entrance of the older Pagan temple corresponded. There is every reason to think that the temple stood north and south, like the so-called temple of the Sun at Palmyra (Fig. 92, p. 101), which measures about 20 by 11 m. (65 by 36 ft.), and has its main axis set accurately north and south. These points have already been noticed by others.[3]

We cannot be certain about the fate of the temple, which came under the enactments of Theodosius the Great against the Pagans.[4] The Paschal Chronicle [5] tells us that he did not merely disestablish the temples, but destroyed them: 'The illustrious Constantine, while he was emperor, only closed the Pagan shrines and temples: but this Theodosius went on to destroy them, including the great and celebrated temple of Balanius at Heliopolis, with its columns made of three drums of marble apiece, which he converted into a Christian church; and in the same way he made the temple at Damascus a Christian church. And the Christian cause was much

[1] Op. cit., p. 254. [2] Op. cit., p. 17. [3] Spiers, op. cit., p. 2.

[4] Haenel, *Codices Gregorianus Hermogenianus Theodosianus. De Paganis sacrificiis et templis*, lib. xvi, tit. x, 7-12. [5] *Corpus script. hist. byz.*, vol. i, p. 561.

FIG. 85.—Damascus. Mosque of Walid during restoration. Eastern vestibule (VIII cent.).

FIG. 86.—Damascus. Mosque of Walid under restoration. Western vestibule (VIII cent.).

FIG. 87.—Damascus. Remains of the arch called the 'Bab al-Barid.'

FIG. 88.—Damascus. Mosque of Walid. Kiosk reproducing the ancient treasury of the mosque.

FIG. 89.—Damascus. Mosque of Walid. Details of mural decoration (VIII cent.).

FIG. 90.—Damascus. Mosque of Walid. Window with lattice (VIII cent.).

FIG. 92.—Palmyra. 'Temple of the Sun' (I and III cents.).

FIG. 91.—Cairo. Mihrab in the Mosque of Qalaun (1279-1290).

advanced in his reign.' Malalas (670),[1] on the other hand, mentions only the transformation of temples into churches: (Theodosius) 'abolished (κατέλυσε) the great and famous temple at Heliopolis called the Trilithon, and made it a Christian church. And in the same way he made the temple at Damascus a Christian church, and many others.' Now the remains of the church of Theodosius at Baalbec, the ancient Heliopolis, discovered in the course of the recent excavations,[2] show that it was not the grand temple of Jupiter, built by the Emperor Antoninus ('At Heliopolis, a city of Phoenicia in the Lebanon, he built a great temple to Jupiter; to be accounted as one of the wonders of the world'[3]), that was transformed into a church, for the latter, on the contrary, stood in the great court of the altar in front of the sanctuary, and there is nothing to show whether this was, or was not, still intact at the time (Fig. 93, p. 105).

One may always argue that, after the temple of Damascus came into the hands of the Christians, the cella was demolished, and a church, on a larger scale than the cella, erected with old materials. The passage quoted above from the Paschal Chronicle implies such enlargement. That rebuilding took place is evident, when it is considered that the temple apparently had the same form as other contemporary ones in Syria, for instance, the temple of Jupiter and Bacchus at Baalbec (II and III centuries) and the so-called temple of the Sun at Palmyra (I and III centuries). Yet it cannot have been a building with several equidistant rows of columns, as some have thought, nor a basilica with nave and aisles. And it cannot have had an internal length of 139 m. (about 450 ft.), seeing that the sanctuary of the colossal temple of Baalbec is only about 45 m. (145 ft.) in length.

The result of the works, apparently begun by Theodosius I and finished by Arcadius, was a church of ample size, as we shall see presently from Arculf's account, of great beauty, and unequalled in the region of Damascus, as we read in Eutychius:[4] 'Now it was a very fair church which had not its like in all the territory of Damascus.' But it was not a basilica with nave and aisles of equal breadth and a length of nearly 139 m. (450 ft.), as has been generally inferred. It must be remembered that such an enormous length would exceed

[1] *Corpus script. hist. byz.*; Ioannes Malalas, *Chronographia*, pp. 344, 345.

[2] *Jahrbuch des Kaiserlich Deutschen Archäologischen Instituts*, 1901, pp. 133-159; 1902, pp. 87-123; Puchstein, Schulz, Krencker, *Ausgrabungen in Baalbek*.

[3] *Corpus script. hist. byz.*; Ioannes Malalas, *Chronographia*, p. 280.

[4] Migne, *Patr. gr.*, vol. cxi, col. 1120; Eutychius, *Annales*.

that of the great church of St. Simeon Stylites at Qalat Simaan (V-VI centuries), which is little more than 96 m. (315 ft.); that of the famous but now almost entirely destroyed abbey church of Cluny (XI and XII centuries), which reached to about 135 m. (443 ft.), a building which in its day was without a rival in the Christian world; and, thirdly, that of the mosque of Cordova, which has a length of more than 130 m. (427 ft.). In fact there would not be a very great difference between its length and that of the largest Catholic church in the world, the present St. Peter's at the Vatican, which reaches 186 m. (612 ft.). The patent anomaly of a church of this form and of such a length has before now aroused suspicion.[1]

The orientation of the church of Damascus is not known, as there is no reference to it. Appearances are in favour of its having been towards the west. In my 'Lombardic Architecture' I dealt with the question of the orientation of apses, and discussed what is known about it. I here return for a moment to the subject, with some additions and corrections.

After the Edict of Milan (313), one of the most important new departures in the history of mankind, the great basilicas erected for Christian worship in Rome had their apses turned to the west, as is shown by those of St. Peter at the Vatican and St. John Lateran, built by Constantine the Great. This plan was, apparently, followed by his immediate descendants, at least in the case of the more important churches, where there was no reason against it on local or architectural grounds. And so the church of the Holy Sepulchre at Jerusalem was orientated towards the west, while the contemporary church of the Nativity at Bethlehem was set in the opposite direction. Exceptions to this are very rare. I may mention the primitive basilica of St. Menas (its remains have been recently disinterred in the holy city of Kharb Abu Mina in the Mareotic region) which was founded in the time of Constantine (306-337) and Athanasius the Great (296-373), Archbishop of Alexandria, and consecrated under Theodosius I (378-395) and the Patriarch Theophilus (385-412). It possesses an apse, curvilinear both inside and out, flanked by two niches measuring 1.60 by 0.70 m. (5 ft. 3 in. by 2 ft. 3½ in.), and turned to the east.[2]

As late as the reign of Theodosius I the original Christian basilica which he erected at Baalbec—'the great and celebrated temple of Balanius at Heliopolis, with its columns made of three drums of marble apiece, he

[1] Fergusson, *A History of Architecture*, vol. ii, pp. 505, 506.

[2] Kaufmann, op. cit., vol. i, pp. 40-103.

FIG. 93.—Baalbec. Ruins of Temples (II and III cents.).

FIG. 95.—Entrance to the Cave Temple at Karli (I cent. B.C.).

converted into a Christian church'[1]—was designed with its principal and two subordinate apses, semicircular both internally and externally, turned towards the west. The change to the east, as now to be seen, was the result of a later alteration when the central apse became a pentagon externally, after the Ravennate type, which I was the first to point out and establish.[2] That form did not originate in the East, as some persist in asserting;[3] nor did it come from Egypt, for the apse of the Constantinian church of St. Menas just mentioned, is semicircular on both sides. Nor do the recent excavations on the Mount of Olives at Jerusalem prove that apses with polygonal exteriors made their appearance before the last part of the IV century. Without entering on the question of the name of the basilica, of which some meagre remains have come to light and have been thought to belong to the church of the Ascension built by Helena and Constantine,[4] it appears to me that they are so fragmentary and show such variety of work that the conclusions based on them are of a very uncertain character. My doubts are confirmed by two capitals believed to be of the same date as the church, one of basket-work out of which grow cauliculi and acanthus leaves, the other of Corinthian type with stiff plain leaves.[5] Both are of poor workmanship, and not comparable nor contemporary with the Constantinian capitals in the church of the Nativity at Bethlehem. Not to say that, if we confine ourselves to ascertained facts, the wicker basket capital, Byzantine in style and type, is never found (unless the contrary be proved) before the V century.

But to resume. It was the Church of Ravenna which made the eastward orientation a fixed rule, possibly out of opposition to its powerful rival the Church of Rome. It first appears in the primatial see of Ravenna in the time of Archbishop Ursus (370-396).

My very reasonable theory of the western orientation of the church of the Baptist, together with the existence, in the eastern part of the outer wall on the south, of the mihrab mentioned above, presumably the work of Muawiya, and, thirdly, the triple entrance near the middle of that wall, which before the time of Walid was used by Christians and Moslems alike, can

[1] *Corpus script. hist. byz.; Chronicon Paschale*, vol. i, p. 561.

[2] Rivoira, op. cit. (Loescher), vol. i, pp. 26, 27; vol. ii, pp. 15, 16; (Hoepli), pp. 7, 8, 328, 329; (Heinemann), vol. i, p. 8; vol. ii, pp. 13, 189.

[3] Brutails, *Précis d'Archéologie du Moyen-Age*, p. 42.

[4] *Revue Biblique internationale*, 1911, pp. 219-265; P. Vincent, *L'église de l'Éléona.*

[5] Ibid., 1911, pl. vi, 1; pl. vii, 1.

all throw considerable light on the problem of the true position of the two buildings.

In my opinion this entrance, not exactly at the centre of the wall of Byzantine times, and therefore somewhat out of the axis of Walid's transept, formed originally the access to the enclosure within which the Christians erected: on the west, the basilica with its front turned, according to the usage of the time, to the east; on the east, the buildings connected with the new cult. At a later time, and after the Moslems had established a mosque facing the church, this entrance, until the days of Walid, gave access to the common enclosure, to the church, and to the mosque.

This inference is not weakened by the discovery of the head of St. John the Baptist when Walid was demolishing the buildings, for in the oldest account of the find, that of Ibn al-Fakih, written about 903, and the source used by the later writers, there is no mention of the spot where it took place, but only of that in which the caliph ordered the re-interment of the relic, viz. the fourth arch of the first row of columns on the east side of the transept;[1] the place, in fact, where the saint's shrine stands to-day.

That the church of the Baptist and the mosque formed two buildings, near to one another but distinct—the ordinary view being that one half of the same basilica was apportioned for Christian, and the other for Moslem worship — has been established by Caetani[2] from the earliest chroniclers, and by the aid of the text of Arculf (about 670), a passage of such importance that it must be repeated here: 'et in honorem sancti Iohannis Baptiste ibidem grandis fundata est ecclesia. Quedam etiam Sarracenorum ecclesia incredulorum, et ipsa in eadem civitate, quam ipsi frequentant, fabricata est.'[3]

Several pieces of evidence point to the fact that the Ummayyad mosque was afterwards erected as a new building, with the exception of a part of the outer wall of the great rectangle, and that it did not retain anything whatever of the Pagan temple or Christian church, apart from the fragment of the outer wall of that rectangle and reused materials taken from those structures. In the place of prayer the colonnades were arcaded from the beginning; and all the larger arches in the building were of horse-shoe form, and sprung from capitals carrying pulvins of various orders, design, and workmanship.

[1] Le Strange, *Palestine under the Moslems*, pp. 233, 234.

[2] *Annali*, vol. iii, 1, pp. 344-391.

[3] Tobler, op. cit., vol. i, pp. 185, 186; *Arculfi Relatio de Locis Sanctis.*

Now in Syria, in Roman times, the colonnades of temples carried architraves. One instance is the temple of Jupiter at Baalbec, begun by Antoninus Pius (138-161) and finished by Philip the Arabian (244-249),[1] where, although the broken arch is found in the stoa of the great court, the colonnades of the temple proper are designed to carry architraves only. This system was copied in the first great Christian basilicas of Syria and Palestine. And so the church of the Nativity at Bethlehem (327-333) had from the beginning architraves surmounting the colonnades of the nave.[2] The principle was applied to colonnades generally, with an occasional exception when a wider interval between the columns was arched over. The colonnades at Palmyra (II and III centuries) provide instances.

Moreover, Syria, at the time in question, was a stranger to the use of the Ravennate pulvin. This feature, characteristic originally of Ravennate, and then of Byzantine architecture, appeared for the first time in the old Basilica Ursiana at Ravenna (370-384) and in San Giorgio Maggiore at Naples (367-about 387), and there is no proof that even as late as the reign of Arcadius had it started on its journey to the East.[3]

Again, what are we to say of the horse-shoe arch, used as an element of construction, and applied uniformly to all the larger arches of the entire edifice? Where are there, we ask, not merely in Syria, but in the Roman and Byzantine empires, before the first Arab conquests, buildings of known date which contain colonnades with arches of that form?

Walid's intention in the construction of his mosque was, as Muqaddasi[4] shows, to outdo the greatest Christian churches, just as previously Abd al-Malik (685-705) had endeavoured to eclipse the Anastasis with the Holy Sepulchre by his Dome of the Rock at Jerusalem. At the same time he wanted to follow the traditional plan of the Prophet's mosque at Medina—an open court, partly occupied by a roofed-in space devoted to prayer, and accessible to the faithful from the court. Accordingly his building was designed as a basilica in the form of a parallelogram, the front side of which

[1] Rivoira, op. cit. (Loescher), vol. ii, pp. 535-538; (Hoepli), pp. 51-53; (Heinemann), vol. i, pp. 48, 49.

[2] Ibid., op. cit. (Loescher), vol. ii, pp. 24-27; (Hoepli), pp. 338-341; (Heinemann), vol. ii, pp. 20-22.

[3] Ibid., op. cit. (Loescher), vol. i, pp. 11-25; vol. ii, pp. 43-45; (Hoepli), pp. 8-18; (Heinemann), vol. i, pp. 10-18.

[4] Op. cit., pp. 22, 23.

consisted of an open arcade looking on the court. The transept, which in a cruciform Christian basilica stood in front of the apse, he set on the axis of the sanctuary, so that it might lead the eye up to the mihrab, the position of which was indicated by the important central dome.

All this was quite original, and it is not surprising that when the Caliph Mamun (813-833) saw the mosque he was astonished to find that it was built on a design which had no prototype,[1] and that Edrisi called it the most singular mosque in existence so far as its plan and arrangements were concerned.[2] The novelties were these: the plan of making the building only three aisles deep, just like a basilica with nave and aisles; the dome rising in the centre of the place of prayer; the two-storied arcades occurring both in the place of prayer and in the cloister round the court. But, above all, the horse-shoe arch, used for the first time as a constructive element. Noticeable, too, was the mihrab, perhaps the work of Muawiya and incorporated in Walid's edifice, for it was the prototype of its kind, derived from the apse of the Christian basilica, and taking the place of the big stone of the qibla.

About the origin and development of that distinctive feature of Moslem architecture, the horse-shoe arch, and about the Moslem style generally, vague theories have been from time to time put forward, supported by scanty, inconsistent, and often uncertain evidence. These theories are easily attacked and refuted. Recently a new one has come on the field, which suggests that the horse-shoe arch style originated in Visigothic Spain. A considerable number of monuments are adduced in support, it has all the appearance of explaining the facts, and, moreover, some of the works in which it is set forth are masterly.

Hence I feel obliged to make a conscientious, extended, and patient examination of the evidence produced in its favour, in order to see whether the whole or part of it can survive the attacks of a serious criticism, and a fresh examination of the buildings on which it is based. This examination will form the subject of Part II of this book. For the present we will confine ourselves to a summary of the origins of the horse-shoe arch.

Its discovery took place in ancient times. The earliest instances are to be found in India, where we see it (combined with the ogee or 'cyma reversa' arch), for instance, in the cave of Lomas Rishi, a few miles from Gaya in

[1] Maqrizi, *Histoire des Sultans Mamelouks de l'Égypte*, vol. ii, 3, p. 276.

[2] Edrisi, (Jaubert), *Géographie*, vol. i, p. 351.

FIG. 96.—Façade of the Cave Temple at Nasik (I or II cent. B.C.).

FIG. 94.—Entrance to the Cave Temple of Lomas Rishi near Gaya (III cent. B.C.).

FIG. 103.—Amman. Outer gateway of the Citadel (VII-XII cent.).

Bengal (Fig. 94, p. 112), dating from about 257 B.C., that is to say, in the reign of Asoka (273-232 B.C.); in the temples of Bhaga and Karli, in the province of Bombay (Fig. 95, p. 106), ascribed respectively to the II or III and the I centuries B.C.; and in the temple of Nasik, in the province of Bombay (Fig. 96, p. 111), to which a date is given in the I or II century B.C. We find it again in the bas-reliefs at Buddh-Gaya (put up in the III century B.C.), at Bharhut (part of which bear the date 185-173 B.C.), and at Sanchi in the State of Bhopal (set up in the II century B.C. or the I century A.D.).[1]

It was examples such as these which led the way to the constructive horse-shoe arch (not merely given that form by a gypsum-mortar addition), and not those at Ctesiphon, as Choisy maintains.[2] But in India it is not used as an element of construction before the Moslem conquest.[3] Till then it was only employed in a decorative way.

If we could accept the recently made assertion[4] that the horse-shoe arch —and the pointed arch too—were brought to Egypt by Indian workmen, we might infer that it was they who introduced it in Walid's mosque. Such a deduction is, however, excluded by what the monuments of India, either still standing, or represented in painting or sculpture, tell us about their knowledge and traditions in matters of planning, construction, and equilibrium. The same reasons are fatal to another statement,[5] to the effect that in the VIII and IX centuries the architects of India were, perhaps, unequalled in the world. How one would have liked to have seen these masters, with their knowledge and traditions, travel to the shores of the Bosphorus or to Germany in order to design and carry out, for instance, the rebuilding of St. Irene at Constantinople (VIII century) and the erection of Charles the Great's round church at Aachen (796-804) (Figs. 97, 98, pp. 115, 116)!

The instances of still earlier date which Dieulafoy, on the basis of a purely arbitrary dating of the monuments, believes that he has discovered in

[1] *Atti del Congresso internazionale di Scienze storiche* (Roma, 1-9 Apr. 1903), vol. vii; PULLÉ, *Riflessi indiani nell'arte romaica*, pp. 111, 112. FERGUSSON, *History of Indian and Eastern Architecture*, pp. 84-99, 108-122. DE BEYLIÉ, *L'architecture Hindoue en Extrême-Orient*, pp. 34, 51, 53. VINCENT A. SMITH, *A History of Fine Art in India and Ceylon*, pp. 19, 20, 69-71, 74. FERGUSSON, BURGESS, *The Cave Temples of India*, pp. 29-33, 38-40, 184, 232-242, 272-275.

[2] *Histoire de l'architecture*, vol. i, p. 132.

[3] FERGUSSON, *History of Indian and Eastern Architecture*, p. 120.

[4] HAVELL, op. cit. pp., 6, 7.

[5] Ibid., p. 21.

Persia, are very far from being so. Thus the date of the four archivolts with a radius exceeding the semicircle (three being made so by moulding in cement, while only the fourth is constructive) in the palace or castle of Firuz Abad,[1] must be brought down more than a thousand years. Elsewhere[2] I have stated the reasons derived from the history, plan, and construction of the building, which demonstrate the impossibility of the date given to it by Dieulafoy, viz. the reign of Xerxes I (486-465 B.C.), or of Artaxerxes I (465-425 B.C.),[3] and I am not alone in thus reducing its age.[4]

I may add here, that among the ruins of Hatra on the Tigris, ascribed to the first three centuries of the Christian era, the well-known palace not merely contains no trace of the Romano-Campanian pendentive, but has not a vestige even of a dome. Its square or rectangular rooms have barrel vaults only; and the hemispherical vault which Dieulafoy[5] has given to one of them is quite conjectural.

Consequently, we must come down to the erection of the palace or castle of Chosroes I (531-579) at Ctesiphon, the port at which the merchandize of India arrived, in order to find, according to Choisy, anything approaching a horse-shoe arch (Fig. 99, p. 117). This building consists, in its present state, of a vast hall covered by a barrel vault of elliptical outline, flanked by eight smaller halls which, like the other, are rectangular. It was built by workmen sent by Justinian (527-565), according to the tradition preserved by Theophylactus Simocatta (638)—'They say that the emperor Justinian provided Greek marble for Chosroes the son of Cabades, and skilled builders and workmen accomplished in the construction of roofs, and that he built a palace for Chosroes in the Roman style, situated not far from Ctesiphon.'[6] Among the craftsmen may, perchance, have been some from Ravenna, considering the occurrence of blank arcading at the top of the walls. Arched corbel courses used decoratively in architecture, the archetype of which I discovered in a tomb of the II century on the Via Praenestina near Rome, at the place known

[1] DIEULAFOY, *L'Art antique de la Perse*, vol. iv, p. 37.

[2] RIVOIRA, op. cit. (Heinemann), vol. i, pp. 24, 25, 193-195.

[3] DIEULAFOY, op. cit., vol. iv, p. 75.

[4] DE LASTEYRIE, *L'architecture religieuse en France à l'époque romane*, pp. 270-272. DE MORGAN, *Mission scientifique en Perse. Recherches archéologiques*, vol. ii, pp. 341-360, Kasr-é-Chirin. PERROT, CHIPIEZ, *Histoire de l'Art dans l'antiquité. Perse*, pp. 561-588.

[5] Op. cit., vol. v, pp. 15, 16.

[6] *Corpus script. hist. byz.*; THEOPHYLACTUS SIMOCATTA, *Historiae*, p. 217.

FIG. 97.—Aachen. Palace Chapel (796-804).

FIG. 98.—Aachen. Palace Chapel (796-804).

FIG. 99.—Ctesiphon. Façade of the Palace of Chosroes I (531-579).
(From DIEULAFOY, *L'Art antique dans la Perse*, vol. v. pl. iii.)

FIG. 102.—Ajanta. Interior of Cave Temple XII (200 B.C.-150 A.D.).

FIG. 100.—Rome. Tomb on the Via Praenestina (II cent.).

FIG. 101.—Rome. House of Caligula on the Palatine. Hanging gallery (37-41).

as 'Acqua bollicante' (Fig. 100, p. 118)—a form derived from pensile arches designed to carry balconies, such as that in the House of Caligula on the Palatine (Fig. 101, p. 118) erected after 37—were developed by the School of Ravenna, and their occurrence in Western Asia is very rare in ancient times.[1] I say in Western Asia, because in India decorative blank arches, of an Indian type of course, were used both internally and externally from early times. Thus the fronts of the cave temples at Nasik and Karli were so treated as early as the I or II century B.C. The cave temple of Ajanta numbered XII was decorated in this way at some time between about 200 B.C. and 150 A.D.[2] (Fig. 102, p. 117).

With regard to the occurrence of the horse-shoe arch at Ctesiphon, I find that it is not really constructive, the semicircular (and, exceptionally, the pointed) arch being used systematically throughout the building; but is only given that form by means of the plaster.

We are on safe ground when we come to the well-known cruciform structure forming an outer gateway to the citadel of Amman (Fig. 103, p. 112), the erection of which was dated by Dieulafoy either at the end of the Sassanian epoch (226-651), or else in the first years of the Hijra (622),[3] but is now fixed in the Arab period,[4] and consequently after the capture of Damascus (636), which took place before the conquest of the old Ammonite capital. Conder[5] thinks that it may have been built by the Caliph Mamun (813-833), but certainly not before the VII century, and, perhaps, in the time of the Crusades, on account of the decorative blank arcading (which he suspects was carved in the stonework after the building was finished) with its saw-tooth ornament, and shafts recalling those in the arcading of the Dome of the Rock at Jerusalem.

The gateway at Amman, with its examples, not only of the horse-shoe arch, but also of hood-shaped pendentives, gives rise to some observations on the deserted castles or palaces of Western Asia, to some of which, such as those of Sarvistan and Firuz Abad, mythical dates have been assigned. These

[1] RIVOIRA, op. cit. (Hoepli), pp. 36, 37; (Heinemann), vol. i, pp. 36, 37.

[2] VINCENT A. SMITH, op. cit., p. 275.

[3] Op. cit., vol. v, pp. 102, 103.

[4] HOUTSMA, BASSET, *Encyclopédie de l'Islām*, Ammān, p. 336. Publication of the Princeton University; BUTLER, *Archaeological Expedition to Syria in* 1904-1905; *Ancient Architecture in Syria*, Div. ii, p. 41, 'Ammân.'

[5] *The Survey of Eastern Palestine*, 1889, pp. 60-63; *The Adwân Country*. Ibid., *Heth and Moab*, p. 158.

observations have been suggested to me by De Morgan's[1] recent study on the buildings of Chosroes II (591-628) at Qasr es-Sherin, and by an article written by Lammens.[2] The buildings at Qasr es-Sherin are the most important in the whole of Persia for giving the complete general plan of a royal palace and its dependencies. They show that the rooms on the ground floor were barrel-vaulted, only those in the upper floors having ceilings; and that the conical squinch was used, as in the case of a square hall covered by an oval cupola, now partly fallen in, recalling similar constructions at Sarvistan and Firuz Abad, and also of smaller rooms.

Now to judge by dated buildings, those erected by the Achaemenids at Susa, Persepolis, and in the valley of Polvar-rud, were without vaulting. The Sassanids (226-651) were the first to introduce it into Persia, under Roman influence. Before their time the vault had no place in buildings. Nor had the Greek influence, which came in with the conquests of Alexander the Great, any effect in this direction; for the Greeks, though they were acquainted with vaulting, rejected it as a form of roofing, because it was not in keeping with their artistic ideals.[3] Their unequalled sense of form made their architectural work decorative rather than constructive. It was the Romans, with their innate architectural sense, who caused the arch and the vault to prevail, who developed their combination, and brought them to perfection in their baths and mausoleums.

Moreover, there is no instance of a vault with ovoidal outline in the great palace and temple buildings of Persia and the neighbouring countries earlier than the palace of Chosroes I at Ctesiphon. Thus the ruins of the palace at Hatra on the Tigris, dated in the first three centuries of our era,[4] contain only semicircular barrel vaults.[5] The Assyrians were acquainted with the form, but apparently made use of it only in subterranean water courses, as for instance at Khorsabad, and there is scarcely any instance of it in buildings above ground.

As for a dome in the true sense—not merely courses of stone or brick, each projecting a little beyond the other, as in the tombs or so-called treasuries of Atreus and Clytemnestra at Mycenae (Fig. 104, p. 127)—with an

[1] Op. cit., vol. iv, 2, pp. 341-357.

[2] Université Saint-Joseph, Beyrouth, *Mélanges de la Faculté orientale*, vol. iv; *La Bádia et la Hira sous les Omaiyades*, pp. 91-112.

[3] De Morgan, op. cit., vol. iv, 2, p. 347.

[4] Dieulafoy, op. cit., vol. v, p. 13.

[5] Andrae, *Hatra.*

ovoidal outline, and of large span, I have found no recorded instance before this one of Chosroes II, perhaps introduced for the first time in this part of Asia by the craftsmen sent to Ctesiphon by Justinian, but employing a traditional local curve though the principle embodied was foreign.

The conical cupola had already made its appearance in San Vitale at Ravenna (526-547), unique in its construction and lightness, which still excites our admiration. That dome, with the rest of the church, was the creation of the brain of Julianus Argentarius, and the minds and handiwork of the craftsmen of Ravenna, who were not partly of Greek origin, as has been asserted recently,[1] though without supplying the necessary evidence: a practice which is more convenient than convincing. My statement has the support of, among other things, the planning and equilibrium of the building which have no parallels in any earlier or contemporary structures in the East; the dome of terra-cotta tubes, inserted one inside the other and coiling round in a spiral up to the crown, a Ravennate feature invented by the Campanians, developed by the Romans, and raised to its highest expression at Ravenna; the pyramidal roof surmounting and protecting the dome from the weather, a device which marks a departure from the Roman custom of leaving the outer face of a dome exposed or covering it with a roof in contact with it, and at the same time contains the germ of the double dome; the style of the masonry; the grace and elegance of its architectural forms, qualities unknown even to the architect of SS. Sergius and Bacchus at Constantinople (527-536).[2]

The dome of St. George at Ezra (515-16) with its boldly ovoidal form (Fig. 105, p. 122), constructed of light concrete materials, a little more than half the thickness of the walls of the drum on which it rests, is clearly of a different date from the rest of the church, which is built entirely of stone without the use of mortar. It is due to rebuilding.

De Vogüé, in his imaginative reconstruction of the original dome of the cathedral of Bosra (511-12), a church almost contemporary with the last, decided, not without good reason, upon a hemispherical instead of a conical outline.[3] His account states that the windows at the base of the dome are the earliest example of this method of lighting. Nothing could

[1] Diehl, *Manuel d'Art byzantin*, pp. 174-176.

[2] Rivoira, op. cit. (Loescher), vol. i, pp. 27, 28, 35, 36, 57-79; (Hoepli), pp. 18-20, 40, 61-82, 96, 97; (Heinemann), vol. i, pp. 18-21, 39, 56-84; vol. ii, p. 22.

[3] *Syrie centrale*, vol. i, pp. 61-67.

be farther from the truth, for it had been applied centuries before at Rome in the imperial age, as may be seen from Montano,[1] and from the sketch of a tomb still perfect in the days of Serlio (1475-1552) (Fig. 106),[2] and shown by Montano to have stood on the Via Appia Antica. Not to speak of the still surviving examples on a grand scale, represented by the Nymphaeum of the Licinian Gardens (253-268) and the Mausoleum of Santa Costanza (326-329).

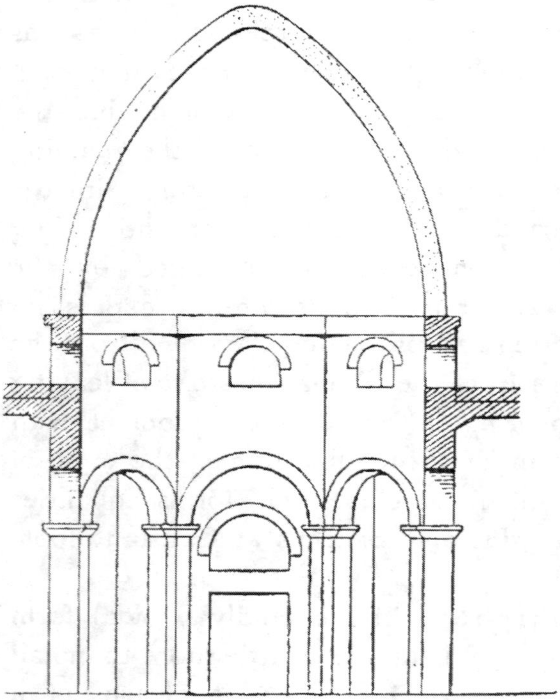

FIG. 105.—Ezra. Section of the church of St. George (515-16).

FIG. 106.—Rome.—Tomb on the Via Appia Antica.

(From SCAMOZZI, *Tutte l'opere d'Architettura di Sebastiano Serlio*, fogl. 63.)

It is true that a much earlier instance of a conical cupola has been cited in the case of the Marneion at Gaza. But it never had any real existence. From the meagre, ambiguous, and disconnected bits of description which Mark the Deacon gives of the important round temple of the Cretan

[1] *Scielta de varii tempietti antichi*, tavv. 29, 30, 34, 38, 42, 43; *Raccolta de tempii e sepolcri disegnati dall' antico*, tavv. 3, 5, 7, 13, 15, 22, 23, 37, 38, 39, 40.

[2] SCAMOZZI, *Tutte l'opere d'Architettura di Sebastiano Serlio*, fogl. 63.

Zeus, ascribed with considerable probability to the II century,[1] all that can be gathered is that the central structure, which had more than one entrance, and stood in an open court surrounded by a two-aisled portico, had the form of a ciborium with a wooden roof, for Mark says that this central part or cella was destroyed by fire, and that a burning beam fell on the official who was superintending the work of destruction, and killed him.[2] In short, there must have been a cylindrical structure of masonry with a conical wooden roof, like the drum of Santo Stefano Rotondo on the Caelian at Rome. The suggestion had previously been made that the author of the *Life of St. Porphyry, Bishop of Gaza*, used the word κιβώριον in the sense of a baldacchino or canopy of some kind; and the same writer thought that, in any case, the dome of the Marneion, if it existed, was of the usual form, that is to say spherical, and not elliptical.[3]

The Assyrian builders were unquestionably acquainted with both the hemispherical and the ovoidal cupola, as is shown by the well-known bas-relief of Kuyunjik (Nineveh) discovered by Layard.[4] But it has been pointed out by others, and the observation has lately been repeated,[5] that the buildings there represented are related to the houses of the present day in the villages of Syria and Northern Mesopotamia, which are roofed with small cupolas of sun-baked bricks set in rings, each projecting beyond the last, and were, perhaps, of the same kind. This way of making a cupola of masonry with each course projecting a little beyond the one below it, is of very early origin. The Etruscans were acquainted with it in the VII century B.C., as is proved by the tomb of the 'Diavolino' from Vetulonia, which has been reconstructed in the garden of the Archaeological Museum at Florence.[6] Here the dome of the cella has raccords in courses projecting one beyond the other (Fig. 107, p. 127). In any case we know nothing of the construction of cupolas such as those represented on the bas-relief, nor how they were supported. The only thing that seems to be certain is that they were

[1] *Proceedings of the British Academy*, vol. v; Hill, *Some Palestinian Cults in the Graeco-Roman Age*, p. 15, n. 1.

[2] Hill, *The Life of Porphyry, Bishop of Gaza, by Mark the Deacon*, pp. 75-87, 140.

[3] Ibid., *Some Palestinian Cults in the Graeco-Roman Age*, p. 15, n. 1. Ibid., *The Life of Forphyry, Bishop of Gaza, by Mark the Deacon*, pp. 85, 86.

[4] *A Second Series of the Monuments of Nineveh*, pl. 17.

[5] *Journal of Hellenic Studies*, vol. xxx, pp. 77-79; Bell, *The vaulting system of Ukheidar*.

[6] Milani, *Il R. Museo Archeologico di Firenze*, vol. i, pp. 282, 283.

designed to cover very small areas, for no vestige of a dome has hitherto been discovered in any of the great Syrian and Chaldaean remains.

Lastly, pendentives either with conical vaults or in the form of niches have not as yet been found, recognizable as such, in Western Asia, or in Egypt, earlier than those at Qasr es-Sherin mentioned above, though it may be conjectured that this example reached Persia by the route which we have suggested, and possibly through craftsmen from Ravenna or South Italy, where the Ravennate niche-pendentive and the hood-shaped pendentive first came into use.

The assertion that, wherever and whenever the vaulted pendentive appears, it denotes decided Oriental influence, is quite arbitrary.[1] Elsewhere I have traced the origins of this form of pendentive,[2] and my view has won acceptance.[3] I will only remark here that there is a general confusion between the pendentive with a simple vault, and the niche-pendentive consisting of a more or less elongated recess. The oldest specimens which we possess of the vaulted and niche forms are to be found in San Giovanni in Fonte (V century) adjoining the cathedral of Naples (Fig. 108, p. 127), and in San Vitale at Ravenna (VI century) (Fig. 109, p. 125). The nearly contemporary instance of a niche-pendentive, said to exist in the dome of the three-lobed choir of the church of the Dair al-Ahmar, or Red Convent, near Sohag in the Thebaid, is not of the date assigned to it, viz. in the early or mid V century; and that on account of the analogies presented by the building known as the Dair al-Abiad, or White Convent.[4] Nor does it belong to the time of Helena († 328), the mother of Constantine the Great, the traditional founder of the latter institution.[5] The well-known early church of St. Menas at Kharb Abu Mina follows the lines of the sanctuaries of the Constantinian age in Egypt, that is to say, it has a semicircular apse, flanked by two small recesses. As late as the reign of Arcadius (395-408) the imposing church of the Virgin, erected at the end of St. Menas, had only a simple semicircular apse.[6]

Moreover, even if we accepted this date, and allowed that the original

[1] VAN BERCHEM, STRZYGOWSKI, *Amida*, p. 262.

[2] RIVOIRA, op. cit. (Loescher), vol. ii, pp. 602-605; (Hoepli), pp. 235-242; (Heinemann), vol. i, pp. 71, 191-199.

[3] DE LASTEYRIE, op. cit., pp. 270-272.

[4] DE BOCK, *Matériaux pour servir à l'archéologie de l'Égypte chrétienne*, pp. 39-67, pl. xxvi, xxviii.

[5] BUTLER, *The Ancient Coptic Churches of Egypt*, vol. i, pp. 351-359.

[6] KAUFMANN, op. cit., pp. 40-103.

structure remained untouched in the Moslem conquest, and survived what was worse, Caliph Hakim's (996-1020) mania for destruction,[1] it has undergone such a series of restorations and rebuildings at different periods, that it has become a perfect enigma.

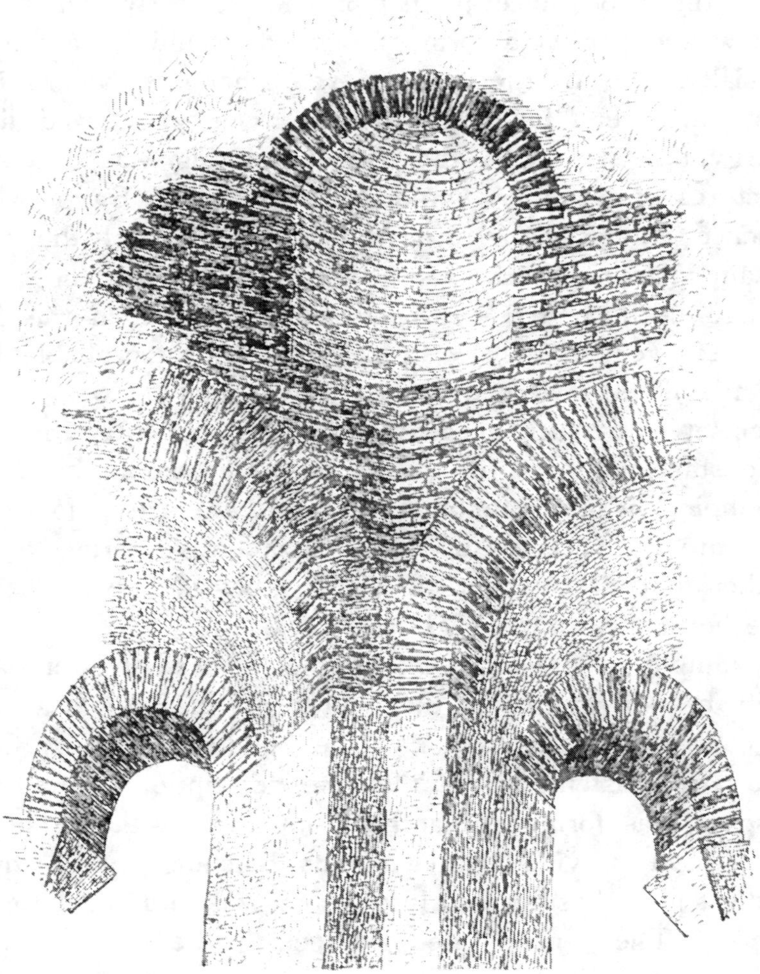

FIG. 109.—Ravenna. San Vitale. Pendentive of the dome (526-547).

With regard to the dome, anyone who looks at the exposed masonry on the exterior (Fig. 110, p. 128) will see at once the extensive rebuilding in the drum, and the complete reconstruction of the cupola. In the interior, too, the remains of the niches are clearly of a late Moslem period, as are the

[1] LANE-POOLE, *A History of Egypt in the Middle Ages*, p. 127.

decorative colonnettes belonging to them (Fig. 111, p. 128). My opinion is confirmed by a recent work,[1] in which the author states that both the Dair al-Abiad and the Dair al-Ahmar originally had wooden roofs, and that the three-lobed choir at the east had no dome over its square central space.

In any case, the appearance in Egypt, in the early years of the IV century, of so new and perfect a form of raccord, would be a very singular anomaly. Especially, too, in the land of the Pharaohs, where before the Roman conquest the great buildings had flat ceilings, curved lines being foreign to the Egyptian style, and the use of vaulting was exceptional and confined to structures of secondary importance.[2] And in Egypt where, even under the influence exercised by the vaulted buildings of the conquerors, there is no certain instance of the use of the pendentive, the rudimentary form of which had been created by those same Romans in the II century and was not yet evolved in the IV, a task which was probably left to the Campanians. If the reverse were the case, the Roman builders would surely have availed themselves of such a useful discovery, and after the transfer of the capital to Constantinople the Byzantine craftsmen would have diffused it over the new empire, which cannot have been the case, for the simple reason that there are no instances of (1) the pendentive formed of a simple conical vault taken out of a spherical surface before the V century; or (2) of the niche form before the VI.

The other example of a vaulted raccord, of somewhat later date, which Millet[3] thinks he has discovered in the church of St. Sergius at Gaza (VI century), in the course of a description of the building given by Choricus of Gaza, never had any existence. All that the description shows is that the square central space was formed of arches supporting walls as high as the arches themselves, and provided with columns reaching up to the start of the roof; that the square base passed into an octagon, and the latter into the circle of the dome.[4] The general inference seems to be that the central space had columns at the angles intended to carry the projecting raccords of the drum and the dome. But there is no foundation for saying that there were hood-shaped or niche pendentives, decorated moreover with columns. Nor is there any information as to whether the dome was of wood or of masonry.

[1] SOMERS CLARKE, *Christian Antiquities in the Nile Valley*, pp. 145-171.

[2] PERROT, CHIPIEZ, op. cit., *L'Égypte*, pp. 112, 530.

[3] *Revue Archéologique*, 1905, pp. 99, 100; *L'Asie Mineure nouveau domaine de l'Histoire de l'Art.*

[4] BOISSONADE, *Chorici Gazaei Orationes Declamationes Fragmenta*, pp. 83-88.

FIG. 108.—Naples. San Giovanni in Fonte. Pendentive (V cent.).

FIG. 104.—Mycenae. 'Treasury of Atreus.

FIG. 107.—Florence. Archaeological Museum. Tomb from Vetulonia, showing one of the raccords (VII cent. B.C.).

FIG. 110.—Church of the Dair al-Ahmar near Sohag. Dome (after 1020).
(From DE BOCK, *Matériaux pour servir à l'Archéologie de l'Égypte chrétienne.*)

FIG. 111.—Church of the Dair al-Ahmar near Sohag. Niche-pendentive of the dome (after 1020).
(From DE BOCK, *Matériaux pour servir à l'Archéologie de l'Égypte chrétienne.*)

FIG. 112.—Milan. San Lorenzo Maggiore (VI-XVI cent.).

FIG. 115.—Rome. Villa Mattei. End of sarcophagus (III or IV cent.).

FIG. 116.—Rome. Villa Mattei. The other end of sarcophagus (III or IV cent.).

I pass over the other instance cited by Millet[1] of the church of Khoja Kalessi in the region of the Taurus, because it possesses no indications of date. That given to it by him and by others is purely arbitrary. Moreover, it contains no trace of raccords.

I must also omit the squinches given to San Lorenzo at Milan,[2] for they are non-existent, the dome being simply the continuation of the drum (Fig. 112, p. 129). How the original dome was supported we do not know precisely. It was only after the catastrophes of 1071 and 1124 that hood-shaped pendentives in tiers were introduced; and these, again, disappeared in the reconstruction which followed the disaster of 1573.[3] San Lorenzo is not a secular building of the III-IV centuries, as Archinti held,[4] but a church of the VI century, as I have demonstrated, and others have confirmed.[5]

The important ruins of Qasr es-Sherin may therefore serve, in default of fresh discoveries, as a touchstone for the dating of a number of desert palaces or castles, as well as of others in the cities of Western Asia, provided with conical domes or hood-shaped pendentives.

This test receives confirmation from the article by Lammens referred to above. According to him, the Lakhmid princes of Hira used to send their children into the centre of Arabia to be out of the way of fevers and infectious diseases. The Sassanid kings, too, had their heirs brought up by these Lakhmid vassals of theirs, in the desert castles of Havarnaq and Sadir. The Arab conquerors, accustomed as they were to the free air of the desert, fearful of epidemics, and anxious to maintain the purity of their language, took a long time to get accustomed to city life. So much so that, in the first century of the Hijra, the Asrafs of Syria retired into the desert for a sojourn after the winter rains. And under the Ummayyads, every caliph, the members of the reigning house, and the chief officials, all had their 'badia' or residence in the desert. Hence it is under that dynasty, responsible as it was for the erection of so many admirable religious edifices, that we may place the principal movement in the construction of monumental fortified palaces in the desert.

[1] *Revue Archéologique*, 1905, pp. 93-109; *L'Asie Mineure nouveau domaine de l'Histoire de l'Art.*

[2] Van Millingen, *Byzantine Churches in Constantinople*, p. 78.

[3] Rivoira, op. cit. (Loescher), vol. i, pp. 79-81; (Hoepli), pp. 83-85; (Heinemann), vol. i, pp. 72-74.

[4] *Stili nell' Architettura*, vol. ii, p. 86.

[5] *Politecnico*, 1911, nn. 11-12; Monneret de Villard, *La chiesa di San Lorenzo in Milano.*

Among these must be reckoned the nameless but imposing structure at Mshatta (each side of the square of the outer wall measures about 145 m., or 477 ft.), the foundation of which is put at about the year 612 by Dieulafoy,[1] while Strzygowski gives it a still earlier date in the IV century.[2] On the other hand, it is possible to place it, with considerable probability, in the caliphate of Yazid II (720-724), for it is known that this effeminate ruler expressed the intention of building a 'qasr' to which he might retire alone with his favourite Hababa, but did not finish it, perhaps because the works were interrupted by her tragic death, soon followed by his own. As a matter of fact, the castle of Mshatta was left unfinished and uninhabited; and the Abbasides saw no need for venting their hatred of the abhorred Ummayyads by its destruction.

The light shed by Qasr es-Sherin, together with the story told by Lammens, thus make it possible to suggest a date for—to give one instance—the grand fortified palace of Ukhaidir, which has been ascribed to one of the early caliphs,[3] or else has been thought to belong to the time of the Lakhmids and, perhaps, to be actually the castle of Havarnaq (built in the first years of the V century by a Greek architect, Sinimmar: a great dome was erected in the middle of the VIII century[4]), or else that of Sadir.[5] A more approximate date would be either in the reign of Chosroes II or in the time of the early Abbasides, omitting the Ummayyads who (as Father Lammens informs me) built their castles in Syria, not in Mesopotamia.

For similar reasons the smaller palaces of Firuz Abad and Sarvistan, and also the domed structure at Farakh Abad, may be assigned to an epoch not earlier than the reign of Chosroes II, and with even greater probability to Moslem times.

With regard to Firuz Abad, I must call attention to the anachronism of ascribing it to the epoch of the Achaemenids (688-330 B.C.), for blank arcading is freely used in its decoration; whereas in that period, although the Persians and Assyrians used rectangular panelling in the decorative treatment of walls,

[1] Op. cit., vol. v, p. 94.

[2] *Jahrbuch der Königlich Preuszischen Kunstsammlungen*, 1904; SCHULZ, STRZYGOWSKI, *Mschatta*, pp. 205-373.

[3] BELL, *Palace and Mosque at Ukhaidir*, p. 135.

[4] AMARI, op. cit., vol. iii, 2, pp. 825, 828, 829.

[5] CHASSINAT, *Mémoires publiées par les Membres de l'Institut Français d'Archéologie orientale du Caire*, vol. xxviii; MASSIGNON, *Mission en Mésopotamie*, pp. 1-20.

they were not acquainted with the system of arcading, which was a Roman invention.[1]

To return now to the horse-shoe arch. The earliest dated instance of a constructive arch of this form in Syria, and appearing there only as an exceptional and individual feature, was formerly to be found in the church of Dana on the Euphrates, illustrated by Texier and Pullan,[2] now no longer in existence. In it the frontal arch of the apse and its vault had a radius larger than that of a semicircle. Its date was the year 540.

It has also been suggested that one of the churches of Zebed in the same region, viz. the eastern one, in which the plan of the apse is larger than a semicircle,[3] forms a parallel to the one at Dana. But we know nothing about its date; and all that can be said about it is that its construction may be connected with that of its sister church at Zebed on the west, which bears the date 511.

In Cappadocia examples are to be found of churches and tombs excavated in the rock, where the entrance is surmounted by a horse-shoe arch; and these have been ascribed to the centuries of the Christian persecutions, and therefore to a time before the Edict of Milan (313). Nor do they stand alone, for in the well-known tomb at Urgub, also cut in the rock, and dated in the IV century, the horse-shoe arch was freely used in one range of openings in the façade, this range being surmounted by two others of blank arcading.[4] There is no certain proof of the date of any of these caves, and it has been suggested on good grounds that paintings which they contain are not earlier than 930.[5] Not to speak of alterations which may have taken place under Moslem rule. However this may be, the façade in question cannot be as old as the IV century, and must have been executed under Moslem influence. It would be too strange an anomaly to find such a singular decorative motive remaining for so many centuries as an individual and sporadic instance, with no attempt to copy it, and ignored by the Byzantine craftsmen.

In the Byzantine empire and the kingdom of Persia there is no dated

[1] RIVOIRA, op. cit. (Loescher), vol. i, pp. 5-9; (Hoepli), pp. 21-26; (Heinemann), vol. i, pp. 23-25.

[2] *Byzantine Architecture*, pp. 173, 174.

[3] BUTLER, *Publications of an American Archaeological Expedition to Syria in* 1899-1900. *Architecture, Sculpture, Mosaic and Wall-Painting in Northern Central Syria and the Djebel Haurân*, pp. 303, 305.

[4] TEXIER, *Description de l'Asie Mineure*, vol. ii, p. 76, pl. 89, 90. TEXIER, PULLAN, *Byzantine Architecture*, pp. 4, 40, pl. iv.

[5] Ibid., p. 40.

building with decorative blank arcading earlier than that which appears at Ctesiphon. And as it was in 540 that Ravenna fell into the hands of Belisarius, it seems to be a not improbable conjecture that it was brought to the new Persian capital by craftsmen from Ravenna, where it enjoyed such popularity.

At Urfa, the Roman Edessa, in Mesopotamia, there is a square minaret, believed to have been the bell-tower of a church of the Virgin erected in the time of Justinian (527-565), which has horse-shoe arches. But Garovaglio dates it in Arab times,[1] and De Beylié[2] suspected, with good reason, that it belonged to the age of the Crusades. The counts of Edessa held the district between 1098 and 1144.[3] A record is to be found in Caetani[4] of an order given by the Caliph Muawiya, after a destructive earthquake in 678, for the restoration of the churches of Edessa, and also of the wreck of the ancient church of the city by another violent earthquake in 681-82. Hence, supposing that there were any bell-towers there, they cannot have belonged to the time of Justinian.

To the XII century, again, must be ascribed another bell-tower at Urfa with an octagonal base, formerly belonging to the church of the Forty Martyrs, but also converted into a minaret, which has been wrongly assigned to the V and VI centuries. It recalls the polygonal minaret at Anah on the Euphrates, which is decorated with sunk panels, and is believed to date from the early centuries of the Moslem era.[5]

In Syria and Palestine the oldest certain record of a great bell-tower on a large scale is of the one belonging to the Holy Sepulchre at Jerusalem, erected between 1160 and 1180.[6] I may mention with regard to this tower that, in a miniature of the XIII century, the church is represented with a pair of similar towers.[7]

In Lycaonia, that is to say at Binbir Kilisse, there are remains of ancient churches, ascribed to the times before the Arab invasion of about 700, in which the horse-shoe arch is freely used.[8] But this ascription, though it

[1] Garovaglio, *Viaggio nella Siria Centrale e nella Mesopotamia*, tav. xxxiii.

[2] *Prome et Samara*, pp. 67, 68.

[3] Lane-Poole, *Saladin and the Fall of the Kingdom of Jerusalem*, tab. i.

[4] *Chronographia*, pp. 637, 701.

[5] De Beylié, *Prome et Samara*, pp. 67, 68.

[6] Barnabé Meistermann, *Nueva Guia de Tierra Santa*, p. 86.

[7] Heisenberg, *Grabeskirche und Apostelkirche, zwei Basiliken Konstantins*, vol. i, taf. xi.

[8] Ramsay, Bell, *The Thousand and One Churches*, pp. 14, 41-50, 71-99, 117-126, 147-151.

may represent the opinion of its authors, is not supported by any certified date. Such being the case, I would refer the reader to what has been said by others on the subject.[1]

In Italy the re-entrant arch in ancient times barely made a beginning here and there as a sporadic motive, sometimes due to the necessities of the plan, as, for instance, in the villa known as the 'Sette Bassi' on the Via Latina near Rome (II century), as I have pointed out elsewhere.[2] In the central block of these important ruins are to be seen a domed vestibule of about 6 m. (19 ft. 9 in.) in diameter, and a room with a niche at the end of 1.80 m. (nearly 6 ft.) in diameter, where this arch is used in plan (Figs. 113, 114). The brick stamps fix the date of erection in the years 100-133. In the detached block to the north-west there may also be seen a cruciform room with an apse at its end which is of horse-shoe form. The brick stamps give the year 134.

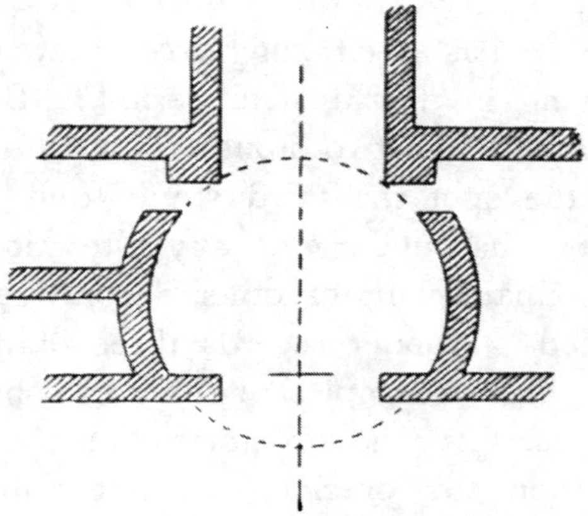

FIG. 113.—Rome. Villa called 'Sette Bassi,' on the Via Latina. Plan of a vestibule (II cent.).

Otherwise it appears occasionally in carving, as in the sarcophagus of the III or IV century in the Villa Mattei on the Caelian at Rome (Figs. 115, 116, p. 130).

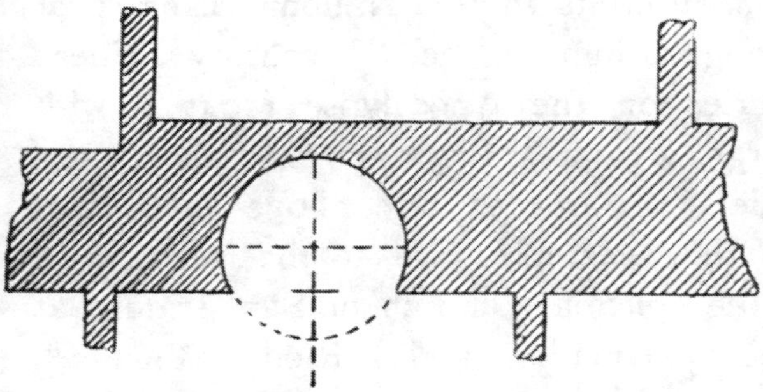

FIG. 114.—Rome. Villa called 'Sette Bassi,' on the Via Latina. Section of a wall with horse-shoe niche (II cent.).

The Iberian peninsula contains some ancient examples of the decorative use of the form, going back to the II or more probably the III century. For instance, the Pagan gravestone from León (Fig. 117, p. 140) in the National Archaeological Museum at Madrid, and two more of the same kind in the Archaeological Museum (formerly

[1] DE LASTEYRIE, op. cit., pp. 17, 18.

[2] RIVOIRA, op. cit. (Loescher), vol. i, pp. 221, 222; (Hoepli), p. 393; (Heinemann), vol. ii, pp. 58, 59.

the convent of St. Mark) at León, exhibit in relief, respectively, an arch enclosing a whorl, two smaller arches flanking a larger one, and two arches of equal size, all of the horse-shoe form. A cinerary urn of the Roman period, from Bausen, in the valley of Arán, has similar arches represented on it.[1]

It has been suggested that these Iberian gravestones received their carving in the Moslem period.[2] But even though this might have been the case with the two stones in the Museum at León, no one who has examined on the spot the third stone from León, now at Madrid, can think, I hope, that it has undergone any alteration.

Spain contains other decorative examples belonging to the early Christian period. Hübner records three of the VI century.[3]

Early examples of the horse-shoe arch are also to be found in illuminated manuscripts, though not of such ancient date as those in buildings. I may mention the precious Evangeliarium, written in Syriac by Rabula in the monastery of Zagba, in Mesopotamia, in the year 586,[4] where the nineteen Canons have arcades of horse-shoe arches in pairs, in threes, and in fours, enclosed within a single arch. But the illuminated leaves of parchment bound with the text, some of which are evidently later additions, belong to different dates and hands, and are, apparently, in every case, the result of later insertion. The Crucifixion which appears on one of these leaves has been ascribed to various centuries between the VIII and the XI.[5]

Next come the no less precious manuscripts in the National Library at Madrid: of the Bible (950); an Evangeliarium of the XI century; Fuero juzgo (1058); St. Beatus, Commentaries on the Apocalypse (1047); with ornamentation of open arcades, a large arcade between two smaller ones, arcades enclosed in a single arch, tiers of arcades one above the other, always with the horse-shoe arch. Other examples are to be seen in a Bible (X century) in the archives of the collegiate church of San Isidoro at León, one page of which (reproduced by Amador de los Rios y Villalta[6])

[1] Puig y Cadafalch, De Falguera, Goday y Casals, *L'arquitectura romanica a Catalunya*, vol. i, p. 248.

[2] Cabrol, *Dictionnaire d'Archéologie chrétienne et de la Liturgie*, fasc. xii, Baños. Leclercq, col. 191-198.

[3] *Inscriptiones Hispaniae Christianae, Supplementum*, Lusitania, nn. 304, 311, 312, 318.

[4] Laurentian Library, Florence.

[5] Morini, *Origini del culto alla Addolorata*, App. D.

[6] Museo Español de Antigüedades, vol. ix, pp. 521-532, *Página de una Biblia del siglo X que se conserva en el Archivo de San Isidoro de León.*

shows five arches of this form. It is specially noticeable in the Codex of Eude and Emeteri in the cathedral of Gerona (975). Another example may be seen in the 'Lex Salica' (794) in the library of the ancient abbey of St. Gall.

THE CONGREGATIONAL MOSQUE OF IBN TULUN AT QATTAI (CAIRO), begun in 876-77, or more probably in 872-73, by Ibn Tulun (868-883) at Qattai, the suburb which he built to the north of Fustat, was finished in 879. The latter date is confirmed by the inaugural inscription built into one of the piers near the qibla.

It was the third mosque of its kind erected in the Moslem capital of Egypt. The first was that of Amr, which we have already dealt with. The second was that of Askar, built in 785-86 in the suburb of Fustat known as al-Askar. It was enlarged in 826-27, and is mentioned in 1123-24, but no trace of it remains.

The architect appears to have been a Christian, and some think that he was actually a Copt, Ibn Katib al-Fargani. I note in passing that Ibn Tulun during his caliphate could not find in his dominions anyone capable of fortifying Acre in the same manner as Tyre—the work demanding a knowledge of hydraulics—and entrusted the task to an architect, Abu Bakr, the grandfather of the geographer Muqaddasi,[1] which shows that his noble profession was practised and honoured in Palestine, and that the Coptic architects were not the repositories of science that some have supposed.

It was the first building on a large scale in Egypt in which brick piers were used instead of columns. In the grave disorders of the caliphate of Mustansir (1035-1094) it was seriously damaged, and an inscription tells us that under him the north-east gate of the outer wall was restored in 1077. It is also known that in his time a mihrab was erected in the middle of the first line of piers, towards the court; and that work was going on in the building under the Caliph Hafiz (1130-1149). Mansur Husam (1296-1298) carried out important restorations and enlargements. Under Nasir Mohammed (1293-94, 1298-1308, 1309-1340) two minarets were restored. These lesser minarets stood at the ends of the mihrab wall, and the one at the eastern angle still exists (Fig. 118, p. 139). More work was executed in 1365-66. In 1389-90 the northern walk of the cloister by the great minaret was restored. Work was again going on in 1524. Finally, in 1711 the mosque

[1] Op. cit., p. 30.

was made into a fortified place, and soon afterwards into a wool factory. In the XIX century it became a hospital for the poor. Of late a careful restoration of the building has been in progress.[1]

The mosque of Ibn Tulun which, through all its vicissitudes, has undergone no essential change, is a rectangle of 140 by 116 m. (about 460 by 382 ft.), enclosed on three sides by double circuit walls, the space between which forms outer courts (Fig. 119, p. 142). The inner wall, strengthened on the outside by buttresses at the corners, is lined on three sides by double arcades with piers. The fourth or southern side, the place of prayer, has five rows of similar supports forming five bays in depth and seventeen in length, the central one leading to the mihrab. The outermost of these rows fell in 1877 (Figs. 120, 121, pp. 141, 142). The range facing on to the court has now disappeared, and only four of the original rows of piers remain.

The building was not a direct copy of the mosque of Samarra in Mesopotamia, as has been asserted.[2] As a matter of fact, the mosque of Samarra, erected by the Abbasid caliph, Mutawakkil (847-861), to replace a former one built by Mutasim (833-842), and still existing in the shape of extensive ruins, possesses only one enclosure wall of 220 by 168 m. (about 725 by 553 ft.), strengthened on its outer face by massive buttresses crowned by round turrets. There seem to have been ten ranges of supports on the south, three or four on the north, four or five on the east and west. Apparently these supports were columns which, it has been suggested, were of wood,[3] and I think rightly, as no vestige of them has survived.[4] Moreover, the mosque built by Mansur (754-775), the founder of Baghdad, was of sun-baked bricks with a flat roof supported by tree trunks. Harun al-Rashid (786-809) rebuilt

[1] CHASSINAT, *Mémoires publiées par les Membres de l'Institut Français d'Archéologie orientale du Caire*, vol. vii; SALMON, *Études sur la topographie du Caire*, pp. 12-27. LANE-POOLE, *A History of Egypt in the Middle Ages*, pp. 63, 65. HERZ, *Catalogue raisonné des monuments exposés dans le Musée National de l'Art arabe* (Le Caire), pp. xxv-xxx, 6-9. BOURIANT, *Mémoires publiées par les Membres de la Mission Archéologique Française au Caire*, vol. xix, pp. 27-39; VAN BERCHEM, *Matériaux pour un Corpus inscriptionum arabicarum. The Journal of the Royal Asiatic Society*, 1891, pp. 527-562; CORBETT, *The Life and Works of Ahmad ibn Tūlūn.* BUTLER, *The Arab Conquest of Egypt*, pp. 341, 342.

[2] CHASSINAT, *Mémoires publiées par les Membres de l'Institut Français d'Archéologie orientale du Caire*, vol. vii, p. 13; SALMON, *Études sur la topographie du Caire.* LANE, op. cit., p. 590.

[3] BELL, *Amurath to Amurath*, pp. 231-235.

[4] But see E. HERZFELD's recently published *Erster vorlaüfiger Bericht über die Ausgrabungen von Samarra*, pp. 6-13, which modifies the statement above.

Fig. 118.—Qattai (Cairo). Mosque of Ibn Tulun. One of the smaller minarets (XIII or XIV cent.).

FIG. 117.—Madrid. National Archaeological Museum. Pagan gravestone (III cent.).

FIG. 123.—Qattai (Cairo). Mosque of Ibn Tulun. Great minaret.

FIG. 120.—Qattai (Cairo). Mosque of Ibn Tulun. Interior (IX cent.).

Fig. 119.—Qattai (Cairo). Mosque of Ibn Tulun. Outer wall (IX cent.).

Fig. 121.—Qattai (Cairo). Mosque of Ibn Tulun. Interior (IX cent.).

it with fire-baked bricks.[1] Again, in the mosque of Gedda on the Red Sea, ascribed to the latter caliph, Ibn Jubair[2] saw two columns of ebony. The existence of pillars of combustible material at Samarra would explain Ibn Tulun's wish, as reported by Maqrizi, 'to erect a building which may last even if Misr were burned by fire or submerged by flood';[3] in other words, to make use of supports in his mosque which were not of wood, as in that at Samarra, which he had seen when he was at the caliph's court there. Besides, the multifoil arch occurs at Samarra, and is still to be seen in the windows of the south wall of the mosque; but it is never found in Ibn Tulun's building.

The mosque is orientated in the direction of Mecca.

The outer face of the walls of the internal arcades, which are quite 1.60 m. (5 ft. 3 in.) thick, was ornamented by large niches alternating with windows, between smaller niches. The arches of the large niches and of the windows, which are not splayed, spring from dwarf angle shafts.

The piers, both in the cloisters and in the place of prayer, are rectangular in shape with four engaged angle columns, and rest on high bases. The walls carried by the arches are pierced above the piers by openings with angle shafts, which have both a constructive and a decorative purpose. The arcades were roofed with flat ceilings.

The pointed horse-shoe arch is used throughout, as is the bell-shaped capital with leaves.

Walls, piers, columns, and arches are all of brick set in thick layers of mortar, and everywhere covered with several coats of stucco. The bands of stucco decoration on the walls and arches are noticeable.

Originally the walls were everywhere crowned by the curious battlements, many portions of which survive.

The original mihrab (Fig. 122, p. 145) is an interesting object. It is placed in the middle of the end wall of the sanctuary, still, as a whole, in its original form. The mosaics of the niche are ruinous. The marble shafts in front, with their capitals and bases, are antiques. The capitals of the basket pattern, or funnel-shaped with complete undercutting, have no relation either in form or style to the stucco capitals of the mosque, and may be assigned to the age of Justinian.

[1] Le Strange, *Baghdad during the Abbasid Caliphate*, pp. 34, 35.

[2] Op. cit., pp. 47, 48.

[3] Chassinat, *Mémoires publiées par les Membres de l'Institut Français d'Archéologie orientale du Caire*, vol. vii, p. 14; Salmon, *Études sur la topographie du Caire*.

The domed structure in the court was erected by Mansur Husam (1296), as we learn from the inscription which it bears. Le Strange[1] is wrong in thinking that it was built as a mausoleum for Ibn Tulun, and only later furnished with a basin for ablutions.

The mosque was provided with a great minaret set towards the north between the cloister and the outer wall, to the left of the main axis of the building. It was the part of the sacred edifice which affected the imagination of the Moslems most forcibly; and in form it is unique among the minarets of Cairo (Fig. 123, p. 140). The only notices relating to the structure after its foundation which have come down to us are its attempted demolition in the caliphate of Hakim (996-1020), and later, in the year 1596-97, the removal of the vessels on its summit intended to hold grain for fowls and pigeons. In its present condition it appears, so far as I can judge, to be untouched in its main features, consisting of a large square base of blocks of a hard limestone with an external staircase, out of which rises a cylindrical tower with stairs winding round its exterior. How it was finished at the top we do not know. The two polygonal stories with internal staircase, which now crown the building, are a later alteration.

The anomaly now to be seen of ranges of two-light openings with pronounced round horse-shoe arches, instead of pointed horse-shoe arches, is due to the fact that they are a later insertion, as is shown by the materials used in them. To the period of this alteration will belong the communication now existing between the minaret and the roof of the cloister. It may all be connected with the work carried out in this part of the mosque in 1389-90.

In the next place, the use of stone for the minaret, while brick is exclusively employed in the mosque, need cause no surprise. In fact, when the mosque of Hakim (990-1003) was built after the pattern of this one, the same system was followed. Moreover, one must remember the great bulk of the minaret and its height (which may have been considerable, like that of the one at Samarra), requiring the use of a harder material, which was easy to procure by robbing ancient buildings, a resource not available at Samarra.

It has been suggested that this minaret was copied from the ancient Pharos of Alexandria, erected by Sostratus of Cnidus in the reign of Ptolemy II, Philadelphus (285-247 B.C.). It had a square base, above which rose an octagonal stage, and above that a circular one supporting a lantern. The

[1] *Palestine under the Moslems*, p. 95.

FIG. 122.—Qattai (Cairo). Mosque of Ibn Tulun. The principal mihrab (IX cent.).

FIG. 124.—Venice. San Marco. Mosaic of the XII century, showing the Pharos of Alexandria.

FIG. 125.—Tagiura. Mosque (XVI cent.).

FIG. 126.—Tagiura. Mosque (XVI cent.).

staircase was internal.[1] This lighthouse was partly demolished under the Caliph Walid I (705-715), considerably damaged by the earthquake of 955,[2] and restored afterwards. Ibn Jubair[3] says that the base measured more than 50 cubits, and that the height exceeded 150 fathoms. On the summit was a mosque. The tower fell in the XIV century,[4] but an interesting representation of it is to be seen in a mosaic (XII century) at St. Mark's, Venice (Fig. 124, p. 145).

On the other hand, as far back as the XI century, it has been believed that the minaret was copied from the one at Samarra.[5] This theory is the more probable one, and it is confirmed by the minaret of the mosque of Mutawakkil (847-861). The latter as designed had a spiral form, recalling, with its external staircase, the ancient staged towers of Mesopotamia known as 'zigurrats.' The base, which is low and ruinous, appears to have been of square shape. Its height exceeds 50 m. (about 165 ft.), and it is crowned by a kiosk with a hexagonal base and a spherical cupola, ornamented with niches which have pointed arches and piers. It too was placed at the north side, outside the court of the sacred edifice.[6]

One has only to compare the two minarets in order to be struck at once by their close relationship. And one is also profoundly convinced that there could never have been erected at Cairo in the XIII or XIV century a minaret —I am speaking only of the original outlines of the structure—so bare of ornament and of so antiquated a form as that exhibited by Ibn Tulun's.

Another minaret of the type of that of Samarra is to be seen in the mosque of Abudolaf, a few kilometres from that city.[7] It is evidently copied from the one at Samarra, and like it has a spiral form. It rises from a base measuring 12.50 by 10.80 m. (about 42 by 36 ft.) and 2.50 m. (8 ft. 2 in.) in height, decorated with narrow niches having horse-shoe arches. The upper part has fallen.

[1] CHASSINAT, *Mémoires publiées par les Membres de l'Institut Français d'Archéologie orientale du Caire*, vol. vii, pp. 25-27; SALMON, *Études sur la topographie du Caire*. BUTLER, *The Arab Conquest of Egypt*, pp. 389-400.

[2] BUTLER, op. cit., pp. 389-400.

[3] Op. cit., pp. 10, 11.

[4] BOURIANT, *Mémoires publiées par les Membres de la Mission Archéologique Française au Caire*, vol. xix, pp. 473-492; VAN BERCHEM, *Matériaux pour un Corpus inscriptionum arabicarum*.

[5] CHASSINAT, *Mémoires publiées par les Membres de l'Institut Français d'Archéologie orientale du Caire*, vol. vii, pp. 25-27; SALMON, *Études sur la topographie du Caire*.

[6] BELL, *Amurath to Amurath*, pp. 231-235. DE BEYLIÉ, *Prome et Samara*, pp. 115-118.

[7] DE BEYLIÉ, *Prome et Samara*, pp. 119-124.

It is thought by some that the small minaret at the south-east angle of the mosque of Ibn Tulun, corresponding to another which has disappeared at the south-west angle, dates from the IX century. But its advanced form is against this, and it must be connected with the works of Mohammed Nasir.

The chief interest of the mosque of Tulun for our purpose is that it is the first building in which the pointed horse-shoe arch was systematically used. For it has yet to be proved beyond the range of doubt that the remains of an ancient aqueduct ascribed by Corbett[1] to Ibn Tulun, and two or three years earlier than the mosque, are really such.

It has been thought that the form was used before this in the Nilometer on the island of Roda, the history of which, as told by Marcel in his *Mémoires sur les Meqyâs de l'île de Rouda,* and repeated by Van Berchem, is as follows. Built in 714-716 by the Caliph Suliman, and restored by Mamun in 814-15, it was repaired in 847-48 under Mutawakkil, and in 861-62 under Mustansir; again in 1092 and 1766-67; and finally in 1799-1800.[2] From this account, and from the inscriptions on the building, the inference may be drawn that the ancient portion of the enclosing wall, with the boldly outlined pointed horse-shoe arches of the recesses, belongs to the caliphate of Mamun. Lane-Poole,[3] on the other hand, says that it was erected in the year 861 by the governor Yazid, and improved by Ibn Tulun in 873. However this may be, the Nilometer apparently takes precedence over the mosque of Tulun in regard to the use of the pointed horse-shoe arch. The original building was entrusted to an architect who came from Fergana.[4]

The pointed horse-shoe arch assumed in time, after being set up on a dado, as in the mosque al-Azhar at Cairo, the light and elegant forms exhibited, for instance, by the mosque of Tagiura near Tripoli, built, according to information obtained from Dr Aurigemma, by Murad Agha in 1550[5] (Figs. 125, 126, p. 146).

The origin of this constructive feature is to be sought in India, where

[1] *The Journal of the Royal Asiatic Society*, 1891; pp. 531, 532, 540; *The Life and Works of Ahmad ibn Tūlūn.*

[2] BOURIANT, *Mémoires publiées par les Membres de la Mission Archéologique Française au Caire*, vol. xix, pp. 18-22; VAN BERCHEM, *Matériaux pour un Corpus inscriptionum arabicarum.*

[3] *A History of Egypt in the Middle Ages*, pp. 26, 43, 63, 65.

[4] SALADIN, *Manuel d'Art musulman*, vol. i, p. 88.

[5] AHMED EN NAIB, *Kitab el Manhal*, p. 189.

FIG. 127.—Mamallapuram. Ganesa Ratha (VII cent.).

FIG. 128.—Mamallapuram. Bhima Ratha (VII cent.).

FIG. 130.—Ajanta. Interior of Cave Temple XIX (VI-VII cent.).

FIG. 129.—Ajanta. Façade of Cave Temple XIX (VI-VII cent.).

FIG. 134.—Cairo. Ruins of the Mosque of Hakim (X and XI cents.).

FIG. 131.—Cairo. Mosque al-Azhar (X-XIX cent.).

it appears in monuments belonging to the time of the flower and expansion of the art of Gandhâra, a period, according to Foucher, which begins before the second half of the II century, and extends at latest to the year 600.[1] Its culmination was between the years 50 and 150 or 200 of the Christian era.[2] Interesting specimens of the constructive and decorative use of the form are to be found in the 'rathas' or small temples (VII century) at Mamallapuram, not far from Madras, known as the 'Seven Pagodas,' each one carved out of a block of granite.[3] Two of these shrines, the Ganesa Ratha (Fig. 127, p. 149) and the Bhîma Ratha (Fig. 128, p. 150), are here illustrated. In India it is also found combined with the 'accolade' or ogee arch, which I describe as the 'cyma reversa arch.'

In Western Asia the simple pointed arch had already appeared as a constructive feature, in—to mention only dated buildings—the palace of Chosroes I (531-579) at Ctesiphon, and in the minaret and mihrab in the mosque of Samarra (847-861).

It may be noticed here that from the horse-shoe arch and the 'cyma reversa' or ogee arch was developed the bulbous or Tartar cupola, early specimens of which on a small scale are to be seen in the stûpas or dâgabas of Buddhist temples cut in the rock; for instance, in the cave temples of Ajanta numbered XIX (Figs. 129, 130, pp. 150, 151) and XXVI. These caves, twenty-nine in number, are dated between about 200 B.C. and 642 A.D. The two just mentioned appear to have been made between 500 and 642.[4] Burgess puts cave XIX at the end of the V century.[5]

THE MOSQUE AL-AZHAR AT CAIRO, begun in 970, at the command of the Caliph Muizz (952-975) by his secretary, an emancipated slave, Jauhar al-Rumi († 992), the subduer of Morocco (959), the conqueror of Egypt and founder of Cairo (969), was finished in 972, and was the first mosque to be erected in Cairo. The fact was still attested in the days of Maqrizi († 1444) by the inscription to be read on the dome to the right of the minbar, in which Jauhar was described as a Sicilian.

The roof, originally low, was raised at a later time to the extent of a

[1] FOUCHER, *L'Art gréco-bouddhique du Gandhâra*, pp. 40-42.
[2] VINCENT A. SMITH, op. cit., p. 99.
[3] Ibid., p. 36.
[4] Ibid., pp. 274, 275.
[5] BURGESS, *History of Indian Architecture*, pp. 150, 151.

cubit. Four of the Fatimite caliphs (909-1171) executed repairs. It suffered seriously from the earthquake of 1303, but was repaired. More restorations took place in 1325 and 1360. The Sultans Qait Bey (1468-1495) and Ghuri (1500-1516) erected the two minarets still standing at the middle of the west side and at the south-west angle of the court. None of the mosque's minarets are contemporary with the foundation. In 1595-96 the building underwent considerable alterations, and was repaired.

In its present state it is the result of important modifications, and forms a group of mosques of various dates,[1] especially of the XVIII and XIX centuries (Figs. 131, 132, pp. 152, 155). Nevertheless, in the oldest part, i.e. in five of the nine aisles running north and south, the central aisle may, on the whole, be regarded as original. In fact the archivolts of its arcades, together with the piers of the first range towards the court, have inscriptions from the Koran in Carmathian characters of the Fatimite period, some of which seem, according to Van Berchem, to be as old as the foundation of the mosque. To this range, then, we must give some attention.

The walls which support the wooden roof have been tampered with, as is shown by the occurrence of round-headed windows. Moreover, the interesting stucco vine reliefs in the lower part clearly belong, both in design and execution, to more than one period. The arcades, on the other hand, with borrowed Roman or Byzantine columns, and pointed arches of elongated form, were all built at the same time. Their importance lies in the form of the arches. These arches are pointed, the curves becoming straight at the key. Those in the nave are set up on high impost blocks, while those in the aisles are raised by means of pedestals. This type of arch, derived from the Indian 'cyma reversa arch,' is known as the Persian arch. The fact, however, remains that Persia, so far as we know at present, contains no dated examples earlier than those in the mosque al-Azhar, and it appears to be of Egyptian origin. I describe it as 'the pointed mixtilinear arch.' We do not know the name of the architect who invented this new form. But remembering that its introduction corresponds to the Fatimite conquest,

[1] HERZ, op. cit., pp. xxxiv and xxxv. LANE-POOLE, *A History of Egypt under the Saracens*, pp. 99-104, 117, 242, 276, 302, 324. BOURIANT, *Mémoires publiées par les Membres de la Mission Archéologique Française au Caire*, vol. xix, pp. 43-50; VAN BERCHEM, *Matériaux pour un Corpus inscriptionum arabicarum.* LANE, op. cit., pp. 599, 600. NASIRI KUSRU, op. cit., p. 135. *Journal Asiatique*, 1891, i, pp. 424-429, 441; VAN BERCHEM, *Notes d'Archéologie arabe.* LANE-POOLE, *The Story of Cairo*, pp. 124, 125.

FIG. 132.—Cairo. Mosque al-Azhar. Side of the court and minarets.

FIG. 135.—Cairo. Mosque of Hakim. Interior of the dome of the mihrab (X and XI cents.).

FIG. 136.—Cairo. Mosque of Hakim. Southern minaret (X, XI, and XIV cents.).

and that in the great mosque of Kairawan, as far back as the days of Ziyadat Allah I (816-837), round horse-shoe arches were raised up on high bases, it seems to me not improbable that it originated in the desire to combine the pointed arch, which in its horse-shoe form had been brought into vogue in Egypt by Ibn Tulun, with the high imposts at Kairawan, the seat of the Fatimids in Barbary before they attained to the caliphate of Egypt. Nor does it seem an unnatural conjecture that it was Jauhar, not only a distinguished general but also a man of letters and therefore of culture, who suggested the form to some Christian architect of Egypt; and that, under these circumstances, the designer of the building, wishing to endow it with some distinctive feature marking the accession of a new dynasty, modified the pointed arch of Tulun's time under the influence of the Indian 'cyma reversa' or ogee arch.

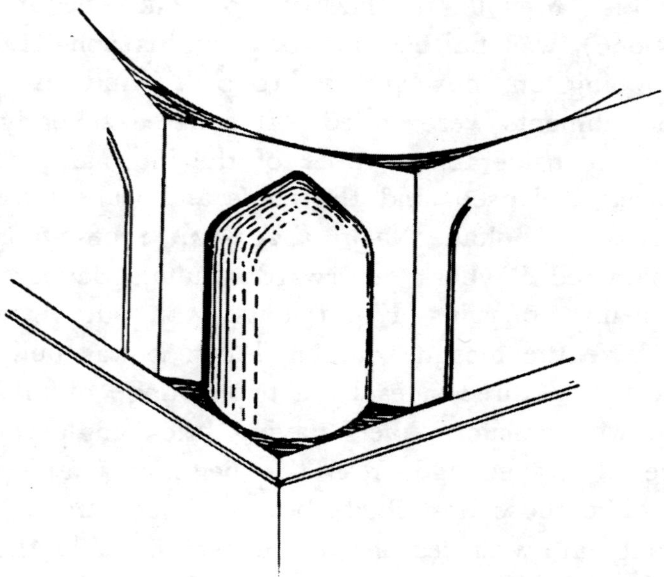

FIG. 133.—Cairo. Mosque al-Azhar. Pendentive of the dome.

Before leaving the mosque al-Azhar I must point out that its well-known cupola does not belong to the original structure. Its pendentives in the form of elongated niches projecting from the face of the walls like canopies (Fig. 133), of the same type as those which we saw in the congregational mosque of Walid at Damascus, point to a date subsequent to that of the mosque of Hakim, also at Cairo (990-1003), in which short niche pendentives recessed in the thickness of the walls are employed, following the pattern of the prototypes in San Vitale at Ravenna. Those in our mosque seem to have been suggested by the examples in the Cappella Palatina, Santa Maria dell' Ammiraglio, and San Cataldo at Palermo; which, until the contrary be proved, may be taken as the prototypes of the species, and in their turn are the offspring of the elegant though dwarf pendentives in the vestibule of the mihrab of Hakam II at Cordova.

The Sicilian pendentives, the inner construction of which is revealed by those in San Cataldo, where the walls have been stripped, have nothing in common with the pendentives consisting merely of a vault taken out of the thickness of the wall, which I describe as 'hood-shaped' or 'Romano-Campanian.' The latter are sometimes elaborated like those in Ibrahim II's dome at Kairawan; and at a later date the Lombards used them in tiers, as may be seen in the cathedral of Piacenza.

THE MOSQUE OF HAKIM AT CAIRO, begun in 990 by the Caliph Aziz (975-996), was finished in 1003 by his son Hakim (996-1020). Work was still going on, however, in 1010-11; and in 1012-13 the decorations and embellishments were added. It suffered severely in the earthquake of 1303, when a considerable number of the internal piers fell, the upper part of the minarets collapsed, and the roofs and walls were damaged. It was restored under the Sultan Nasir (1293-94, 1298-1308, 1309-1340) by the Emir Mohammed Baybars, afterwards Sultan Baybars II (1308-09).[1] At present it is a mass of ruins (Fig. 134, p. 152), but we will give a short account of it.

Like the mosque of Ibn Tulun it was built with piers. The court was enclosed on three sides by a triple range of arcades, now for the most part gone, with cruciform piers having brick angle columns without capitals. The place of prayer had from the beginning a depth of five bays divided by piers like those described above. The piers at the end of each series were rectangular with lesenas or pilasters. All the piers were connected by wooden ties; but this device, considering the nature of the piers themselves, must have been due to Baybars. The pointed arch of slightly horse-shoe form is used throughout, and the imposts of the arches are made of wood.

The arches run, as in the mosque of Ibn Tulun, from east to west, and start from isolated piers or half wall-piers. In the spandrels are openings, as in the mosque of Tulun. There were flat ceilings. The piers were built of brick with thick layers of mortar. The outer walls show that they have been repaired or rebuilt in places where a mixture of stone and brick occurs. These were the restorations due to the catastrophe of the XIV century.

[1] LANE-POOLE, *A History of Egypt in the Middle Ages*, pp. 117, 123, 129, 276, 302. BOURIANT, *Mémoires publiées par les Membres de la Mission Archéologique Française au Caire*, vol. xix, pp. 50-54; VAN BERCHEM, *Matériaux pour un Corpus inscriptionum arabicarum*. *Journal Asiatique*, 1891, i, pp. 429-442; VAN BERCHEM, *Notes d'archéologie arabe*.

FIG. 137.—Cairo. Mosque of Hakim. Northern minaret (X, XI, and XIV cents.).

FIG. 138.—Cairo. Minaret of the Mosque of Salih Ayyub (1240-1249).

FIG. 139.—Osia. Temple of the Sun (VIII cent.).

FIG. 140.—Palermo. Cappella Palatina (XII cent.).

FIG. 141.—Bhuvanesvar. Temple of Muktesvara (IX or X-XIII cent.).

It will be noticed that over the ends of the central bay and the two last bays to east and west, three domes were set, that in the centre still surviving and parts of those which flank it at the angles of the building. The former, rising in front of the mihrab, rests on three arches and part of the southern outer wall. The square base passes into the octagon of the drum by means of four pendentives with short niches (Fig. 135, p. 156). The drum supports the conical cupola, which has four windows at its base and eight above.

The presence of the typical Ravennate pendentive demands a closer examination of the dome. If we look at the nave to which it belongs, we notice that the piers have been altered in order to increase their resistance to the pressure of the dome. And if we climb a ladder to examine the exterior of the cupola at close quarters, we find that the bricks are not exactly like those in the rest of the building, and that they are sometimes set in herring-bone fashion. This gives rise to a doubt as to whether the cupola belongs to the date of the foundation, and is not rather the result of an alteration. But in spite of this, and not forgetting what has been done in the way of repair and reinforcement, probably after the disaster of 1303, in order to preserve it, I think that it retains its original form. In fact the plainness of the pendentives is quite in keeping with the simplicity of the bell-shaped capitals below, and with the absence of ornament in the piers throughout the mosque. To judge by the simple niche pendentive which survives in one of the two domes at the ends of the building, and is identical in form with the four belonging to the central cupola, this dome, too, together with its fellow which has disappeared, must belong to the time of Aziz and Hakim. The lesena, however, in the south wall, which carries the transverse arch, is of later date than the original building, so that the dome itself must be ascribed to the work of Baybars.

At the angles of the north wall of the court were set the two minarets, the tops of which fell in the earthquake of 1303 (Figs. 136, 137, pp. 156, 159). Each has a square basement of courses of large limestone blocks, accurately cut and set in mortar. It is lighted by rectangular windows, and contains a spiral staircase. Upon this is set an octagonal story, above which rises the cylindrical minaret. When the latter fell, Baybars enclosed the surviving parts within clumsy basements, making a staircase in the space between the old wall and the new; and at the top he built the fanciful polygonal brick towers still to be seen, crowned by cupolas of irregular shape. The cupolas were inspired by the one belonging to the minaret of the mosque tomb of Salih Ayyub (1240-1249), finished in 1243-44[1] (Fig. 138, p. 159)—supposing that it is the original, the upper part of the minaret having been restored[2]—and both were derived from the no less bizarre forms found in Indian buildings, such as the temple of the Sun at Osia in the State of Jodhpur, belonging to a group of sacred edifices dating from the VIII century (Fig. 139, p. 160), and the shrine of Muktesvara at Bhuvanesvar in the district of Puri in Orissa (Fig. 141, p. 162), one of the earliest religious structures in that reign, dated between the IX or X and the XIII centuries.[3]

Special attention must be drawn to two features in the mosque of Hakim: the compound piers and piers with angle columns, and the niche pendentives.

The compound piers are of the Lombardic type, but with this difference, that they are not designed as the starting-point of a whole group of members, as only longitudinal arches spring from them. Their outline was intended to render the piers less heavy to the eye, and make them more pleasing. Elsewhere I have dealt with the origin and development of compound piers.[4]

The niche pendentives are the earliest dated specimens of their kind, freely and clearly defined and visible, which I have met with in the Moslem world. The earlier form used in the bay in front of the mihrab in the mosque of Cordova (961-976) consists of an angle recess within a pensile cusped framing arch. The history of this Romano-Ravennate element will also be found in my previous work.[5]

It is not easy to say from what source the architect of the mosque of Hakim derived these pendentives, so characteristic of Fatimite architecture, of which the only earlier attested examples in existence are those constructed by Julianus Argentarius to carry the dome of San Vitale at Ravenna (526-547). It is only too true that nearly all the Moslem buildings were destroyed during

[1] Bouriant, *Mémoires publiées par les Membres de la Mission Archéologique Française au Caire*, vol. xix, pp. 102-110; Van Berchem, *Matériaux pour un Corpus inscriptionum arabicarum.*

[2] Herz, op. cit., p. xlv.

[3] Vincent A. Smith, op. cit., pp. 25-32.

[4] Rivoira, op. cit. (Loescher), vol. i, pp. 291, 315, 316; vol. ii, pp. 107, 110, 187, 488, 489; (Hoepli), pp. 86, 214-216, 220, 244, 282, 283, 307, 408; (Heinemann), vol. i, pp. 75, 176-178, 181, 199, 228, 248; vol. ii, p. 70.

[5] Ibid. (Loescher), vol. i, p. 76; vol. ii, p. 604; (Hoepli), pp. 79, 80, 236, 237; (Heinemann), vol. i, pp. 71, 193.

FIG. 142.—Palermo. Santa Maria dell' Ammiraglio or Martorana (XII cent.).

Fig. 143.—Palermo. San Cataldo (XII cent.).

the Norman conquest of Sicily (1060-1091).[1] And even if those of Palermo, which capitulated in 1072, were spared[2] and aroused the admiration of Edrisi (1154),[3] not one of them is now in existence. However, when Roger II (1130-1154) in 1132 began to erect that jewel of art, the Cappella Palatina at Palermo (Fig. 140, p. 161), the dome was sprung from elegant projecting angle niches which showed an advance on those of Hakim. The same procedure was followed when George of Antioch built Santa Maria dell' Ammiraglio, now known as the Martorana, at Palermo (1143)[4] (Fig. 142, p. 165). I note in passing that originally this church was of such beauty that Ibn Jubair, who saw it in 1184, calls it 'unquestionably the fairest building in the world.' Its campanile, too, with variegated marble columns adorning its stages, excited great admiration.[5] The cupola of the small church of San Cataldo (1161) close to the Martorana, also rests on niches of the same kind (Fig. 143, p. 166).

All these buildings at Palermo, together with the castles or palaces of La Zisa and La Cuba (1180), are to be ascribed to the craftsmen of Sicily. No surprise need be felt at their exhibiting inscriptions in Arabic, Greek, and Latin, for all three languages were spoken there.[6] The assertion often made that these structures are due to Byzantine or Arabic workmen, is mere conjecture. The type of pendentive used in the domes now proves that this was not the case. Besides, it is incredible that Sicily was devoid of native craftsmen in the XII century, when the cathedrals of Cefalù, Monreale, and Palermo bear witness to the existence of such by their style of architectural decoration which was not practised at that time outside Sicily. In any case, how can the work of Greek artists be traced, for instance, in the mosaics of the Cappella Palatina containing figures seated after the Moslem fashion?

I may remark here that the question of the presence of Greek craftsmen in Italy, which seems to be attested by inscriptions in the official language, by monograms, and by names, has never yet been dealt with properly or exhaustively. I commend it as a subject of research, and will merely add that it was not only in Roman times that ancient Greek colonies existed in Italy, keeping up the use of Greek names and the Greek language, and

[1] AMARI, op. cit., vol. ii, p. 450.
[2] Ibid., vol. iii, 1, pp. 131, 132.
[3] EDRISI (Amari, Schiaparelli), *L'Italia descritta nel 'Libro del re Ruggero,'* pp. 25-27.
[4] AMARI, op. cit., vol. iii, 2, p. 656.
[5] IBN JUBAIR, op. cit., pp. 331, 332. SALINAS, *Trafori e vetrate nelle finestre delle chiese medioevali di Sicilia.*
[6] AMARI, op. cit., vol. iii, 2, pp. 856, 857.

sometimes preserving their municipal autonomy and Greek laws; but that as late as the Middle Ages, and in parts not under Byzantine rule—the duchy of Amalfi, to give one instance—the civil year was regulated according to the Greek calendar. Moreover, it has a special bearing on our case that, after Leo III the Isaurian (717-740) had separated Sicily from the Diocese of Rome, the Greek language was introduced in religious services, together with the Greek liturgy. It is obvious, too, that the Norman conquest of Sicily found a population which had thoroughly assimilated the Greek language and Greek customs.[1] Hence it is possible that many buildings ascribed to craftsmen who are supposed to have been brought from the East, were really, on the contrary, the productions of Italian workmen, who had nothing Oriental about them except an origin or a tradition which may have been centuries or even thousands of years old, or the use of an alien language imposed on them by the arbitrary will of a ruler.

The mosque of Hakim is almost the last of the new mosques on a grand scale, of quadrangular plan, with rows of columns, flat roofs, a single dome in front of the mihrab, and sometimes a second rising above the central aisle, and a colonnaded court, the whole following the pattern of the prototype at Medina.

From the second half of the X century onwards the trade of the East was, almost exclusively and on a great scale, in the hands of Venice, Pisa, and Amalfi, with their fleets of galleys.[2] These relations with the West, intensified at a later date by the Crusades, were followed by the introduction in the East of types of sacred buildings which departed from the traditional pattern of Islam, and exercised an undoubted influence on Moslem architecture.

On the other hand, through the influence of the East, these relations gave the impulse to the creation of the Pointed style which enriched the West with so many wonderful cathedrals and abbeys; for it was by grafting the pointed arch of Islam on to the Lombardic vaulted basilica that the Transitional style, from which the Pointed style sprung, was inaugurated in Durham cathedral (1093-1133)[3] (Fig. 144, p. 169). It was these relations, too, which inspired the parti-coloured facing of sacred buildings; for though the Romans had introduced it in walls and sometimes in arches, they used it only for constructive or

[1] SINOPOLI DI GIUNTA, *La badia regia di Santa Maria Latina in Agira*, pp. 20-23.

[2] SCHLUMBERGER, *L'épopée byzantine à la fin du dixième siècle*, vol. i, p. 239.

[3] RIVOIRA, op. cit. (Loescher), vol. ii, pp. 210, 450; (Hoepli), pp. 468, 614; (Heinemann), vol. ii, pp. 123, 124, 242.

FIG. 144.—Durham. Nave of the Cathedral (1093-1133).

FIG. 145.—Church of San Miniato al Monte near Florence. Façade (XI, XII, and XIII cents.).

Fig. 146.—Church of San Miniato al Monte near Florence (about 1018-1062).

FIG. 147.—Tunis. Zituna Mosque. Minaret (1894).

FIG. 148.—Tripoli. Mosque of the Camel, with minaret and domes.

economical reasons, whereas the East adopted it as a Christian fashion as well, first in churches, and later in mosques. Its introduction into Italy was due to the Tuscans by way of Pisa (the cathedral has recently been discussed by Goodyear[1] and Supino[2]), and they too were the first to clothe even the exteriors of churches with splendid marble inlays, and enrich them with elaborate arcading. One of the earliest examples of the style is the church of San Miniato al Monte, near Florence, rebuilt about 1018, and probably finished about 1062 (Figs. 145, 146, pp. 170, 171). The older part of the façade, only the lower part of which goes back to the XI century, the upper evidently belonging to the XII and XIII, was copied by the architect of the front of the parish church of Empoli (1093).[3] The decorative use of inlaid marbles was derived from the indigenous style of decoration in the interiors of late Roman and early Christian buildings; but in a different atmosphere it assumed a new and distinctive outward appearance.

To all this may be added the unquestionable change both in architecture and art observable in the Seljuk period (1055-1300), under Central Asiatic influence. The flat-roofed mosque then assumed various forms. The true or false vault was introduced, the number of cupolas was increased, the principal dome obtained an elongated form, means were adopted to give greater importance to the façade which was also brought into relation with the internal divisions of the building, and the architectural decoration became generally more extensive and varied.

Under the inspiration of these new ideas the minaret also started on a fresh career. As we have seen, it was originally a plain square tower, like those in Walid's mosques at Damascus and Medina, and in that of Bishr at Kairawan. The square form took deep root, so that in Spain it remained in vogue down to the end of the Moslem dominion; and in some countries—Morocco, Algeria, Tunis, Libya—it still retains its pre-eminence, the other forms being less frequent. As recently as 1894, when it became necessary to rebuild the old minaret of the Zituna mosque at Tunis, the ancient square shape was retained (Fig. 147, p. 172).

Subjoined is an illustration (Fig. 148, p. 172) of the minaret belonging to the mosque of the Camel at Tripoli, traditionally supposed to have been erected after the capture of the city, which took place shortly before Omar fell under

[1] *The Bulletin of the Brooklyn Institute of Arts and Sciences*, vol. vi, 1911.

[2] R. Accademia delle Scienze dell' Instituto di Bologna, 1913, *La costruzione del Duomo di Pisa.*

[3] Supino, *Gli Albori dell' arte fiorentina*, pp. 64-67.

an assassin's dagger at Medina (644).[1] Nothing short of extensive testing of the masonry could decide whether this mosque, which I examined early in 1911, preserves anything of the original structure. The columns have been taken from older buildings, and have damaged capitals of similar origin with abaci. The arches above them are of various forms: pointed horse-shoe, pointed and stilted, and semicircular (Figs. 149, 150, p. 175).

In the IX century the square form was sometimes combined with the cylindrical by raising on a lofty four-sided basement a round tower with an external staircase winding round it. The union was effected in Mesopotamia, and the minaret of Samarra is an example of it on the grand scale. The new style of minaret was adopted at Qattai, the suburb of Fustat founded by order of Ibn Tulun in 868; but it did not enjoy a long or prosperous career in Egypt, nor did it spread thence to other countries. Moreover, it had no extension in Syria. We know, for instance, that about the year 985 the Syrian minarets were still being built of the square form.[2]

This Mesopotamian type, however, was the forerunner of the square-based minaret surmounted by a spiral cylinder with an octagonal base, like the two ancient minarets in the mosque of Hakim; and also of the other form with a square base supporting a spiral column—just like the columns of Trajan (113) and Marcus Aurelius (about 176) at Rome—an early example of which is afforded by the minaret of Khosrugird, near Sebzewar, in Persia, of the year 1110,[3] which has an artistic character, for the bricks of the shaft are arranged so as to make a decorative pattern on the surface. The form was also accompanied by the use of niches to adorn the base and summit, as may be seen at Samarra and Abudolaf; and a beginning was thus made in the decorative treatment of minarets. And so the new minaret seen by Muqaddasi at Damascus (about 985) was covered with mosaics,[4] while that of Abd al-Rahman III at Cordova (945-46) exhibited every kind of embellishment.[5]

We saw in our description of the congregational mosque at Kairawan how the practice of decorating the exterior of minarets coincided with the ornamental treatment of bell-towers. But, for all its embellishment, the minaret, to judge by those which we have mentioned at Cairo, does not seem to have departed from the traditional form till the end of the X century.

[1] CAETANI, *Chronographia*, p. 261.
[2] MUQADDASI, op. cit., p. 75.
[3] CURZON, *Persia and the Persian Question*, vol. i, pp. 269-271.
[4] MUQADDASI, op. cit., p. 21.
[5] EDRISI, *Géographie*, vol. ii, pp. 62, 63.

FIG. 149.—Tripoli. Court of the Mosque of the Camel.

FIG. 150.—Tripoli. Mosque of the Camel.

Fig. 151.—Delhi. Qutb Minar (XIII and XIV cents.).

The earliest literary evidence for the new type of minaret is to be found in Ibn Jubair under the years 1183 and 1184. Referring to the three belonging to the great mosque of Medina, he draws a distinction between towers and minarets—'this holy mosque has three minarets: two are small and have the appearance of towers, the third has the form of a minaret'[1]—from which it may be inferred that the upper part of the latter was of cylindrical form with an internal staircase. In fact, our traveller in his account of the mosque at Mecca says that the six minarets described by him as of square shape half-way up, the other half being a spiral column, were of singular forms.[2]

It was then, apparently, in the XI century that, in imitation of the minarets of the mosque of Hakim, steps were taken towards emancipation from the traditional, universally accepted, square type of minaret, and there were substituted forms which gradually assumed varied and singular shapes; shapes which were sometimes thoroughly artistic and picturesque, but in other cases quite extravagant; and the tendency was always towards greater and even excessive slenderness. This type in its telescopic form we find represented on the grandest scale by the Qutb Minar at Delhi, some 75 m. (about 245 ft.) in height, which was erected in 1232, the two highest stories being rebuilt in the XIV century[3] (Fig. 151, p. 176). To a large extent these forms were made possible by the fact they had not to contain the bells which were required in Christian worship.

It is true that instances of slender cylindrical minarets of a date earlier than the XI century have been alleged; but they are not really of that age. I may mention—to take one instance—the minaret at the eastern angle of the mosque of Ibn Tulun at Qattai, which is clearly not of the same date as the mosque itself, though it is built of brick.

An early and interesting example of the new type of mosque is

THE MOSQUE AL-AQMAR AT CAIRO, erected by the Emir Ibn al-Bataihi in 1125 under the Caliph Amir (1101-1130), and restored in 1397.[4] The orientation is towards Mecca.

[1] Op. cit., p. 181.

[2] IBN JUBAIR, op. cit., p. 73.

[3] *East and West*, 1907, pp. 1200-1205; VINCENT A. SMITH, *Who built the Kutb Minar?*

[4] BOURIANT, *Mémoires publiées par les Membres de la Mission Archéologique Française au Caire*, vol. xix, pp. 67-71; VAN BERCHEM, *Matériaux pour un Corpus inscriptionum arabicarum*. *Journal Asiatique*, 1891, ii, pp. 46-58; VAN BERCHEM, *Notes d'archéologie arabe*. LANE-POOLE, *A History of Egypt in the Middle Ages*, pp. 117, 166.

It is reached through a court surrounded by arcades with piers and columns fitted with ancient Corinthian capitals. Next comes the place of prayer, which is divided into three aisles by eight columns with capitals as above. The central dome has fallen, and only the drum remains. The shafts belonging to the mihrab have plain bell-shaped capitals, and stand on bases formed like the capitals, but inverted. The arches are of the pointed ogee or 'cyma reversa' form and stilted, and have wooden imposts. The original roof, to judge by what remains of it, consisted of brick vaulting.

The most interesting feature is the façade, which indicates the arrangement of the interior, and has bold effects of light and shade obtained by its deep recesses. It is also richly ornamented (Fig. 152, p. 179). One of its various decorative forms is that of stalactites, the earliest instance preserved in Egyptian Moslem architecture.[1] The side walls were also embellished on their outer faces.

The original minaret, being out of the perpendicular, was demolished in 1412. The one to the left of the façade is modern.

We have no information about the architect of this mosque with its church-like appearance. But the ornamentation of the arches in the façade connects it with the gates of al-Futuh (1087) (Fig. 153, p. 179), opened at the same time as that of an-Nasr (1087) (Fig. 154, p. 180), and of az-Zuweleh (1091) (Fig. 155, p. 180), in the new Fatimite walls of Cairo built under Mustansir (1035-1094). Now the design or conception of these gates seems to have been due, together with the walls, to John the Monk; and their construction to three architect brothers, supposed to have been brought from Edessa by the Armenian emir, Badr al-Jamali (1073-1094).[2] Hence it is possible that the architect was a Christian from Armenia, whence, perhaps, he brought the idea of stalactite decoration. As a matter of fact, I have found no instance in Western Asia, in existing buildings of certain date, of either the stalactite or stalagmite design used as an architectural decoration, or in the form of a raccord, earlier than the erection of the mosque of Ani in Armenia. The mosque was built by order of Manutchê (1072-1110) after Alp Arslan's capture of the city (1064). The minaret was a latter

[1] Herz, op. cit., pp. xxxvi-xxxix.

[2] Bouriant, *Mémoires publiées par les Membres de la Mission Archéologique Française au Caire*, vol. xix, pp. 61, 62; Van Berchem, *Matériaux pour un Corpus inscriptionum arabicarum*. Lane-Poole, *A History of Egypt in the Middle Ages*, pp. 152, 153.

FIG. 152.—Cairo. Façade of the Mosque al-Aqmar (XII cent.).

FIG. 153.—Cairo. Gate al-Futuh (1087).

FIG. 154.—Cairo. Gate an-Nasr (1087).

FIG. 155.—Cairo. Gate az-Zuweleh (1091).

FIG. 156.—Ani. Mosque (1072-1110).

Fig. 157.—Cairo. Mosque of Muayyad. Pendentive of the dome (1412-1421).

Fig. 159.—Rome. Columbarium in the Vigna Codini (10 A.D.).

addition[1] (Fig. 156, p. 181). The specimen of stalagmite[2] in the traditional tomb of Zobaide, the favourite wife of Harun al-Rashid (786-809), at Baghdad, belongs to a reconstructed cupola,[3] which, even if it were a copy of one of 786-809, would be nothing short of a phenomenon from both the constructive and the artistic point of view, without a predecessor, and without immediate descendants. According to Saladin[4] it was restored in 1051, and again in the XIII and XVI centuries. Le Strange[5] says that it is not the tomb of Zobaide at all, but a comparatively modern building. Again, the similar example known as the tomb of Ezekiel near Baghdad, and thought by Texier to be the copy of an older cupola,[6] really belongs to the early Seljuk period. And it was under the Seljuks that, according to Pullé, the art known as Saracenic came into existence in Persia.[7]

In Sicily the Cappella Palatina at Palermo (1132) contains an early and exquisite example of stalactite ornament in the pendentives of the nave roof (Fig. 140, p. 161). Another of the same kind is to be found in the castle of La Zisa near the same city, the work of William the Bad (1154-1166), and partly also of William the Good (1166-1189).[8] An interesting specimen of the same motive applied to the supports of the domes is to be seen in the mosque of Muayyad at Cairo (1412-1421) (Fig. 157, p. 182).

Still it must be remembered that these two decorative motives, consisting of an accumulation of niches or of arched recesses, seem to have sprung from the honeycomb or cellular design; and, therefore, it is not unreasonable to suppose that all three were developed in the same countries.

With regard to the honeycomb design, which is thought probably to have been diffused under the early Abbasides (750-1258),[9] there is nothing to substantiate De Vogüé's[10] theory that it was derived from the rudimentary raccords, such as those of the chapel of Umm ez-Zeitun in Syria (282), where

[1] LYNCH, *Armenia, Travels and Studies*, vol. i, pp. 376, 377.

[2] LANGENEGGER, *Die bankunst des Irâq*, pp. 115-120.

[3] DE BEYLIÉ, *Prome et Samara*, pp. 32, 33.

[4] *Manuel d'Art musulman*, vol. i, pp. 108, 320.

[5] *Baghdad during the Abbassid Caliphate*, pp. 161-165, 350-352.

[6] TEXIER, PULLAN, *Byzantine Architecture*, p. 1.

[7] *Annuario della R. Università di Bologna*, 1911-12; PULLÉ, *Le conquiste scientifiche e civili dell'Italia in Oriente, dall' antichità ai tempi nuovi.*

[8] AMARI, op. cit., vol. iii, 2, pp. 818, 819.

[9] DE BEYLIÉ, *Prome et Samara*, pp. 113, 114.

[10] *Syrie Centrale*, vol. i, pp. 41-45.

we see overhanging the square base of the dome the polygonal outline which is multiplied stage by stage and gradually merges in the circle of the cupola (Fig. 158). This system, first introduced in the dome, was afterwards applied to other parts of buildings.

It might equally well be said that it was suggested by some columbarium of the type of one of those in the Vigna Codini on the Via Appia at Rome, belonging to the year 10 A.D.[1] (Fig. 159, p. 182). But it is much more probable that it originated in the use of niches with cusped arches.

FIG. 158.—Umm ez-Zeitun. Chapel. Raccord of the cupola (282).

All the changes which we have mentioned reached their full development at a later date in Constantinople, under the Ottoman dominion, in the imposing mosques modelled on St. Sophia: of Mohammed II (1451-1481), erected between 1463 and 1469 and almost entirely rebuilt between 1768 and 1771; of Bajazet II (1481-1512), built between 1489 and 1497 (Fig. 160, p. 185); of Suliman the Magnificent (1520-1566), erected between 1550 and 1556 (Fig. 161, p. 185), the creation of the celebrated Albanian architect Sinan, of striking grandeur and dignity, and unrivalled save by the mosque of Selim II (1566-1574) at Adrianople, which was the work (1568-1574) of the same builder;[2] and, lastly, of Ahmed I (1603-1617), raised between 1608 and 1614 (Fig. 162, p. 186). In all of them the dome is the principal feature.

* * *

We will conclude the first part of this book with a short but instructive account, bearing directly on our subject, of some of the older characteristic religious buildings of Armenia. They have sometimes been invested with

[1] LANCIANI, *The Ruins and Excavations of Ancient Rome*, p. 333.

[2] LAUNAY, *L'architecture ottomane*, pp. 42, 81-86.

FIG. 160.—Constantinople. Mosque of Bajazet II (1489-1497).

FIG. 161.—Constantinople. Mosque of Suliman the Magnificent (1550-1556).

Fig. 162.—Constantinople. Mosque of Ahmed I (1608-1614).

an antiquity to which they have no claim, and this has been made the basis for hypothetical origins and influences in matters both of construction and decoration; whereas, if assigned to their true dates, they will be found to possess undoubted and remarkable features which we will try to place in a clear light. These features constitute a real and individual style—a style which is the most complete representative and the highest expression of a nation, small indeed in numbers, but which concentrated all the nobler sentiments in its ancestral faith. A style which, by its adoption of the Roman or else the Romano-Byzantine plan, indicates on the one hand its connection with Roman architecture, and on the other the relations of the Armenian people with the Greek Empire. But the variations and innovations which it displays betray the jealous care of the Armenians to avoid becoming the servile followers of the Byzantines, and still less their subjects.

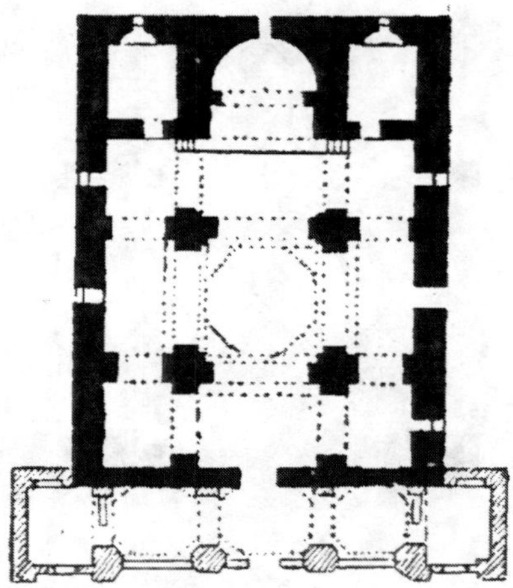

FIG. 163.—Etschmiadzin. Plan of St. Gaiana (VII cent.).

At the head of the list must be placed the churches said to have been founded in the last thirty years of the III century by St. Gregory the Illuminator, who is supposed to have occupied the episcopal see from 302 to 332, and to have died about the year 336.[1] These are, at Vagharshapat, the modern Etschmiadzin, St. Gaiana, St. Rhipsima, the Shoghagath or Effusion of Light, and the cathedral. Next come the church of the Holy Cross at Usunlar, and the primatial church of Aghthamar, connected with the name of an illustrious member of the ancient family of the Arzruni. They are followed by the churches of Ani erected under the Bagratids at a time when Armenia was more united and prosperous than usual. These latter buildings, owing to their ascertained dates, may be used as trustworthy guides in our estimate of those of Etschmiadzin, and of other Armenian churches.

THE CHURCH OF ST. GAIANA NEAR ETSCHMIADZIN.—On the spot pointed out by the legend as the scene of the martyrdom of the Roman Saint Gaiana

[1] BROSSET, *Collection d'Historiens arméniens*, vol. ii; SAMOUEL D'ANI, *Tables chronologiques*, pp. 366, 367, 372.

and her two companions, the Apostle of Armenia, with the help of his followers and under his own direction, built a chapel with the stones, brick, and cedar wood which he had collected for the purpose.[1] The existing building is ascribed to the episcopate of Ezra (628-640). The porch in front was added in 1687.[2]

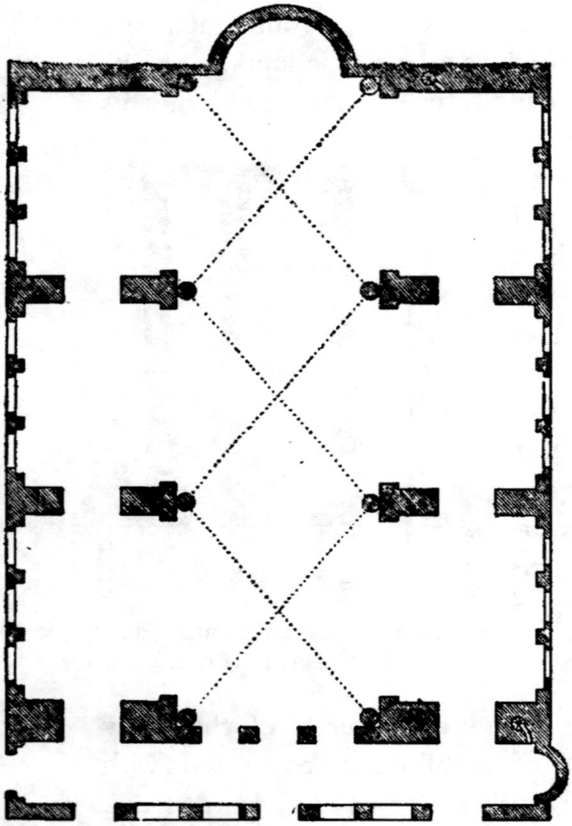

FIG. 165.—Rome. Plan of the original 'Basilica Nova' of Maxentius, or Basilica of Constantine (IV cent.).

The plan is a rectangle measuring internally about 21.40 by 14.50 m. (70 by 47 ft.), and terminated at the east by a semicircular apse flanked by two chapels (Fig. 163, p. 187). In the centre rises a dome with a polygonal drum lighted by four windows, and supported by four isolated piers. It is crowned by a conical roof of masonry (Fig. 164, p. 191). The walls, where they have not been rebuilt, are of concrete with facings of coursed and carefully cut and laid stone. The walls are over 1.50 m. (nearly 5 ft.) thick. On the whole, except for the outer roofs, which, like the rest, are of tufa, and bearing in mind sundry restorations, the structure seems to be all of one date. But what is that date?

The plan shows unquestionable Byzantine influence, and must be later than the erection of several churches in Western Armenia by the orders of Justinian (527-565).[3] For the type of church with a rectangular outline and central dome was a Byzantine development, though its plan was derived from the tepidarium of the great Roman baths, with its central hall flanked by six smaller ones,[4]

[1] AGATHANGELOS (Armenian Mechitarists of Venice), *Storia*, pp. 99, 137, 138.

[2] LYNCH, op. cit., vol. i, pp. 270, 271.

[3] *Corpus script. hist. byz.*; PROCOPIUS, *De aedificiis*, vol. iii, pp. 253, 254.

[4] *British and American Archaeological Society of Rome*, 1910; RIVOIRA, *The Roman Thermae.*

or, again, from the 'Basilica Nova' of Maxentius (310-312)[1] (Fig. 165, p. 188), the model for St. Sophia at Constantinople; together with suggestions obtained from Roman tombs and baptisteries, and also from the Christian buildings of Ravenna.

I produce in this connection a very interesting though imperfect plan of a Roman building, made by Fra Giocondo, and now in the Uffizi at Florence (No. 3932) (Fig. 166), showing a central dome with a narthex in front of it, surrounded by rooms, some of which are cross-vaulted and others domed; the whole being enclosed by a square outer wall, and forming an actual Roman prototype of the Byzantine church plan.

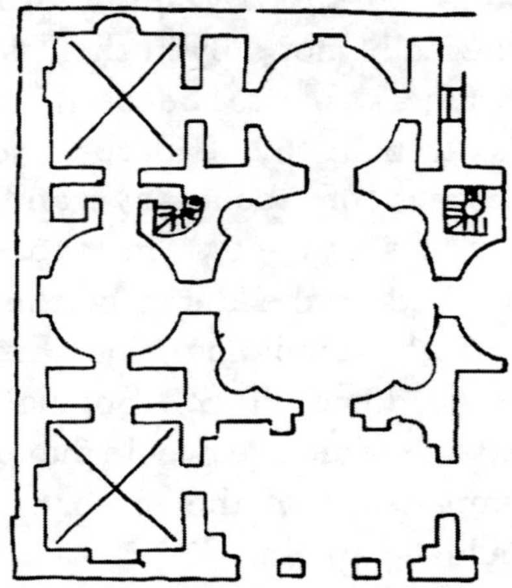

FIG. 166.—Mutilated plan of a Roman building.

I have used the word 'influence' only, because the ancient churches of Etschmiadzin, Aghthamar, and Ani have an individual character. Among other points, it may be noticed that they had no narthex, an adjunct which, so far as can be seen, was not adopted before the second half of the XII century. The church of the Saviour at Sanahin (961) provides the first dated example of a narthex, for we know that in 1181 the patriarch John erected a porch at the entrance of the church, and was buried in it.[2] The new feature does not seem to have become established at once, for though we are told that the 'Mother of Light' or Shoghagath at Bagnaïr, built by Sembat II (977-989)[3] (Fig. 167, p. 192), possessed a narthex when the primate Basil II (still living in 1207) was buried there,[4] nevertheless, in 1215 and 1217 respectively, the churches of Saghmosavank and Johannavank were designed without a narthex.

The narthex has been regarded as the special property of the Byzantines, whereas it appears in innumerable Roman imperial buildings in various shapes, especially the rectangular, and the form with a niche or apse at either end, as may be seen from existing examples or from drawings.

[1] RIVOIRA, op. cit. (Loescher), vol. i, pp. 71, 72; (Hoepli), p. 76; (Heinemann), vol. i, p. 66.

[2] *Mémoires de l'Académie impériale des Sciences de Saint-Pétersbourg*, 1863, vol. vi, n. 6, pp. 77-81; BROSSET, *Monastères arméniens d'Haghbat et de Sanahin.*

[3] BROSSET, *Deux Historiens arméniens;* KIRACOS [XIII century], *Histoire d'Arménie*, p. 47.

[4] TCHAMTCHEAN, *History of Armenia* [in Armenian], vol. iii, chronological table.

Moreover, the simple plan of the church compared with those of St. Rhipsima and the cathedral, points to a date earlier than the two latter churches. And again, the absence of the characteristic V-shaped niches on the exterior, apparently a creation of the X century, compels us to date it earlier than that century. Lastly, the VII century was a period of building activity on the part of the primates of the Armenian Church, so much so that Narses III (640-661) was surnamed 'the builder.'[1] Hence we may accept the years 628-640 as the period to which St. Gaiana belongs.

The height of the drum as seen from outside seems to be against this date. In the Byzantine world the dome rose from a drum which was low externally, not only in the first half, but also in the second half of the VI century. Instances are to be seen at Constantinople, in St. Sophia, where the dome was rebuilt by Isidorus the younger between 558-563; SS. Sergius and Bacchus of about 527; and St. Mary Diaconissa, founded by the patriarch Cyriacus (593-605) in 596. It is true that doubts have been raised[2] as to whether the dome of the last church be not, as a whole, the result of a Turkish rebuilding; but its drum seems to form a transition between that of the dome of St. Sophia and that of St. Irene, also at Constantinople, and the structure would have to be tested in a number of places, and careful comparisons of the masonry made, before a decisive answer to the question could be given.

It was not till well on in the VIII century that the Byzantines thought of raising their domes on fairly pronounced drums lighted by large windows, as the Romans had already done, the Mausoleum of Santa Costanza at Rome (about 326-329) (Fig. 168, p. 192) being an illustration of this. St. Irene led the way in the new fashion at Constantinople (Figs. 169, 170, p. 195).

I have previously stated[3] that St. Irene is the result, not of a mere restoration (following the earthquake which Van Millingen[4] places in 740 and Bury[5] in 739), as some have thought, contrary to the view which has prevailed since Fergusson,[6] but of rebuilding. As long ago as 1900 I

[1] LYNCH, op. cit., vol. i, p. 265.

[2] VAN MILLINGEN, *Byzantine Churches in Constantinople*, p. 186.

[3] RIVOIRA, op. cit. (Loescher), vol. i, pp. 213, 214; (Hoepli), p. 655; (Heinemann), vol. ii, pp. 274, 275.

[4] VAN MILLINGEN, *Byzantine Churches in Constantinople*, p. 89.

[5] BURY, *A History of the Later Roman Empire*, vol. ii, p. 423.

[6] *A History of Architecture*, vol. ii, pp. 452, 453.

FIG. 164.—Etschmiadzin. St. Gaiana (VII cent.).

FIG. 167.—Bagnair. Church of the Mother of Light (X cent.).

FIG. 168.—Rome. Santa Costanza (IV cent.).

had come to this conclusion, essentially on the ground of the form of the dome, and with the help of the notions which I had acquired by prolonged study of the origin and development of dome vaulting. The recent investigations[1] have, as a matter of fact, proved that the only remains of the structure proper of Justinian's St. Irene are some reused columns with poor capitals (which, if they did not bear explanatory monograms, would appear work of the decadence and not of the time of Justinian), and the lower parts of the walls.

In the Moslem world the domes of the VII and VIII centuries occasionally had high drums lighted by large windows, as in the Dome of the Rock at Jerusalem (687-691) and the congregational mosque of Damascus (706-714). These drums, however, were circular in construction, and intended to carry a dome, not of masonry, which, considering the span, would have involved serious problems of weight and thrust, but only of wood.

The dome of St. Gaiana, on the other hand, was designed on a very modest scale, and its base was pierced by a limited number of narrow windows (one for every two faces of the polygon), which made the adoption of this form more easy.

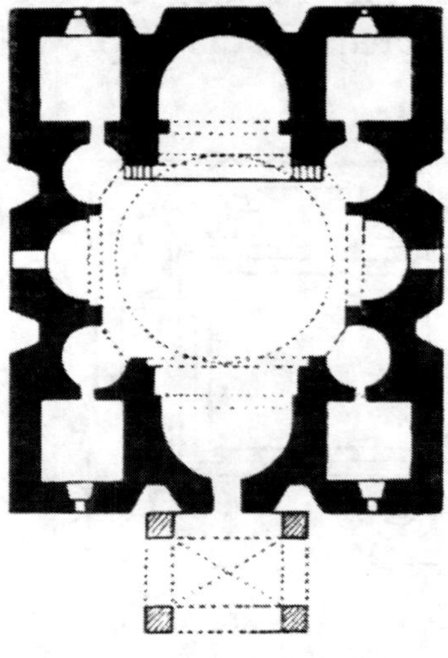

FIG. 171.—Etschmiadzin. Plan of St. Rhipsima (after the VII cent.).

THE CHURCH OF ST. RHIPSIMA, NEAR ETSCHMIADZIN, founded by the Illuminator on the spot where St. Rhipsima and thirty-three companions were said to have been martyred,[2] was rebuilt in 618 by the primate Komitas (617-625). The original building was dark and of mean appearance,[3] and was pulled down.[4] Later information about the structure is deficient until we come to the XVII century.[5]

The existing church, which is orientated in the usual way, has a singular

[1] GEORGE, *The Church of S. Eirene at Constantinople*, pp. 9-75.

[2] AGATHANGELOS, op. cit., pp. 99, 137.

[3] BROSSET, *Coll. d'Hist. arm.*, vol. ii; SAMOUEL D'ANI, *Tables chronologiques*, p. 399. BROSSET, *Deux. Hist. arm.*; KIRACOS, *Histoire d'Arménie*, p. 27.

[4] Bibliotheca Teubneriana, *Des Stephanos von Taron armenische Geschichte*, p. 62.

[5] LYNCH, op. cit., vol. i, pp. 269, 270.

plan (Fig. 171, p. 193). With a rectangular exterior, a four-lobed shape is given to the interior by means of four apses, two larger and two smaller, between which are interposed four circular niches, each communicating with a square room or chapel lighted from the outside. The eastern of the two larger apses contains the altar and has no window. The opposite one serves as the entrance. The internal dimensions are about 23 by 18 m. (75 by 60 ft.).

The western porch dates from 1653. In 1790 a bell-turret in the form of an open spirelet was erected above it. In each of the four external faces of the building are recessed two tall narrow niches with splayed sides and vaulted at the top. Above the centre of the church rises a spacious dome resting on spherical triangular pendentives. Its rather low drum, circular internally and polygonal externally, is lighted by a number of fairly large windows (Fig. 172, p. 196). The masonry of the exterior, where it is original—and a good deal has been rebuilt—is distinguished from that of St. Gaiana by the small size of the stones.

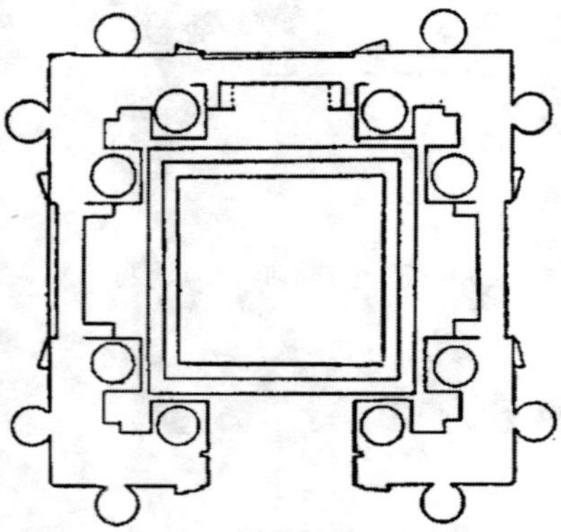

FIG. 173.—Plan of a Roman bath-room.

The plan of St. Rhipsima is another instance of Byzantine influence in its application to a church of the principle of grouping within a quadrangular space the interiors of palace rooms such as the domed apartments in the 'Domus Augustana' on the Palatine; or of Roman tombs with recesses, of the type which we illustrated in connection with the account of the Dome of the Rock at Jerusalem. Moreover, the recesses in the angles recall the plan of a bath-room, formerly existing on the Via Flaminia at Rome, which was sketched by Bramantino[1] (Fig. 173).

In one respect—its complicated internal outline—it seems to be more advanced than St. Gaiana. On the other hand, the isolated supports of the dome in the latter church are an advance on St. Rhipsima. And again, the relatively large windows in the base of its dome put it at a later date than St. Gaiana. The fact that this base is not elevated in the manner usual in Armenia at the beginning of the VIII century, may be due to its diameter, which exceeds 14 m. (46 ft.), it being the largest of all the domes in Etschmiadzin.

[1] MONGERI, op. cit., tav. 68.

Fig. 169.—Constantinople. St. Irene (VIII cent.).

Fig. 170.—Constantinople. St. Irene. Interior looking towards the Narthex (VIII cent.).

FIG. 172.—Etschmiadzin. St. Rhipsima (after the VII cent.).

FIG. 175.—Ani. Church of St. Gregory the Illuminator (1215)

FIG. 176.—Kanligia. Monastery Church of Marmashen (X, XI, and XIII cents.).

The splayed niches of St. Rhipsima, in their turn, are connected with the church of Aghthamar (904-936) which possesses the earliest dated examples.

For all these reasons, St. Rhipsima seems not to belong to the time of the patriarch Komitas. Doubts have previously been suggested about it,[1] though the reasons have not been stated before. What the real date is I am unable to decide. All I can say is that it is later than the VII century.

The Church of the Shoghagath or Effusion of Light, near Etschmiadzin, was founded by St. Gregory on the site of the traditional dwelling of the martyrs, where he himself had resided after his release (301) from the cruel imprisonment at Artaxata to which he had been sentenced by Tiridates (286-341).[2] It is said to have been rebuilt by the primate Narses III between 640 and 649. The western porch with its bell-turret was added in 1693.[3]

The church forms a rectangle of three bays, with a semicircular apse at the east end. Its internal dimensions are nearly 17.50 by 8 m. (58 by 26 ft.). From the centre rises a high cupola with spherical pendentives, covered by the usual conical roof. The drum, polygonal on the outside, is carried on four half wall-piers, and lighted by four fairly large windows.

As with the other churches of Etschmiadzin, no wood or iron is used in the building. The absence of the splayed niches, and the character of the original parts of the external masonry in the body of the church, connect it with St. Gaiana. On the other hand, the height of the dome, the outer surface of which seems to be entirely renewed, places it at a later date than the VIII century.

The Cathedral of Etschmiadzin.—The foundation is ascribed to the Apostle of Armenia, after his return from Caesarea in Cappadocia, to the jurisdiction of which the patriarchs of Armenia were subject down to the reign of Pap (369-374).[4] Later, the Armenian Church became and remained autonomous.

After the ruin caused by the Persians at Vagharshapat, it is supposed

[1] Lynch, op. cit., vol. i, p. 270.

[2] Agathangelos, op. cit., pp. 60, 137, 138.

[3] Lynch, op. cit., vol. i, pp. 271, 272.

[4] Faustus of Byzantium, *Vatican MS.* 9545, bk. v.

that the primate, Narses I the Great (364-383), restored the churches there. But we have definite information that the cathedral was repaired about 483 by the governor of Armenia, Vahan Mamikonean.[1] At this time the residence of the primate was at Dovin. Archbishop Komitas (617-625) in 618 rebuilt the wooden dome in stone. Narses III (640-661) is believed to have done some repairs. It is known that in 1442 there was a restoration by the primate Cyriacus, after Etschmiadzin had once more become the seat of the primacy. When the Shah of Persia, Abbas I (1587-1629), depopulated Armenia in the inhuman manner which is notorious,[2] the cathedral church lost many of its venerated stones which were carried away to New Julfa to form the nucleus of a second Etschmiadzin there. The building remained neglected, but after 1629 it was repaired and the roof rebuilt. The western porch was added later and finished in 1658, and in 1682 the eastern, southern, and northern apses were crowned with open spirelets. Other works were carried out in the XVIII and XIX centuries.[3] The beauty of the church has aroused the admiration of many travellers.[4]

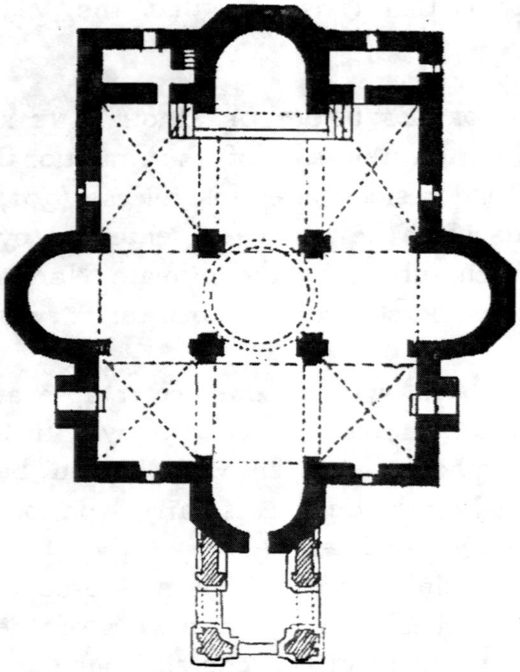

FIG. 174.—Etschmiadzin. Plan of the Cathedral (VII cent. and onwards).

The plan (Fig. 174) is a rectangle, from each side of which projects an apse, semicircular internally and polygonal externally. That on the east, which is flanked by two chambers, contains the principal altar. In the opposite one is a door. The dimensions are about 33.50 by 29.70 m. (110 by 98 ft.). The walls are over 1.20 m. (4 ft.) thick.

The tall dome rises in the centre above four isolated cruciform piers, and

[1] LANGLOIS, *Collection des Historiens anciens et modernes de l'Arménie;* LAZARE DE PHARBE, *Histoire d'Arménie*, vol. ii, p. 352.

[2] BROSSET, *Coll. d'Hist. arm.*, vol. i, pp. 274-303; ARAKEL, *Livre d'Histoires.*

[3] LYNCH, op. cit., vol. i, pp. 261-268.

[4] P. MINAS NURIKHAN, *Il Servo di Dio abate Mechitar ed il suo tempo*, p. 43.

FIG. 177.—Etschmiadzin. Porch of the Cathedral (XVII cent.).

FIG. 180.—Usunlar. Church of the Holy Cross (VIII cent.).

Fig. 178.—Johannavank. Church (XIII cent.).

is developed from spherical pendentives. It is crowned by a conical roof, and the drum, which is polygonal on the outside, is lighted by windows. The whole edifice is of stone. The exterior of the drum is encircled by a gallery with pointed ogee or 'cyma reversa' arches supported by shafts which have traces of spiral carving, framing medallions with heads of saints.

It has been asserted that the building, with the exception of the dome and the spirelets, actually goes back, at least in part, to the reign of Tiridates (286-341). On the other hand, it has been suggested that the main structure belongs to the work of Vahan Mamikonean. A third view prefers to ascribe it to the time of the primate Komitas.[1] The mystery in which the date is involved is rendered still more obscure by our ignorance of the vicissitudes of Etschmiadzin as the seat, first of the archbishops subject to Caesarea, and later of the primates of the Armenian Church from its establishment down to its restoration in 1441. I shall not pretend that I have discovered the clue to guide us in the labyrinth of all the questions, religious, historical, and archaeological, bearing on the history and the construction of the cathedral. Nevertheless, starting from my persistent belief that styles of architecture have always had a development which is rational, gradual, and linked with the past, and not an arbitrary and imaginary one of spontaneous and phenomenal origin, and in the ever faithful company of dated buildings, I will try to discover what is the most probable age to be assigned to it.

That the cathedral of Etschmiadzin does not belong to the time of the Illuminator may be inferred from the fact that the three chapels which he erected there were constructed of stone and brick, perhaps taken from Pagan buildings in the Roman Nor-Kaghak,[2] and roofed with wood.[3] Hence we may conjecture that his cathedral was made of the same materials. Samuel of Ani (XII century) bears witness to the very mean character of these structures.[4]

However this may be, the Apostle of Armenia certainly did not adopt for his church a Christian Romano-Byzantine plan which was only developed in the VI century. Nor can he have introduced the apses with semicircular interior and polygonal exterior, nor an orientation which was still unknown to the Christian world. For the orientation of churches and the polygonal

[1] Lynch, op. cit., vol. i, pp. 263-265. [2] Ibid., p. 287.

[3] Agathangelos, op. cit., p. 137.

[4] Brosset, *Coll. d'Hist. arm.*, vol. ii, p. 399; Samouel d'Ani, *Tables chronologiques*.

apse, the reader may be referred to our account of the great mosque of Damascus.

Moreover, it must be remembered that in those days the Armenians had not long emerged from barbarism. Moses of Chorene (born in the second half of the IV century) states that the arts and sciences were introduced into Armenia between the years 78 and 120 of our era. They would, therefore, have been unable to provide workmen capable of producing masonry like that of the cathedral of Etschmiadzin. Though Tiridates erected at Garni, for his sister Khosrovidukht, a summer residence ornamented with columns and magnificent bas-reliefs, the commemorative inscription being in Greek,[1] that does not prove that the work was done by Armenian hands. Nor is it to be forgotten that under the Sassanid Sapor II (310-379), between 363 and 379, Vagharshapat was mercilessly destroyed,[2] and that the sacred edifices erected there by St. Gregory were certainly not spared. In fact, the cathedral was rebuilt with great magnificence by Vahan Mamikonean. And we cannot ignore the passage in Faustus of Byzantium[3] (395-416) in which he tells how Urhnayr, King of the Albanians, with his army, before joining the Persians of Sapor II in a battle against the Armenians and Greeks, earnestly exhorted his own soldiers to spare the lives of their Greek prisoners in order that they might be available as brickmakers, builders, and masons, for constructing cities and palaces, and for other purposes. The story shows that the Armenians had not made much progress in building, for they are not mentioned in this connection.

I think that it was Komitas who gave the cathedral its present form. His work will not have been confined to mere restoration and a new dome, but can have been nothing less than a reconstruction, for we know that the church was in ruins.[4]

The dome of 618 is not the one now to be seen, though it has been generally believed to be so. Lynch[5] and Bryce[6] suspected a later date, and Dubois thought that it was much more recent than the church.[7] We shall

[1] Moses of Chorene (Armenian Mechitarists of Venice), *Storia*, p. 264.

[2] Lynch, op. cit., vol. i, pp. 301-305.

[3] *Vatican MS.* 9545, bk. v, chap. iv.

[4] Saint Martin, *Mémoires historiques et géographiques sur l'Arménie*, vol. i, p. 116.

[5] Op. cit., vol. i, p. 263.

[6] Bryce, *Transcaucasia and Ararat*, p. 301.

[7] Dubois de Montpéreux, *Voyage autour du Caucase*, vol. iii, pp. 370-376.

see presently that domes with high drums, like that of this cathedral, first began to be erected in Armenia in the early years of the VIII century, and that they were not encircled by blank arcades of elegant form before the end of the X. The vaults, too, at the four angles of the base of the dome must belong to the reconstruction, for in the oldest Armenian churches barrel vaults are regularly used and not cross vaults. Moreover, there is no evidence that either the pointed ogee or 'cyma reversa' arch, or the pointed mixtilinear arch, which came from India, were freely used in other countries before the erection of the mosque al-Azhar at Cairo (970-972). Again, at Ani, the decorative arcading on the exteriors of dated buildings regularly has round arches, with some rare exceptions, as late as the beginning of the XIII century. The church of St. Gregory the Illuminator, erected in 1215,[1] is evidence of the fact (Fig. 175, p. 197). And though in other parts of Armenia we find arches of a different kind used in churches older than the XIII century, such churches are not wholly in their original condition. For instance, the dome with external arcade of triangular arches belonging to the monastery church of Marmashen in Kanligia, near Alexandropol (Fig. 176, p. 198), erected between 988 and 1029,[2] is the result of the extensive restoration of 1225. Lynch had already stated his suspicion that this was so.[3] Lastly, the external masonry facing of the body of the church, where original, is like that of St. Gaiana. That of the dome cannot be verified, as it has been daubed over with plaster and paint.

All this shows that the essential structure of the primatial church of Etschmiadzin may possibly be as old as the VII century. The well-known and often discussed slabs with Greek inscriptions, and the figures of Paul and Thecla framed by rude arches, which Strzygowski[4] has illustrated, afford no evidence of date, as they did not belong originally to the building.

The dome and the vaults at its angles are another matter, and for the reasons stated above cannot be older than the XIII century.

Before leaving the cathedral of Etschmiadzin a passing reference must be made to the bell-turret of its front (Fig. 177, p. 201), and the similar open spirelets surmounting the apses.

[1] Lynch, op. cit., vol. i, pp. 374, 375.

[2] Brosset, *Coll. d'Hist. arm.*, vol. ii; Samouel d'Ani, *Tables chronologiques*, pp. 440, 441. Ibid., *Rapports sur un voyage archéologique dans la Géorgie et dans l'Arménie*, pp. 86, 87.

[3] Lynch, op. cit., vol. i, pp. 131, 132.

[4] *Byzantinische denkmäler*, i; *Das Etschmiadzin evangeliar*, pp. 1-16.

It has been believed that spirelets in the latter position are a traditional Armenian feature, and that the cathedral possessed four from the outset.[1] On the contrary, facts show that as late as the X and XI centuries the Armenian churches were without them. Thus the churches of Gagik (904-936) at Aghthamar, and of the Shoghagath at Khoshavank (928-951), did not originally possess them; and they were absent from the cathedral of Ani (977-1010) and the sepulchral churches of the Bagratids at Khoshavank; all of them important monuments.

Bell-turrets seem to have made their appearance in the first part of the XIII century. The church of Saghmosavank, at the foot of Mount Aragaz, finished in 1215,[2] and designed without a narthex, the existing one being an addition, was not provided with a belfry till 1235, when the south chapel with the library was built.[3] The church also of Johannavank (Fig. 178, p. 202), not far from the last, completed in 1217, was built without one. It was only in 1250-51, when the narthex was added, that a bell-turret was provided in the form of an open lantern.[4] Brosset erroneously substituted for the top of this lantern a kind of ornament carved in relief.

The adoption of this feature is to be ascribed, even if indirectly, to the influence of the Crusades. Its typical form, derived, apparently, from the kiosks surmounting minarets, has been maintained for centuries with the same persistence as other characteristics of Armenian church architecture. Sometimes it took the place of the dome, as in the singular, perhaps sepulchral, church faced with basalt at Haghpat, on the railway between Tiflis and Alexandropol (Fig. 179, p. 207), where the spirelet dominates the whole structure. This church, with its cusped niches and gabled bell-turret, cannot be older than the XIII century.

THE CHURCH OF THE HOLY CROSS AT USUNLAR is situated on the railway between Alexandropol and Tiflis. It was built by the patriarch

[1] LYNCH, op. cit., vol. i, p. 263.

[2] *Nouvelles Archives des Missions scientifiques et littéraires*, 1910; MACLER, *Rapport sur une mission scientifique en Arménie russe et en Arménie turque*, pp. 73, 74.

[3] ALISHAN, *Airarat*, p. 162.

[4] BROSSET, *Coll. d'Hist. arm.*, vol. ii; ZAKARIA, *Cartulaire du S. Asile de Johannou-Vank*, pp. 165-167.

FIG. 179.—Haghpat. Church (after the XII cent.).

FIG. 181.—Rome. Nymphaeum of the Licinian Gardens, called 'Minerva Medica' (253-268).

FIG. 182.—Rome. Mausoleum of St. Helena (IV cent.).

John Oznezi, surnamed the Philosopher (718-728), after his return from the court of the Caliph Hisham (724-743), laden with honours and presents.[1]

The plan follows the usual Romano-Byzantine type: a rectangle containing a large central block, and three smaller bays on either side. The semicircular apse is flanked by two square chambers. The dimensions are over 28 by 11 m. (92 by 36 ft.). The octagonal dome rises above the four piers of the central block, and is carried on hood-shaped pendentives. It has only two narrow round-headed windows, and is crowned by a steep conical roof.

Though Grimm[2] says that the plan appears to have been carried out at one and the same time, I think that the eastern transept, and the arcade forming a narthex at the west end, are due to a later alteration.

The church of Usunlar is a landmark in the history of Armenian church architecture, affording as it does the oldest example of a polygonal cupola of considerable elevation, crowned by a pointed roof (Fig. 180, p. 201).

Rome, both Pagan and Christian, had seen the erection of buildings of grand proportions crowned by domes raised on lofty drums. Evidence of this still survives in the Nymphaeum of the Licinian Gardens (Fig. 181, p. 208); the Mausoleum of St. Helena, also used for the burial of Constantius Chlorus[3] (Fig. 182, p. 208); and in the representations of the Imperial Mausoleum at the Vatican (V century). I would call attention to the illustration of the two rotundas of which the mausoleum was composed: the one, Santa Petronilla, in process of demolition; the other, Sant' Andrea or Santa Maria della Febre, still standing, but only to be destroyed in 1776[4] (Fig. 183, p. 211). At Jerusalem, too, the Dome of the Rock with its high drum had been erected as far back as the VII century.

The Armenians, however, were the first to introduce the practice of setting church domes on high bases, with the result, as Orsi has remarked,[5] that what the cupola lost in diameter it gained in pre-eminence over the subordinate parts of the building. It cannot be said that they borrowed the idea from the Byzantines at the time when Armenia exercised an influence in the

[1] BROSSET, *Deux Hist. arm.*; KIRACOS, *Histoire d'Arménie*, pp. 35, 36. Bibliotheca Teubneriana, *Des Stephanos von Taron armenische Geschichte*, pp. 74, 75.

[2] *Monuments d'Architecture byzantine en Géorgie et Arménie*, iv.

[3] TOMASSETTI, *La Campagna Romana*, vol. iii, pp. 389-393.

[4] RIVOIRA, *Lombardic Architecture*, vol. i, pp. 82, 83.

[5] *Bollettino d'Arte*, 1912, p. 279; *Siberene. S. Severina.*

empire.[1] The Byzantines adopted the feature only at a later date, and in a modified form; in other words, at the beginning of the XI century, after the Armenian architects had ornamented the drum with graceful blank arcading.

Its introduction into the European provinces of the Byzantine Empire may have been due to the presence at Constantinople of the Armenian architect and sculptor, Tiridates, who restored St. Sophia after the serious damage which it suffered in the terrific earthquakes of October 989.[2] The earliest dated instances in those regions are the churches of the Virgin at Salonica (1028) (Fig. 184, p. 212), and of St. Theodore at Athens (1049).

Another instructive feature in the church of Usunlar is the hood-shaped pendentive, as against the traditional Armenian predilection for the triangular form. My theory is that this sporadic instance must be explained by Moslem influence. In his journey to the court of Hisham, under whose sway he had brought his own country, the patriarch John may have had the opportunity of seeing domes supported by pendentives of this type. And his prejudice in favour of the children of Ishmael may have led him to introduce this constructive feature, hitherto foreign to the Armenians, but well known to the Moslem world. In any case we may be sure that it was not Byzantine craftsmen who introduced it in the church of the Holy Cross, for we know that the Greeks were banished from Armenia just at this time.[3]

In the course of his journey the cultured primate may also have derived the suggestion for his tall cupola at Usunlar from some high-set dome of the Ummayyad period, such as that of Abd al-Malik at Jerusalem (687-691), which is known to have had about the same elevation as the present one.[4]

THE CHURCH OF THE CROSS AT AGHTHAMAR stands on the island of the same name in Lake Van, where a monastery had been founded in 653.[5] Apart from some XVIII-century additions, the church is the one erected by Gagik (904-936), Prince of Van, of the family of Arzruni. In

[1] BURY, op. cit., vol. ii, pp. 452, 525.

[2] Bibliotheca Teubneriana, *Des Stephanos von Taron Armenische Geschichte*, p. 190. SCHLUMBERGER, *Epopée byzantine*, vol. ii, p. 627.

[3] BROSSET, *Deux. Hist. arm.*; KIRACOS, *Histoire d'Arménie*, p. 35.

[4] LE STRANGE, *Palestine under the Moslems*, p. 121.

[5] SAINT-MARTIN, *Mém. hist. géogr. sur l'Arménie*, vol. i, p. 140.

Fig. 183.—Rome. The 'Mausoleum Augustorum' at the Vatican (V cent.).
(From a painting in the Vatican Library.)

FIG. 184.—Salonica. Church of the Virgin (1028).

FIG. 185.—Aghthamar. Church of the Cross (904-936).

FIG. 186.—Aghthamar. Church of the Cross. Carving (904-936).

1113 Archbishop David, on his secession from the main Armenian Church, made it his cathedral.[1]

We possess detailed and precise information about its history.[2] The materials used were taken from a fortress on the Assyrian frontier, demolished by Gagik. The work was entrusted to the architect Manuel, whom the prince had previously employed to build, after plans drawn by himself, the wonderful palace in the new city of Aghthamar. The representations of sacred subjects were carried out with the advice of a monk.

We do not know precisely to what country the architect belonged. All we are told is that the ambitious works ordered by the prince on the island were carried out by skilled craftsmen from all parts. It is possible, however, that he may have been an Armenian. The name is a common one in Armenia at the present day. Moreover, the design is too different from that of IX and X century churches of the Byzantines to be ascribed to one of that nation.

The subjects of the decorative carvings included the principal personages of the Old and New Testaments; the Redeemer, before whom stands the founder carrying in his arms the model of the church; lions, bears, boars, bulls, birds, stems bearing grapes, vine scrolls with animals and reptiles. All this corresponds exactly to what we see to-day, and has no parallel in any other Armenian church.

The exterior of the building (Fig. 185, p. 213) is ornamented with carved cornices and bands displaying branches of the vine or other plants with leaves and fruit, either in a simple form or accompanied by human figures sacred and secular, birds, and quadrupeds; pairs of various kinds of animals facing one another; human heads; small corbel arches. The flat surfaces are adorned with scenes from the Bible, figures of saints on foot or on horseback, and other personages, one of whom is seated in the Moslem fashion, while others support, like caryatides, a band forming an arch (Fig. 186, p. 214). There are also pairs of beasts and wild animals facing one another, hippogriffs, projecting heads of animals, birds sometimes pecking at one another, eagles with prey in their talons, winged monsters of Assyrian derivation, fishes, angels holding the Greek cross, seraphs, Latin

[1] SAINT-MARTIN, *Mém. hist. géogr. sur l'Arménie*, vol. i, pp. 140, 141.

[2] BROSSET, *Coll. d'Hist. arm.*, vol. i; TH. ARDZROUNI (X century), *Histoire des Ardzrouni*, pp. 235-241.

crosses, &c. (Figs. 187, 188, 189, p. 217). The interior contains some carved heads of animals both wild and domestic, and also very valuable remains of mural painting (Fig. 190, p. 218).

The church, the dimensions of which are about 16.50 by 12 m. (55 by 40 ft.), has four apses, each apse being flanked by two recesses which form part of the exterior design; and is surmounted by a dome with a high drum, polygonal on the outside, and a conical roof. The whole is built of hewn stone with concrete filling.

The church of Aghthamar throws considerable light on the origin of the Armenian type of church. Thus it affords the oldest example, beyond the reach of controversy, of the tall, narrow, V-shaped niches, looking like stilted hooded squinches, which are one of the characteristics of the type.

These niches are anticipated by three squinch arches still to be seen at Hadrian's Villa near Tivoli (125-135), in the large Baths, the Imperial Palace[1] (Fig. 191, p. 218), and the Greek Library. These squinches are either purely constructive, or both constructive and decorative. It is not irrelevant to point out the error of those—and they are not a few—who maintain that niches generally are an essentially and characteristically Oriental form of decoration; forgetting that, perhaps owing to the fact that in building they employed materials which were easily moulded, and tenaciously hard mortar, no people made such free use of niches for both constructive and decorative purposes as the Romans. One has only to study the actual remains or extant sketches of their sepulchral structures, and the truth of this statement will at once become apparent.

THE CHURCH OF SHOGHAGATH AT KHOSHAVANK, NEAR ANI.—The convent was founded on the Arpa-Chai, a few kilometres from Ani, in the reign of Abbas (928-951), by Armenian priests who abandoned Greek territory in the hope of finding in the dominions of the Bagratids that religious independence which they strenuously maintained and the Byzantine authorities refused to recognize. Its original name was Horomosivank. It was burned by the Moslems in 982, and is supposed to have been restored in 1038 by King John Sembat (1020-1041), who is known to have been buried, like

[1] RIVOIRA, op. cit. (Loescher), vol. ii, pp. 602-604; (Hoepli), pp. 235-237: (Heinemann), vol. i, p. 193.

FIG. 187.—Aghthamar. Church of the Cross. Carving (904-936).

FIG. 188.—Aghthamar. Church of the Cross. Carving (904-936).

FIG. 189.—Aghthamar. Church of the Cross. Carving (904-936).

FIG. 190.—Aghthamar. Church of the Cross. Wall-paintings (904-936).

FIG. 191.—Tivoli. Villa of Hadrian. Imperial Palace, Angle raccord (125-135).

his predecessors who had ruled in Ani, in the royal cemetery of the convent which we are about to describe.[1]

The church, which is orientated in the usual way, is approached through an enclosed vestibule, the vaulting of which is carried by four rows of short columns. This structure is disproportionately large considering the small size of the church to which it leads, and is shown to be a later addition, not only by its construction and by the way in which it is joined to the church, but also by the shape of the isolated supports. Over the middle of its central aisle rises a small cupola surmounted by an open spirelet to hold a bell, which, again, is later than the vestibule, as is proved by its masonry and slightly pointed arches. Moreover, the older Armenian churches did not have the vestibule or narthex. As late as 1215 and 1217 respectively, the church of St. Gregory the Illuminator at Ani and the church at Johannavank were planned without it.

The dimensions are about 16.30 by 10.10 m. (53 by 33 ft.). The cupola with its circular drum is carried by four piers and spherical pendentives. The exterior is relieved by the characteristic splayed niches, but there is no blank arcading. The east end is flanked by two chapels. The one to the south, which is in fair preservation, also has a cupola with circular drum. These chapels are later additions, apparently for sepulchral purposes. The fact that they are additions is betrayed by the difference in the masonry and in the form of the dome roofs; and is confirmed by the cornice of the sanctuary roof being continued at the sides (Fig. 192, p. 223).

Near to the convent, in the old bed of the Arpa-Chai, stand two partly ruined chapels which are also decorated with splayed niches, and are without blank arcading (Fig. 193, p. 223). The larger of the two, and the more perfect, was erected in 1011. Close to it is the tomb of Ashot the Merciful (951-977).

This group of churches suggests several considerations. Above all should be noticed the continuity of a type of domed church with a drum circular on both faces, and not ornamented with blank arcading. Contrasted with this are the neighbouring churches of Ani, which also have circular drums, at least as late as the XIII century, but encircled by one or two ranges of decorative blank arcades. The logical deduction from this is that the conventual church is the original one, and that it came through the catastrophe

[1] Brosset, *Coll. d'Hist. arm.*, vol. ii; Samouel d'Ani, *Tables chronologiques*, pp. 435-437. Lynch, op. cit., vol. i, pp. 387-390.

of 982 unharmed. The fact that it was in every part faced with dressed stones set in very thin beds of mortar would suffice to protect it from the conflagration which consumed the adjoining monastery. It is walls composed of rubble and, still worse, of lumps of tufa, with plentiful use of mortar, which are quickly consumed under intense heat, as I myself witnessed at Constantinople in 1908 during the great fire in Stambul.

This inference is strengthened by the fact that the structure, apart from the vestibule and the chapels, is all of a piece; and that the designers of the other churches at Khoshavank all took it as their model; while the builders of the early churches at Ani were influenced by it, though they added (but not in every case) the embellishment of graceful blank arcading, which was first introduced in the large church at Sanahin, built in 961 (Fig. 194, p. 224).

The other point to notice is that the church has the peculiarity of possessing the earliest dome with a drum of considerable height, circular both internally and externally.

THE CATHEDRAL OF ANI was begun by Sembat II (977-989), at the place which his father, Ashot III (951-977), had converted from a fortress into a royal residence, and was completed in 1010 by the wife of King Gagik I (989-1019), on which occasion the patriarchal see was transferred from Arghina to the new capital.[1] The architect was Tiridates, the designer of the cathedral at Arghina, who flourished in the reigns of the above-named sovereigns.[2]

Within a rectangle of about 32.80 by 19.80 m. (108 by 65 ft.) is contained the plan of a Roman Tepidarium, i.e. a central hall with six lateral compartments, and the addition at the east end of an apse flanked by two apsidal chapels. Above the central bay rose the dome, which has almost entirely disappeared, supported by four compound piers, from which arches are carried across in both longitudinal and transverse directions to half wall-piers, also of compound form. The walls are of concrete, with facings of tufa blocks cut and laid with great accuracy. The exterior is encircled by blank arcading with tall semicircular arches, a few being slightly pointed. With the exception of the façade, each of the other faces is also relieved by a pair of

[1] BROSSET, *Coll. d'Hist. arm.*, vol. ii; SAMOUEL D'ANI, *Tables chronologiques*, pp. 440-443. LYNCH, op. cit., vol. i, pp. 354, 355, 373.

[2] DULAURIER, *Recherches sur la Chronologie arménienne technique et historique*, vol. i, p. 369. Bibliotheca Teubneriana, *Des Stephanos von Taron armenische Geschichte*, p. 138.

the characteristic splayed niches (Figs. 195, 196, pp. 224, 227). So far as the slight remains enable one to judge, the exterior of the drum of the dome also had blank arcading.

In addition to the windows, the walls are pierced by round openings recessed within concentric circles. I may remark that 'oculi' appear in Italian buildings from a very early period.[1]

The constructional arches of the interior are slightly pointed. The lower part of the apse is embellished by a range of arched niches, some being semicircular and some rather pointed.

The cathedral of Ani contains a wealth of instructive features and suggestions.

(1) The graceful arcading of the exterior—of Romano-Ravennate origin—is the earliest of such an advanced type known to me, with the exception of the church of the Saviour at Sanahin, near Haghpat (built in 961 by the wife of Ashot III,[2] and restored in 1184, 1752, and 1832[3]), where, at a rather earlier date, it appears in the important parts of the structure, but without rising to the free decorative use which we find at Ani.

It was Eastern influence, exercised through the trade of Pisa, which induced the Tuscan builders, not long after this time, to apply arcading of elegant form to their churches, as at San Miniato al Monte, near Florence (about 1018-1062), the culmination being reached in the cathedral of Pisa (XI, XII, XIII centuries) (Fig. 197, p. 228). They did not, however, do so as servile imitators, but, on the contrary, created a form of decoration which was both original and extremely rich in effect.

(2) The remains of the drum make good its claim to be the dated archetype of a dome embellished by an external blank arcade with slender shafts. The Romans, indeed, had sometimes surrounded domes with blank arches, either plain or springing from columns, such as are shown in the Vatican Latin MS. 3439, f. 85,[4] among drawings of fragmentary reliefs of the imperial epoch (Fig. 198, p. 228), or as may be seen on the tomb known as 'la Conocchia,' near Santa Maria Capua Vetere (Fig. 199, p. 228). These arcades, however, have not the elegant form of the Armenian ones.

[1] Rivoira, op. cit. (Heinemann), vol. ii, p. 224.

[2] Brosset, *Coll. d'Hist. arm.*, vol. ii; Samouel d'Ani, *Tables chronologiques*, pp, 436, 437.

[3] *Mémoires de l'Académie impériale des Sciences de Saint-Pétersbourg*, 1863, vol. vi, n. 6, pp. 77-81; Brosset, *Monastères arméniens d'Haghbat et de Sanahin.*

[4] Vatican Library.

And outside Armenia there was no attempt to apply them to domes in a refined form with slender shafts and bases before the first quarter of the XI century, the first church to set the fashion being that of the Virgin at Salonica (1028). Its example was followed in many other instances, for example St. Theodore at Athens (1049). We are told, indeed, of earlier cases, but only on the strength of assumptions. I may cite, among others, that of the Holy Apostles at Salonica, assigned to about 1012;[1] whereas comparison with analogous buildings shows that it cannot be dated before the second half of the XI century[2] (Fig. 200, p. 229).

In Italy, in the days when the tall drums of the Roman style with their decorative architectural treatment came back into fashion, the minds of the craftsmen turned either towards mere imitation, as in the case of the tomb of Bohemond at Canosa (1111-1118),[3] where the cupola, encircled by columns, recalls that of the sepulchral edifice of 'la Conocchia' mentioned above; or to embellishments of the drum such as those in the Vatican MS. referred to; or, thirdly, to original designs, such as the polygonal Lombardic cupola, the prototype of which appears to be found in San Michele at Pavia, rebuilt after 1112,[4] which was followed in the cathedral of Piacenza (1122-1233) (Fig. 201, p. 230) and other churches.

(3) In the interior we find piers with compound bases, and pointed arches. The fact has been made the foundation for the most fanciful theories as to the origins of the Pointed style. Now the accumulation of piers and columns as the starting-points for arches and framing arches with a decorative purpose, does not imply any progress towards the creation of a new architectural style with ribbed vaulting, in which every member has its essential place in the plan. Moreover, piers, and, what is more, compound piers (i.e. piers composed of pilasters and columns), had been in use in the West from Roman times onwards; while the pointed arch had been systematically employed by the Moslems as far back as the IX century.

The true origin of the Pointed style was explained in my former work,[5] and the explanation is repeated in the account of the mosque of Hakim at

[1] Bayet, *L'Art byzantin*, p. 140.

[2] Rivoira, op. cit. (Heinemann), vol. i, pp. 155, 156.

[3] Avena, *Monumenti dell'Italia Meridionale*, p. 95.

[4] Rivoira, op. cit. (Loescher), vol. ii, pp. 199-201; (Hoepli), pp. 302-306; (Heinemann), vol. i, pp. 244-247.

[5] Ibid., *Le origini dell'Architettura lombarda. Lombardic Architecture.*

FIG. 192.—Khoshavank. Church of Shoghagath (X cent.).

FIG. 193.—Khoshavank. Chapels near the convent.

FIG. 194.—Sanahin. Churches.

FIG. 195.—Ani. Cathedral. North side and west front (977-1010).

Cairo in the present volume. Armenia had no share in starting or facilitating its career.

I may note that compound piers had been employed in Armenia, earlier than the primatial church of Ani, in the cathedral of Arghina near that city, between 974 and 977:[1] the work, as we saw, of the architect Tiridates (Fig. 202, p. 230).

In taking leave of the cathedral of Ani I would draw attention to the fact that the principal characteristic of the churches founded under the dynasty of the Bagratids was architectural ornament, not figure ornament; so much so that the only figures decorating the cathedral in question are two flying eagles (on the west front), recalling the eagle of the Arsacids, from whom those rulers were descended. Gagik, on the contrary, allowed his architect to run riot with a whole host of living creatures represented on the singular church of Aghthamar. It is possible that this artistic discrepancy may be an echo of the hostility between the Bagratids and the Arzruni in the days of Sembat I (890-914) and Gagik (904-936), combined with the desire to avoid imitation of a building for which Gagik had not only contributed the funds but also the ideas, for we are told that his knowledge embraced all subjects, and that he had drawn with his own hand the plans for the new city of Aghthamar as well as for the royal palace.[2]

There is one other characteristic to which I would call attention: the circular form of the high drums and their steep conical roofs, as if they were so many huts of the Latin type (capanna) set on the square central space of the church.

The Chapel of St. Gregory at Ani is said to have been built by the Palavid, Vahram († 1047). The name of the Armenian hero may be read in the inscription over the door. Another inscription in the north wall proves that the church was in existence in 1040.[3] Its date will be the end of the X century or the beginning of the next. The theory of Khanikof,[4] that this was the 'marvellous' church mentioned by Asoghik (X century) and Samuel

[1] Brosset, *Coll. d'Hist. arm.*, vol. ii; Samouel d'Ani, *Tables chronologiques*, pp. 438-440.

[2] Ibid., vol. i; Th. Ardzrouni, *Histoire des Ardzrouni*, pp. 236-239.

[3] Lynch, op. cit., vol. i, pp. 381, 382.

[4] *Revue archéologique*, 1858, pp. 401-420; *Voyage à Ani*.

of Ani (XII century),[1] has been contradicted by the recent discovery of the remains of that building.

In plan the chapel is a somewhat elongated dodecagon. The two axes measure respectively 9.50 and 9.20 m. (30½ by 29¼ ft.). The exterior (Fig. 203, p. 231) is relieved by six of the usual splayed niches. Inside, there are exedras all round the walls, above which rises the circular base of the dome, arcaded on the outside.

It is easy to see that, with the exception of the roof, the plan and essential structure are derived from the tombs and nymphaea of Imperial Rome.

The Chapel of the Redeemer at Ani was built by the Prince Aplkharip, on his return from Constantinople in 1034.[2]

The ground floor is polygonal, the upper part circular. Both parts are encircled on their outer face by blank arcading (Fig. 204, p. 232).

This is another instance of a design derived generally from Pagan Roman sepulchral rotundas.

If we sum up now all that we have said about the early Armenian churches, the following appear to be the results :—

(1) The plan, while related to its Roman and Romano-Byzantine sources, differs from them in the absence of the narthex. This is true, of course, for the ordinary quadrangular plan, for in a few very rare cases the Armenians erected circular annular churches. A celebrated one was built by the patriarch Narses III, and was known as the Zuardnoz, or church of the Angels, near Etschmiadzin. He dedicated it to the Illuminator, but as early as the year 1000 it was a mere ruin.[3]

Recent excavations have laid bare its plan, which was of the Romano-Ravennate type: Roman in its annular form and in its porches; Ravennate by virtue of the exedras with open arcades, which surround the central square space and recall the archetype of that arrangement in San Vitale at Ravenna. This plan, which is here reproduced after Palakian[4] (Fig. 205, p. 233),

[1] Bibliotheca Teubneriana, *Des Stephanos von Taron armenische Geschichte*, pp. 214, 215 Brosset, *Coll. d'Hist. arm.*, vol. ii; Samouel d'Ani, *Tables chronologiques*, pp. 441-443.

[2] Lynch, op. cit., vol. i, p. 383.

[3] Bibliotheca Teubneriana, *Des Stephanos von Taron armenische Geschichte*, pp. 214, 215.

[4] Palakian, *Description of the Ruins of Ani* [in Armenian], p. 47.

FIG. 196.—Ani. Cathedral. South side (977-1010).

FIG. 197.—Pisa. Cathedral (XI, XII, and XIII cents.).

FIG. 198.—Rome. Fragment of sculpture of the Imperial age. (From a drawing in Vatican MS. 3439.)

FIG. 199.—Santa Maria Capua Vetere. Tomb called 'la Conocchia' (II cent.).

FIG. 200.—Salonica. Church of the Apostles (XI cent.).

FIG. 201.—Piacenza. Cathedral (XII and XIII cents.).

FIG. 202.—Arghina. Remains of the Cathedral (974-977).

FIG. 203.—Ani. Chapel of St. Gregory (X or XI cent.).

FIG. 204.—Ani. Chapel of the Redeemer (1034).

reminds one of that of Sant' Angelo at Perugia, which I take from Viviani[1] (Fig. 206, p. 234), a church supposed to date from the V century,[2] but which may very well belong to the first part of the VI.[3]

The round church of Etschmiadzin was afterwards copied by Gagik I (989-1019) when he erected at Ani his church of St. Gregory or of the Angels, finished in 998 or 1000, which has likewise gone to ruin.[4] The excavation of this structure (Fig. 207, p. 238) has revealed a system of strengthening applied to the central part, apparently due, as was suggested to me by Father Gabriel Nahapetian, to the excessive weight of the dome, in which the usual void had not been left between the extrados of the cupola and the pointed roof above it.

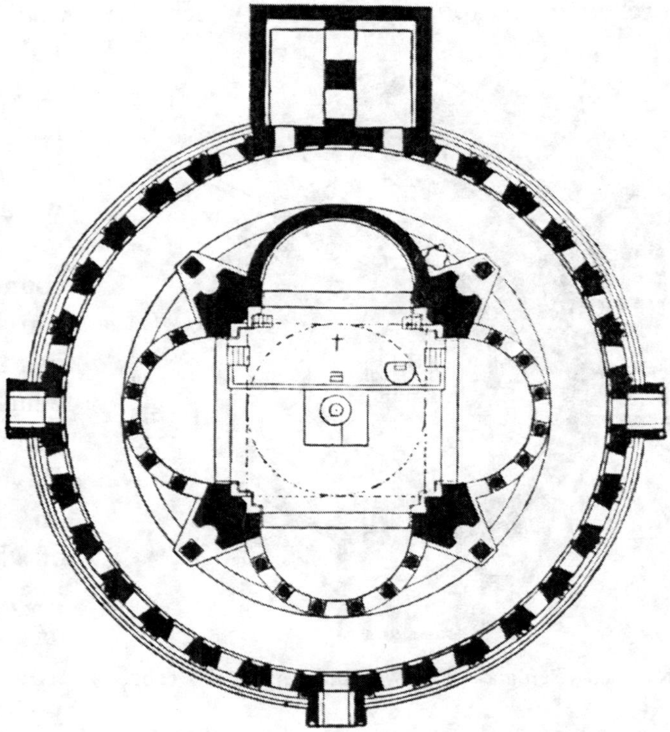

FIG. 205.—Etschmiadzin. Plan of the ancient Church of the Illuminator or the Angels (VII cent.).

The fate of these two rotundas proves that the ordinary compact quadrangular type of Armenian church was better suited to resist earth shocks than the circular annular form. For it is nature even more than time which has proved the worst enemy of the Armenian churches. They suffered little from the pick-axe of the destroyer. I cannot mention, down to the last century, a single church so treated, except the one built by Narses III over

[1] VIVIANI, *Tempio di Sant' Angelo in Perugia*, pp. 5-9.

[2] Ibid.

[3] RIVOIRA, op. cit. (Loescher), vol. ii, pp. 43-45; (Hoepli), pp. 10-12; (Heinemann), vol. i, p. 12.

[4] BROSSET, *Coll. d'Hist. arm.*, vol. ii; SAMOUEL D'ANI, *Tables chronologiques*, pp. 441-443. ALISHAN, *Shirac*, pp. 51, 52.

St. Gregory's grave at Chorvirap, near Erivan, which was ruined by the Moslems.[1]

(2) The masonry follows the Roman tradition, including the bonding stones at the angles. From the same source came the occasional use of pottery jars (amphorae) in the haunches of vaults of large span. The roofs, on the other hand, instead of being covered with tiles or sheets of metal, are constructed of dressed stones. The entire absence of wood enabled many churches to escape the fires to which they would otherwise have inevitably fallen victims in the endless wars and invasions which Armenia had to undergo. To judge by the methods still in use, the stones were dressed with the axe.

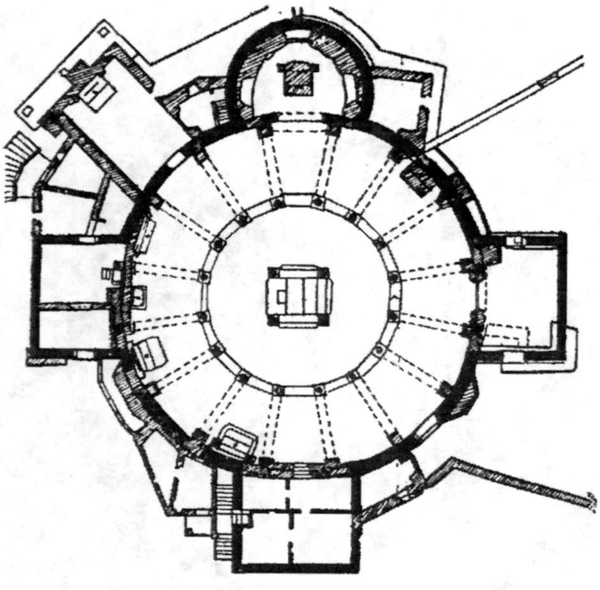

FIG. 206.—Perugia. Plan of Sant' Angelo (VI cent.).

(3) The dome was usually connected with the square central block by means of spherical pendentives. The pendentive which merges in the dome is a Roman invention, perfected at Ravenna, where it was applied on a large scale in the baptistery of Neon (449 or 458-477) (Fig. 208, p. 235); but the form which has a different spherical surface from that of the dome was also a Roman invention, but developed by the Byzantines.[2] It is to this latter species, the earliest example of which (unnoticed by Durm[3]) is to be found in the 'Domus Augustana' on the Palatine (about 85) (Figs. 209, 210, pp. 236, 237), that the triangular Armenian pendentives belong. The hood-shaped pendentive is not used, at least for the domes of churches, with the exception of that at Usunlar. It does appear in secular buildings, but at a late date. Yet Armenia was in touch with, if not under the sway of, Persia, the mythical home of the hood pendentive. The reason

[1] BROSSET, *Deux hist. arm.*; KIRACOS, *Histoire d'Arménie*, p. 31.

[2] RIVOIRA, op. cit. (Hoepli), pp. 29-36; (Heinemann), vol. i, pp. 29-35.

[3] DURM, *Die Baustile. Die Baukunst der Römer*, pp. 285-288.

for its absence is to be looked for in the fact that it only obtained a footing, not merely in Persia, but also in Mesopotamia, Cappadocia, and Syria, at a time when the spherical pendentive had been already adopted by the Armenian builders.

(4) It was in Armenia that domes with high drums were first used in churches, and decorated with blank arcades in which the arches spring from slender shafts. In the earlier examples the interior was polygonal. This bold upward expansion was made possible by the moderate span and compactness of the churches.

(5) Domes with conical roofs entirely constructed of masonry are an Armenian invention. Another Armenian idea was the open lantern or spirelet to hold the bells. It may have been suggested by the pavilions at the tops of minarets, a very early example of which was once to be seen on the minaret of Abd al-Rahman III at Cordova[1] (945-46). It reminds one of the characteristic open lanterns of wood which crowned the two circular cupolas of the famous abbey church of Saint-Riquier (Centula) (793-798), and the tower of the adjoining church of St. Mary[2] (Fig. 211, p. 239).

FIG. 208.—Ravenna. Baptistery of Neon. Vertical section (449 or 458-477).

(6) The Armenian use of continuous blank arcading of elegant form had an influence not only in the East, but also in the West, and in Italy itself, which had given birth to this form of decoration.

[1] EDRISI, *Géographie*, vol. ii, pp. 62, 63.

[2] MABILLON, *Acta Sanctorum Ordinis S. Benedicti*, vol. v, p. 106. RIVOIRA, op. cit. (Loescher), vol. ii, pp. 91-93; (Hoepli), pp. 395-397; (Heinemann), vol. ii, pp. 60, 61.

(7) The round arch continued to be used, even by the side of the pointed form.

The lobed arch and the horse-shoe arch make their appearance only at a late date. An early dated instance of the former is to be found in the narthex (1250-51) of the church of Johannavank. An old example of the latter may be seen in the church of the Trinity at Ticor, near Ani (Fig. 212, p. 238), ascribed by Fergusson[1] to the VII century, though Texier[2] says that it was finished in 1242.

It is not very easy to find one's bearings in coming to a decision about the date of this church. And this doubt about the date prevents us from using it as a touchstone in other cases. The inscription on the lintel of the west door suggests that it was erected by the order of Sahak (Isaac) Kamsarakan, one of the generals of Vahan Mamikonean, who is mentioned in the year 484.[3] On the other hand, the mutilated and transferred inscription in the tympanum of the same door attributes its construction to the patriarch John Mandacuni (480-487).[4] This early date would be confirmed by the existence of an eastern transept, and also by the clumsy internal cupola, a sort of cone ending in a spherical cap, the square passing into the circle by a gradual transition. The drum is low. The date would also be consistent with the absence of decorative blank arcading, and of the splayed niches. Armenian churches later than the V century had cupolas and pendentives of another type, were not provided with a transept, and after the IX century were decoratively treated in the aforesaid way.

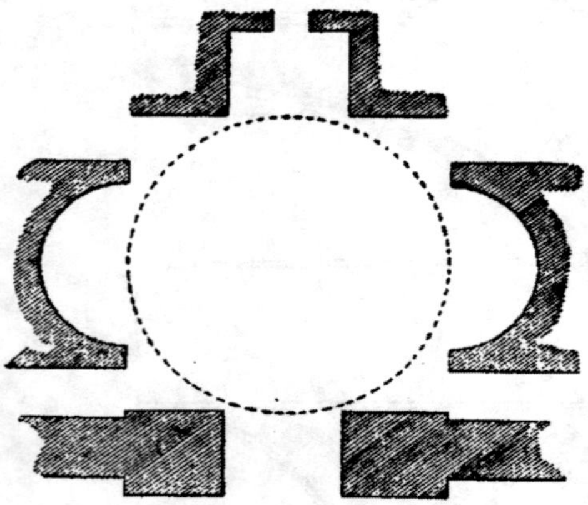

FIG. 209.—Rome. 'Domus Augustana.' Plan of the central room (about 85).

The external masonry, however, of the lower part of the front is clearly of a different date from that of the upper; and the body of the church, which has been strengthened with oak tie beams, in its turn seems to be

[1] *A History of Architecture*, vol. ii, pp. 465, 466.

[2] *Description de l'Arménie, la Perse et la Mésopotamie*, vol. i, p. 120.

[3] TCHAMTCHEAN, op. cit., vol. ii, p. 201.

[4] ALISHAN, *Shirac*, p. 132.

FIG. 210.—Rome. 'Domus Augustana.' Pendentive of the dome in the central room (about 85).

FIG. 207.—Ani. Remains of the Church of St. Gregory or the Angels (finished in 998 or 1000).

FIG. 212.—Ticor. Church of the Trinity.

of a different date from the transept. We thus, apparently, have to deal with more than one period of construction; and this would explain the appearance of windows in pairs in the upper part of the structure, and of a quatrefoil opening in the western gable.

FIG. 211.—Saint Riquier (Centula). View of the ancient churches of the Saviour and St. Richarius, SS. Mary and the Apostles, and St. Benedict (VIII cent.).

(8) The decorative splayed niches, employed by the Romans in construction as well as in decoration, make one wonder why the Armenian architects never found out their use as pendentives or supports for the dome in their earlier churches. And all the more as a sporadic instance of the hood-shaped pendentive was already to be seen at Usunlar. And besides, long before, Julianus Argentarius had, in order to use it like a squinch, lifted the Roman angle niche from the level of the ground floor to that of the dome, and thus produced the niche pendentive. And at a still earlier time the Campanians had, with a similar object, raised aloft the arched head of the angle niche, so that it became the hood-shaped pendentive. This, however, need cause us no surprise, for the vital discoveries of vaulted architecture were essentially the legacy of the West.

PART II

THE leading idea of the second part of this book may be stated as follows. In 711 the forces under the command of Tarik and Julian, aided by treachery, destroyed at a single blow, on the banks of Lake Janda, between Medina Sidonia and Vejer de la Frontera, the army of Roderic and the Visigothic monarchy. After losing his throne, the last King of the Visigoths is believed to have lost his life as well in the battle fought by Musa and Tarik near Segoyuela, in the province of Salamanca (713).[1] In recording the epitaph which marked his grave, his namesake Roderic, the Archbishop of Toledo[2] (1276-1280), invokes on the head of Julian, the contriver of his ruin and of the enslavement of the Iberian peninsula, one of the most vehement imprecations that in the course of my wide reading I have ever met with.

The conquered people was allowed the free exercise of its religion, though the Church was reduced to subjection. And in places where there had been no resistance it retained the use of the sacred buildings which the conquerors left standing, with the exception of those which were turned into mosques. The condition, however, was imposed that no new churches were to be built, and that the existing ones were not to be enlarged. In every one of these buildings the round arch only was to be seen.

But we must not suppose that the Moslems brought with them the horse-shoe arch, which at that time had hardly attained to systematic use, and had appeared only in a tentative form and restricted to the larger arches in

[1] ALTAMIRA Y CREVEA, *Historia de España y de la civilización española*, vol. i, pp. 199, 200. LAMPÉREZ Y ROMEA, *Historia de la Arquitectura christiana española en la Edad media*, vol. i, p. 106. *The Cambridge Medieval History*, vol. ii, pp. 185, 186; ALTAMIRA Y CREVEA, *Spain under the Visigoths*.

[2] *Chronicon rerum gestarum in Hispaniis;* RODERICUS, *De regno regis Roderici*, lib. iii, cap. xix.

the congregational mosque of Damascus (706-714). Nor do we know precisely, for the monuments fail us, when it was introduced into the conquered peninsula. It seems, however, that there was no formal display of the new system of arching in Spain before the erection of the great mosque of Abd al-Rahman I (756-788) and Hisham I (788-796) at Cordova. And everything tends to prove that, as formerly at Damascus the Ummayyad Walid I (705-715) had raised the horse shoe arch to the rank of a constructive system, so now at Cordova another Ummayyad was the first to apply the system brought into being under the auspices of one of his family. It is certain, too, that this systematic use did not make its appearance in the kingdom of Asturias, the mountain fastness of the Visigoths, before the exodus of the Mozarabic monks from Cordova during the fury of the cruel persecution of the Christians there, begun by Abd al-Rahman II (822-852) and continued by Mohammed I (852-886).

Hence, the view of not a few writers, including some of eminence, who assert that the systematic use of the horse-shoe arch was a Hispano-Visigothic invention, has no support in actual facts. It is not worth while to dwell upon the strange theory that the churches built by the Visigoths in Spain followed the Byzantine model because those barbarians coming from the banks of the Danube had made acquaintance with the methods of Eastern architecture.[1]

* * *

The theory that in Spain the horse-shoe arch was systematically used in construction from the VI and VII centuries, through a Roman tradition as old as the II century, is based on a passage in Isidore of Seville (599-636), on late Roman exedras and niches with arches larger than the semicircle, and on erroneous dating of buildings.

The words of Isidore are these: '*Arcus* dicti, quod sint *arcta* conclusione curvati.'[2] This has been rendered: 'They are called arches because the ends are markedly curved inwards;'[3] and this erroneous version has been generally accepted without question. The real meaning is approximately

[1] CLOQUET, *Revue de l'Art chrétien*, vol. iii, p. 98.

[2] MIGNE, *Patrologia latina*, vol. lxxxii; ISIDORUS, Hispalensis episc., *Etymologiae*, XV, viii.

[3] FERREIRO, *Historia de la Santa A. M. Iglesia de Santiago de Compostela*, vol. iii, p. 31.

this: 'Arches were so called because their curve closes up at the keystone.' I leave it to Latin scholars who know something of architecture, and to architects who know Latin, to say which is right.

For the exedras and niches some rare instances are cited,[1] which only prove that the form was used sporadically in the Iberian peninsula. This is precisely what took place in Italy in the imperial epoch, as we noticed in our account of the Ummayyad mosque at Damascus.

Let us now turn to the monuments.

To the Visigothic age (466-711)[2]—by which I mean the period beginning with Euric (466-484) who conquered the whole of Spain except the small district where the Suevi (409-584) had established themselves[3]—is ascribed the double western or Seville gate of Cordova, in existence in 711, where the twin arches, now built up, are of the horse-shoe form (Figs. 213 [p. 243], 214).[4] But the three main points alleged in support of a date not later than the VII century—viz. the prolongation of the curve of the intrados of the arches by a third of the radius beyond the semicircle; the divergence between the curve of the extrados and that of the intrados, the former continuing in an outward direction at the impost; and, thirdly, the stone voussoirs converging towards the centre of the radius—are nullified by the fact that, for instance, the arches of the church of San Juan at Baños de Cerrato, which certainly does not belong to Visigothic times, show the same internal curve, and radiate in the same manner as those at Seville; while the arch of the door into the church, and also the arch of the apse, exhibit a similar divergent curve in the extrados.[5]

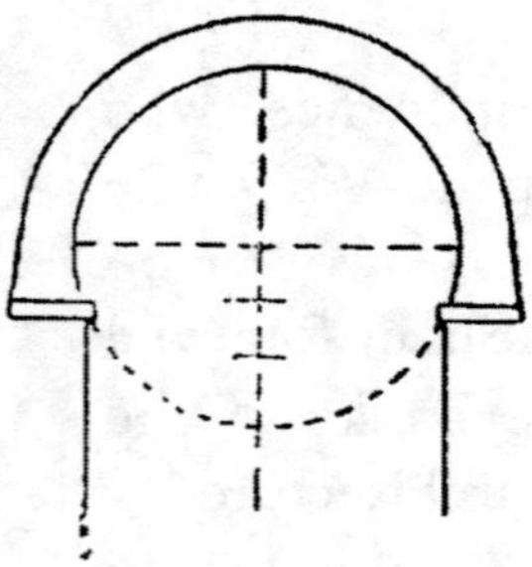

FIG. 214. — Cordova. An arch of the double Western or Seville Gate.

There is another point still to be reckoned with, viz. that the arches of this western gate of Cordova betray to an experienced eye which examines

[1] *Cultura española*, 1906, pp. 735-811; GÓMEZ-MORENO, *Excursión á través del arco de herradura.*

[2] The Spanish chronology of the Suevic and Visigothic kings, as well as of the kings of Asturias, León, Castile, Navarre, and Aragon, is taken from LAFUENTE, *Historia general de España*, vols. ii and iii.

[3] LAFUENTE, *Historia general de España*, vol. ii, pp. 16, 17.

[4] *Cultura española*, 1906, pp. 785-811; GÓMEZ-MORENO, *Excursión*, &c.

[5] Ibid.

Fig. 213.—Cordova. The double Western or Seville Gate.

Fig. 215.—Baños de Cerrato. Church of San Juan Bautista from the south-west (XII cent.).

Fig. 216.—Baños de Cerrato. San Juan Bautista from the south-east (XII cent.).

Fig. 218.—Baños de Cerrato. San Juan Bautista. Nave (XII cent.).

them, as I have done, on the spot, signs of alteration: an event which must have taken place in Moslem times, and after Abd al-Rahman I's architect had introduced in the great mosque of Cordova just this form of arch prolonged for a third of the radius beyond the semicircle.

We have historical notices of the foundation, or rebuilding, or restoration of churches of the Visigothic period, and a few descriptions; but the contemporary chroniclers say nothing about the form of their arches, though this would have been such a departure from the traditional Roman form. Among the churches mentioned[1] are those of St. Martin at Orense, St. Marcian at Évora, St. Eulalia, the Baptistery, and the great church (the Holy Jerusalem) at Mérida, St. Felix at Cordova, St. Romanus at Hornija (Zamora), SS. Peter and Paul and St. Leocadia at Toledo. To these may be added the cathedrals of Tarragona and Valencia, and other churches in the latter city and diocese.[2] Moreover, we know that King Wamba carried out an important restoration of the buildings at Toledo,[3] and among them we may be sure were some churches.

Other churches assigned to the Visigothic age are: San Juan Bautista at Baños de Cerrato (Palencia), the basilica of Segóbriga or Cabeza de Griego (Cuenca), the church of Santa Comba (Columba) or San Torcuato (Torquatus) at Bande (Orense), San Pedro at Nave (Zamora); the baptistery of San Miguel at Tarrasa (Barcelona), the crypt of San Antolin at Palencia, the basilica of Elche, the chapel of Burguillos (Badajoz), the chapel of the Sanctuary of San Miguel in Excelsis near Huarte-Aráquil, the chapel of Arnal (Portugal), the hermitage of SS. Justus and Pastor at Medina Sidonia (Cadiz), the church of Camarzana de Tera (Zamora), the basilica of Guarrazar (Toledo), and the cathedral of Sétabis (Játiva, Valencia).[4]

Of these the only ones which Lampérez y Romea regards as genuine, until the contrary be proved, are: the churches of Baños de Cerrato, Cabeza de Griego, and Santa Comba or San Torcuato at Bande; the baptistery at Tarrasa; the crypt of the cathedral of Palencia; and the basilica of Elche. He also

[1] Lampérez y Romea, op. cit., vol. i, pp. 119, 120.

[2] Puig y Cadafalch, De Falguera, Goday y Casals, *L'Arquitectura romanica a Catalunya*, vol. i, pp. 302, 309, 310.

[3] Flórez, *España sagrada*, vol. v, pp. 165-167. *Chronicon rerum gestarum in Hispaniis*; Rodericus, *De reparatione urbis Toletanae*, III. xi. Migne, *Patr. lat.*, vol. xcvi, col. 1260; Isidorus Pacensis, *Epitome imperatorum*.

[4] Lampérez y Romea, op. cit., vol. i, pp. 143, 144.

ascribes, with more or less foundation, to the Visigothic age: San Pedro at Nave, the chapel of San Miguel in Excelsis, and the church of Camarzana de Tera.

The remaining cases at Burguillos, Arnal, Medina Sidonia, Guarrazar, Sétabis, though they appear to be authentic, are of small importance, both intrinsically, and because very little of them is left.[1] The same writer raises the question whether the Cristo de la Luz at Toledo may not be in part a Visigothic church.[2]

Lampérez y Romea's list of six genuine Visigothic churches may be increased by the addition of San Pedro and Santa Maria at Tarrasa, the sanctuary of which is believed to belong to that period.[3]

Madrazo[4] was the first to draw up a list of this kind, as well as others containing a far larger number of names, though not accepted by some, and even recent, Spanish authorities.[5] He also reproduced the attribution which Ambrogio de Morales[6] had made, as long ago as the XVI century, in the case of San Juan Bautista at Baños and of other churches. However, now that we have come to sifting the list, we will begin with this church. Even if the list almost entirely disappears in the process, this will in no way diminish the interest attaching to the monuments which it included, but will rather stimulate archaeologists to make a fresh start, and enter upon new investigations. In doing so, they must remember that there can be no doubt that in the Visigothic buildings of Spain the traditional Roman round arch was systematically used, and not the horse-shoe arch; and that these buildings had no original character, but rather were, as Lafuente says,[7] a corruption of the Roman style. Besides, Spain is so rich in monuments that there is no need to confer upon any of them an antiquity which they do not possess, or to make her the inventor of a system of construction which really was imported from the East.

THE CHURCH OF SAN JUAN BAUTISTA AT BAÑOS DE CERRATO is the best

[1] LAMPÉREZ Y ROMEA, op. cit., vol. i, p. 144.

[2] Ibid., vol. i, pp. 177-179.

[3] PUIG Y CADAFALCH, op. cit., vol. i, pp. 311-340.

[4] *España, sus monumentos y artes, su naturaleza é historia;* MADRAZO, *Valladolid, Palencia y Zamora*, pp. 331-335.

[5] SELGAS, *Monumentos Ovetenses del siglo IX*, p. 143.

[6] *La Coronica general de España*, lib. xii, cap. 37.

[7] LAFUENTE, op. cit., vol. ii, p. 115.

preserved of the buildings ascribed to the Visigothic period, and also, apparently, the one which has real evidence to support its claim.

Investigations made in the course of the recent restoration, and descriptions of the building which have been preserved, make it possible to settle with fair probability, and with the exception of the external colonnades, what the original plan was like.[1] It was a small basilica, with the usual orientation, possessing a transept, and a porch at the west end. At the east end was a principal apse corresponding to the nave, and two subordinate apses opening from the arms of the transept. The apse on the left served as a baptistery. The font, hewn out of a single block of stone with a diameter of 1.10 m. (3 ft. 7 in.), remains in the church to-day. As to the colonnades outside, we only know that there was once a columned porch.[2]

The original structure has lost the lateral apses, the ends of the transept, and the porch with its columns. Hence the present building consists merely of a nave and aisles, entered through a porch, and terminated by three apses, the lateral ones being formed in the two spaces originally existing between the principal and the secondary apses (Figs. 215, 216, 217, pp. 243, 244, 253).

The porch is a rectangular chamber of 4.25 by 2.80 m. (14 by 9 ft.) with a wooden roof. The raising of the front wall to form a bell-cote is an addition. The inner doorway has undergone alteration. The outer is ornamented on the imposts and circumference with conventional flowers and beads.

The nave, which is 10.80 m. (about 35 ft.) long by 4.67 m. (about 15 ft.) broad between the columns, is divided from the aisles by four arches on either side, supported by eight ancient marble columns of varying size, and by two half wall-piers (Figs. 218, 219, pp. 244, 254). The stone bases of the columns are of different forms and heights, being in some cases of the Attic type, in others consisting only of a torus above a socle.

The capitals are either imitations of the Corinthian, or else Corinthianesque. The latter sometimes have, besides the acanthus leaves, conventional lilies, palm leaves, and cauliculi with ribbed stalks. Among the Corinthian capitals are one or two of good workmanship, especially the one here illustrated with its column and base (Fig. 220, p. 253). The others are more or less of mediocre design and execution.

The capitals are surmounted by plain moulded abaci, of varying height

[1] Lampérez y Romea, op. cit., vol. i, pp. 145-149.

[2] *España, sus monumentos y artes*, &c.; Quadrado, *Valladolid, Palencia y Zamora*, pp. 331-335.

in order to fit the columns. Two, however, which consist of a band and a flat cyma, are ornamented with carving. All are of an easily worked stone. The two half wall-piers are decorated with a band of carving at the impost of the arch.

Both nave and aisles have wooden roofs. The latter formerly had flat ceilings. The holes for the beams can be seen above the columns. The sanctuary has a horse-shoe barrel vault, round the base of which runs a band of conventional foliage and beads, a motive which appears in almost every part of the building—sanctuary, nave, and porch. The two lateral apses, which have pointed frontal arches, are covered by ribbed cross-vaulting of XV-century date, when the free spaces between the apses were closed on the outside and converted into chapels.[1] On the exterior of the walls of these two modern apses traces remain of the horse-shoe barrel vaults of the original lateral apses, and also of the band of carved interlacing which ran below the impost of their vaults.

The walls of the church, where original, are seen to be formed of irregular courses of stone blocks of various size, roughly dressed, with a sparing use of mortar. The exterior face of the walls was unbroken: the two buttresses now to be seen at the east end were added on the construction of the two cross-vaults. The original windows are splayed on the inside, have interlaced ornament, and were filled with lattices (transennae) of geometrical patterns, fragments of which survive. The horse-shoe arch is used throughout.

The erection of the church is ascribed to King Receswinth (649-672) on account of the inscription on a votive stone inserted above the sanctuary arch. A cast of this inscription placed in the porch is here reproduced (Fig. 221, p. 253). The dedication seems to have taken place on January 3rd, 661.

Tradition ascribes the foundation to the fulfilment of a vow or thank-offering by the king for having been cured of the stone from which he suffered, by drinking the water of a spring which rises not many yards from the church.[2] It is well to notice, however, that any therapeutic quality is negatived by chemical analysis;[3] and that the name Baños, apparently, was not given to the place on account of the medicinal properties of the water,

[1] Lampérez y Romea, op. cit., vol. i, p. 146.

[2] *España, sus monumentos y artes*, &c.; Quadrado, *Valladolid, Palencia y Zamora*, p. 331.

[3] *Cultura española*, 1906, pp. 785-811; Gómez-Moreno, *Excursión*, &c.

but because of the existence of a Roman bath there.[1] This bath may have provided the columns used in the nave of the church, as well as the squared stone of which the walls are built.

The date of the inscription has been put as low as the XII century.[2] I leave it to epigraphists to decide whether this be so, and only remark that, even if the stone were as old as the reign of Receswinth, the existing building is not the one which he erected.

As a matter of fact, some of the capitals, not of alien origin, but made expressly for the church, not only display the same manner as the capitals also made expressly for the church of San Miguel at Escalada (913-14) and its porch (1050), but belong to a somewhat more advanced stage of art than those in that porch, and must be dated later than the first half of the XI century. On the other hand, the remaining capitals, imitating the Corinthian, are markedly different from those at Escalada both in design and execution, and the date which suits them will be the first half of the XII century.

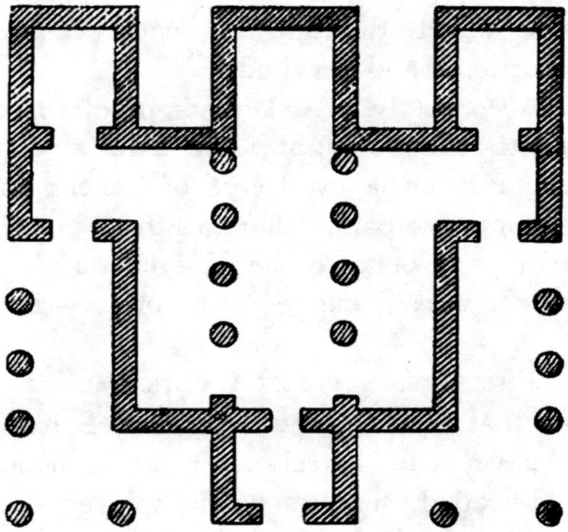

FIG. 222.—Baños de Cerrato. Plan of the original Church of San Juan Bautista (XII cent.).

The plan, again, as set out by the architect Alvarez who restored the building (Fig. 222), plainly belongs to a time later than the epoch of about 1000. The lateral apses projecting from the sides of the arms of the transept are a feature which first appears in the Lombardo-Norman basilica at the beginning of the XI century.[3] The same may be said of the carved bands of geometrically formed flowers and beads derived from classical ornament. No Western artist of the Early Middle Ages could have produced such refined carving as that on the impost bands below the sanctuary vault: not

[1] LAMPÉREZ Y ROMEA, op. cit., vol. i, p. 145.

[2] CABROL, *Dictionnaire d'Archéologie chrétienne*, &c., vol. ii, 1, col. 191-198; LECLERCQ, *Baños.*

[3] RIVOIRA, op. cit. (Loescher), vol. ii, p. 106; (Hoepli), pp. 359, 407; (Heinemann), vol. ii, pp. 34, 69.

even the imported carver who executed the VII-century sarcophagus of St. Theodechildis in the crypt of the church of Saint Paul at Jouarre (Fig. 223, p. 255).[1]

Not to speak of the great, or rather absolute improbability that a building mainly roofed with wood, situated in a bare plain, in a district fearfully ravaged by both Moslems and Christians—the latter had made it a desert by order of Alfonso I (739-756) for defensive reasons—and near to Dueñas and Palencia (both destroyed, the former in the IX century by order of Alfonso III (866-909); the latter in the XI century by decree of Sancho the Great, King of Navarre (970-1035), and only re-established at a later period), can have passed intact through so many centuries of wars, raids, conflagrations, destructions, and servitude.[2]

Accordingly, in default of proof to the contrary, the church of San Juan Bautista must be put at a date later than the resurrection of the neighbouring town of Palencia by decree of Sancho the Great, and at the same time as the erection of the parish churches there in the XI and following century;[3] in other words, it belongs to the XII century. The XII or even the XIII century had been already suggested by other writers on grounds of artistic style.[4]

The Crypt of the Cathedral of Palencia.—It has lately been made clear that the ancient crypt of San Antolin (Antoninus), consisting of a low nave with barrel vault strengthened by transverse arches, and small round-headed windows boldly splayed on the inside, was enlarged by a second structure of which, when I visited it, there was to be seen a rectangular chamber with lateral recesses, roofed with stone slabs laid flat upon horse-shoe arches, and having at the east end a triplet of similar arches supported by two marble columns of alien origin. These columns rest on bases composed of a thick roll, a shallow scotia, and a band; and carry Corinthianesque capitals of very rude and careless workmanship, surmounted by abaci ornamented with conventional flowers.

About the dates of these two structures very different views have been

[1] Rivoira, op. cit. (Loescher), vol. ii, p. 84; (Hoepli), p. 385; (Heinemann), vol. ii, pp. 51, 52. *The Burlington Magazine*, vol. xxi (1912); Rivoira, *Antiquities of St. Andrews*, p. 25.

[2] Dozy, *Histoire des Musulmans d'Espagne*, vol. iii, pp. 24-26. Lafuente, op. cit., vol. ii, p. 153. *España, sus monumentos y artes*, &c.; Quadrado, *Asturias y León*, p. 133.

[3] *España, sus monumentos y artes*, &c.; Quadrado, *Valladolid, Palencia y Zamora*, p. 359.

[4] Michel, *Histoire de l'Art*, vol. i, 2, p. 560; Enlart, *L'architecture Romane.*

expressed. It has been suggested, for instance, that the oldest part—that with the barrel vault—is Roman work going back to the time before the destruction of Palencia (456-57) by King Theodoric (453-466); and that an addition was made to this by order by King Wamba (672-680). Others again, on more reliable grounds, hold that the first building is Visigothic, and that the annexe was added in the XI century.[1]

Palencia, after its second destruction by the Moslems and the final blow which it received from Alfonso I (739-756) about the middle of the VIII century,[2] remained for centuries almost forgotten. The bishopric came to an end, and the diocese was divided in the reign of Alfonso V (999-1027) between the neighbouring bishops of Burgos and León.[3] After Baroaldus became bishop in 693, the see of Palencia remained vacant till 1035, and the existence of an Abundantius[4] Bishop of Palencia in 811 is a matter of controversy.[5] About the year 1030, however, its restoration was decreed by Sancho the Great, King of Navarre, at the advice of Ponce, Bishop of Oviedo (about 1028-1035), and with the aid of the King of León, Bermudo III (1027-1037). The rebuilding of the cathedral seems to have been the first thing taken in hand, for by 1035 Sancho had established a bishop there in the person of Bernard I (1035-1040).[6] A privilege of King Ferdinand I of Castile and León (1037-1065) tells us that the cathedral was of stone—'lapidum honestissima domus'—and that the crypt was rebuilt: 'Postquam est reedificata cripta . . .'[7] Just at the same time tradition connects the memory of King Sancho and the new cathedral with the existence, among the ruins of Palencia, of an old church of rude construction.[8] For me the story is the complement of the historical account, and the two together throw an interesting light on the building which we are considering. The rude structure of the legend will be the first part of the crypt. Who built it I cannot say. The idea that it may have been constructed by King Wamba as a receptacle for the relics of St. Antoninus, which tradition says

[1] LAMPÉREZ Y ROMEA, op. cit., vol. i, pp. 165-167.

[2] FLÓREZ, op. cit., vol. viii, pp. 9, 10, 32.

[3] *España, sus monumentos y artes*, &c.; QUADRADO, *Valladolid, Palencia y Zamora*, pp. 350-358.

[4] GAMS, *Series episcoporum ecclesiae catholicae.*

[5] *España, sus monumentos y artes*, &c.; QUADRADO, *Valladolid, Palencia y Zamora*, pp. 350-358

[6] Ibid., pp. 350-358. FLÓREZ, op. cit., vol. viii, pp. 9, 10, 32.

[7] *España, sus monumentos y artes*, &c.; QUADRADO, *Valladolid, Palencia y Zamora*, pp. 350-358.

[8] MARIANA, *Historia general de España*, p. 487.

that he brought to Palencia from Narbonne,[1] rests on no ground of probability. Not only is it uncertain whether there was any cultus of the saint in the old capital of the Vaccaei before 711, but it seems that the relics were really brought by Sancho from the abbey of Frédelas.[2] Its construction, the apse in particular, is far more suggestive of the barbarous Visigothic period than of the Roman decadence.

When the cathedral was rebuilt, this early chamber was retained; but an opening was broken in the apse at its end in order to connect it with the new crypt or second chamber which, in default of proof to the contrary, may be ascribed to the reigns of Sancho the Great and Ferdinand I, and the episcopate of Bernard I. The difference between the capitals in the crypt at Palencia and those in San Juan at Baños de Cerrato, though all of the same style,[3] is to be explained by the fact that they were produced at different periods.

The Basilica of Cabeza de Griego.—We know that at the end of the XVIII century the remains indicated a basilica in the form of a Tau cross, in which the apse, both in plan and in its frontal arch, the arches which crossed the transept, and those of the doors, were all of the oval horse-shoe form. The columns dividing the nave from the aisles, the bases of which survived, were composed of portions of Roman shafts brought from other buildings, clumsily put together.[4] In their present state these remains consist of little more than the outer walls and those of the apse, together with the foundations of the bases of the columns in the nave.

The discovery therein, among other things, of a fragmentary inscription eulogising a bishop called Sefronius, which is ascribed to the VII century, and also of a sepulchral inscription in Visigothic lettering, referring to the same bishop and to another named Nigrinus—'hic sunt sepulcra sanctorum, Sefronius Episc., Nigrinus Episc.'—together with the form of the arches and apse, have led to the inference that the church is of Visigothic origin, and that Sefronius and Nigrinus were two bishops of the ancient diocese of Segóbriga.[5]

[1] Lampérez y Romea, op. cit., vol. i, p. 166. [2] *Acta Sanctorum*, vol. xl, pp. 340-357.

[3] Lampérez y Romea, op. cit., vol. i, p. 167. [4] Ibid., vol. i, pp. 150-152.

[5] Ibid., vol. i, pp. 150-152. *Boletín de la Real Academia de la Historia*, vol. xiii, pp. 353-388; Guevara, Cornide, Montejo, *Monumentos romanos y cristianos de Cabeza del Griego.*

FIG. 217.—Baños de Cerrato. San Juan Bautista. Porch (XII cent.).

FIG. 220.—Baños de Cerrato. San Juan Bautista. Column at the entrance to the sanctuary (XII cent.).

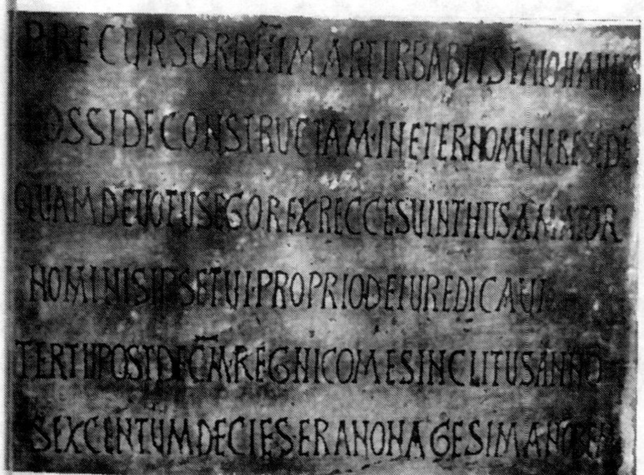

FIG. 221.—Baños de Cerrato. San Juan Bautista. Votive inscription (from a cast).

Fig. 219.—Baños de Cerrato. San Juan Bautista. North arcade of the nave (XII. cent.).

FIG. 223.—Jouarre. Crypt of Saint Paul. Sarcophagus of St. Theodechildis (VII cent.).

FIG. 225.—Bande. Sanctuary of Santa Comba or San Torcuato (IX cent.).

FIG. 226.—Bande. Santa Comba or San Torcuato (IX cent.).

FIG. 240.—Ravenna. Palace of Theodoric. Remains of mosaic pavement (493-526).

FIG. 241.—Ravenna. Palace of Theodoric. Remains of mosaic pavement (493-526).

It has not yet, however, been proved that the Roman ruins in the territory of Cabeza de Griego actually belong to the ancient Segóbriga. Nor does the list of bishops of that diocese printed by Gams[1]—a list which begins with Proculus in 589 and ends in 688 with Anterius—contain the names of Sefronius and Nigrinus. Nor do they appear in the *Acta Sanctorum*.

Moreover, considering that the building was the cathedral of Segóbriga, the existence of inscriptions in Visigothic character is no proof that what was left of the structure in the XVIII century was as old as the Visigothic age, and not rather a reconstruction carried out after the ruin caused by the Moslem conquest. When the rebuilding took place the remains of the Roman columns formerly belonging to the original structure were used again in a clumsy fashion.

It may be that an entirely new church was built, in which were employed columns taken from ruins left by the Moslems, while it was made the receptacle for relics and sepulchral memorials brought from one or more of the churches destroyed in their ravages.

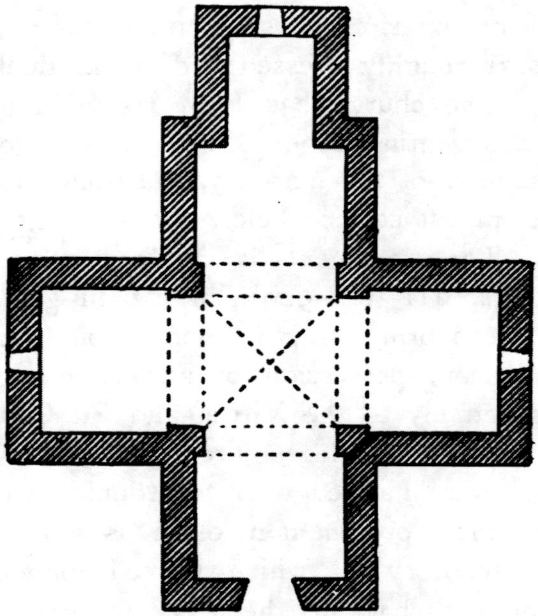

FIG. 224.—Bande. Plan of Santa Comba or San Torcuato (IX cent.).

Whatever the truth may be, the exaggerated form of horse-shoe arch used in the building points to a period some time after the Moslem conquest and the subsequent systematic use of the horse-shoe arch in the Iberian peninsula. In its earlier days that arch had not so pronounced a form.

THE CHURCH OF SANTA COMBA OR SAN TORCUATO AT BANDE is a small building in the shape of a cross with arms of equal length, having at the east end a rectangular sanctuary (Fig. 224). It is covered with barrel vaulting, except the low central tower, which has a cross vault. At the impost of the vaults runs a rudely designed and carved string of cable

[1] Op. cit.

pattern. The arches of the central square space exceed the semicircle by a third of the radius, and the same is the case with the sanctuary arch which springs from a pair of marble columns on either side (Fig. 225, p. 255). These columns, which come from the Roman baths of Bande, and are partly buried under the present pavement of slabs, have Corinthian capitals which may be of the complete decadence of Roman art, or even of the Visigothic period, and have belonged to the original church of the VII century. The sanctuary window has a stone transenna with a reticulation of semicircles. The walls on the exterior are seen to be constructed with irregular courses of large stone blocks roughly dressed and set in thick beds of mortar (Fig. 226, p. 255).

The church has been regarded as a work of the VII century and of the Byzantine type. The evidence for this is: a document, the plan and character of the masonry, the occurrence of the horse-shoe arch, the capitals, the impost cornice below the vaulting, and the transenna in the sanctuary.[1]

The document is a deed of gift which says that in the reign of Alfonso III (866-909), his captain-general, Adoarius, on going to Galicia in order to bring back its population (872), granted to his own brother Adonius, a deacon, possession of an estate on which stood two churches dedicated respectively to the Virgin and St. Columba. These churches, founded more than two centuries before, were out of repair and in an unseemly state; and they were handed over to Adonius with the property on the condition that he should put them in order as soon as he had taken measures to re-people the territory to which they belonged.[2] This document would make our church go back to the VII century.

This date, however, is not so certain as appears at first sight. The presence of the horse-shoe arch does not help to confirm it: rather that form would show that the present building is later than the Moslem invasion of the Iberian peninsula. Nor is it supported by the carved impost at the base of the vaulting in the church or sanctuary, nor even by the transenna in the latter, for the stringcourse might be mediaeval in date, and the transenna either Roman or mediaeval. The capitals, again, are equally inconclusive, as they were not made expressly for the structure in which we find them.

We come next to the plan in the form of an equal-armed cross. What are we to say of this?

[1] Lampérez y Romea, op. cit., vol. i, pp. 153-156.

[2] Ibid.

This form of cross, wrongly described as *Greek* in contrast to the *Latin* cross with unequal arms, is not in fact of Byzantine origin as is so generally asserted. On the contrary, it is derived, like the 'Latin' cross, from plans of tombs and other structures of the Roman imperial epoch. I have dealt with this point elsewhere;[1] and, without taking the trouble to search,

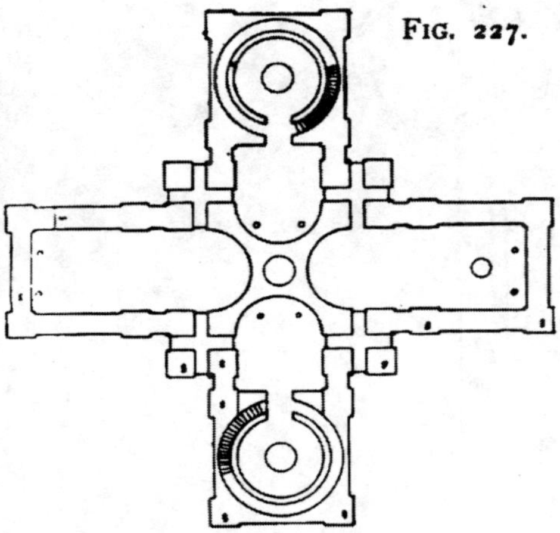

FIG. 227.

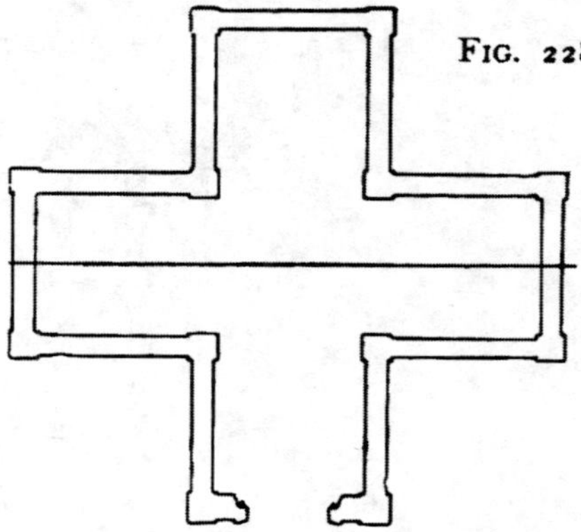

FIG. 228.

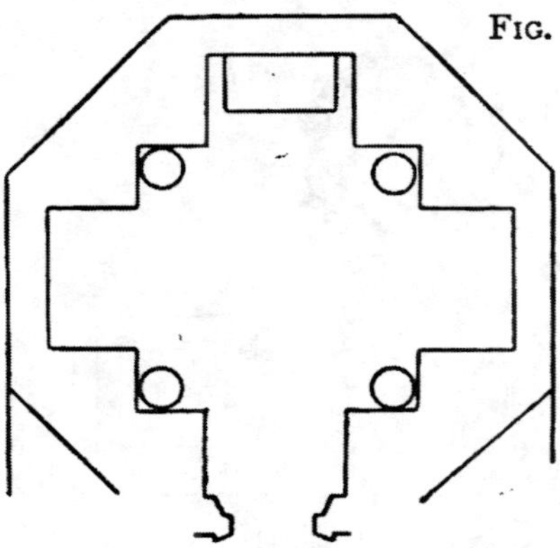

FIG. 229.

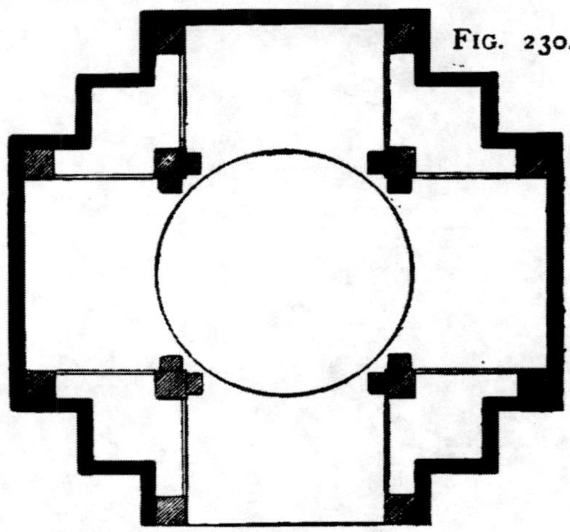

FIG. 230.

FIGS. 227, 228, 229, 230.—Plans of Roman cruciform buildings.
(From MONGERI, *Le rovine*, &c., tavv. 18, 32, 41, 65.)

as I have done more than once, through the drawings in the Uffizi at Florence and other collections outside Italy, anyone can assure themselves of its correctness by simply glancing at the designs of Serlio,[2] Montano,[3]

[1] RIVOIRA, op. cit. (Hoepli), p. 28; (Heinemann), vol. i, p. 28.

[2] SCAMOZZI, *Tutte l'Opere d'architettura di Sebastiano Serlio.*

[3] *Raccolta de tempii, e sepolcri disegnati dall'antico; Scielta de varii tempietti antichi.*

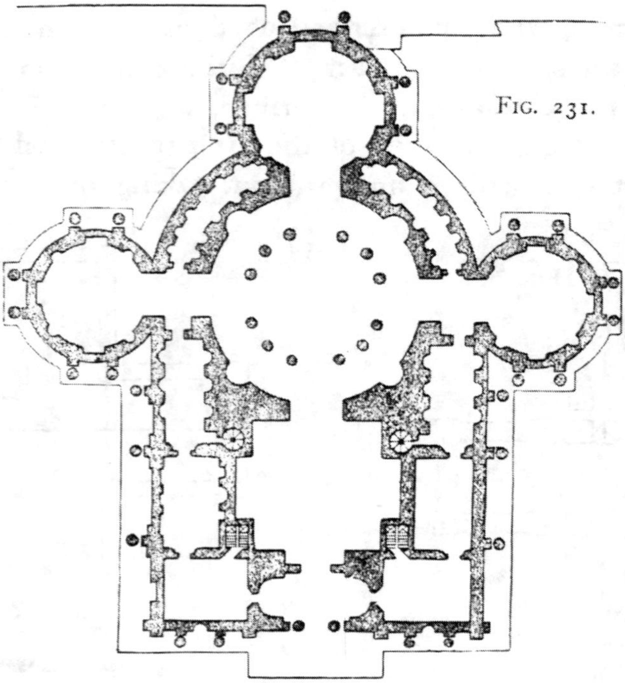

FIG. 231.

FIG. 232.

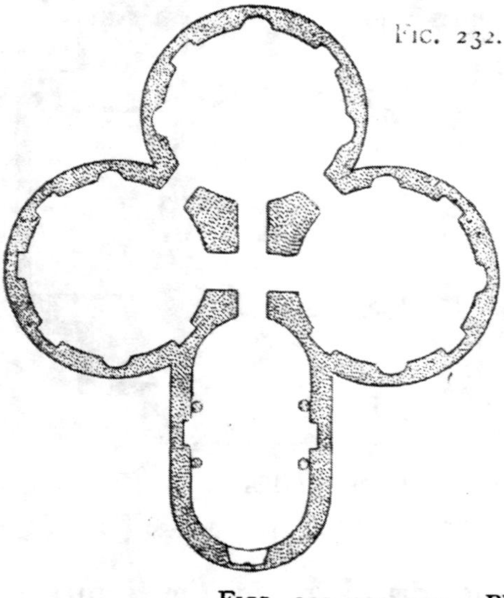

FIG. 233.

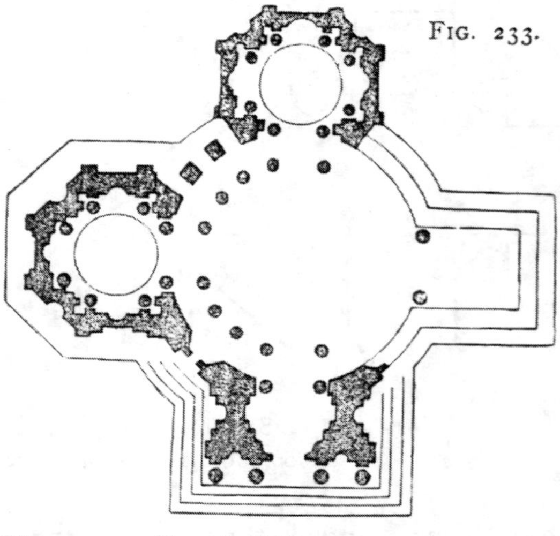

FIGS. 231, 232, 233.—Plans of Roman cruciform buildings.
(From MONTANO, *Raccolta*, &c., tavv. 4, 18, 28.)

Bramantino,[1] and the Vatican Barberini MS. 4424.[2] Specimens of the plans

[1] MONGERI (Studi del Bramantino), *Le rovine di Roma al principio del secolo XVI.*
[2] HÜLSEN, *Il libro di Giuliano da Sangallo.*

of such buildings, with equal or unequal arms, and of simple and elementary form as well as of complex variety—one having the appearance of four basilicas united at the apsidal ends—are here illustrated, the examples being taken

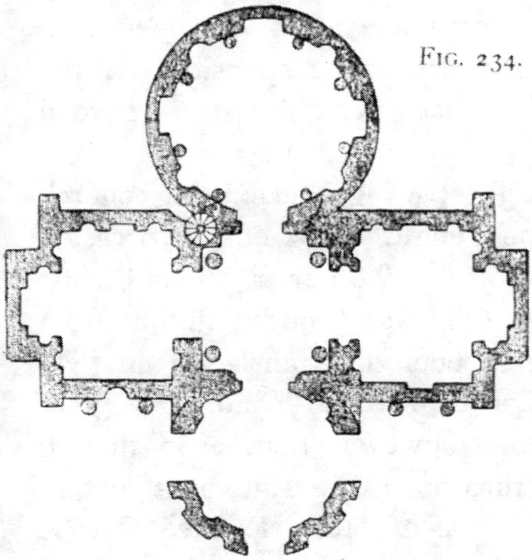

FIG. 234.

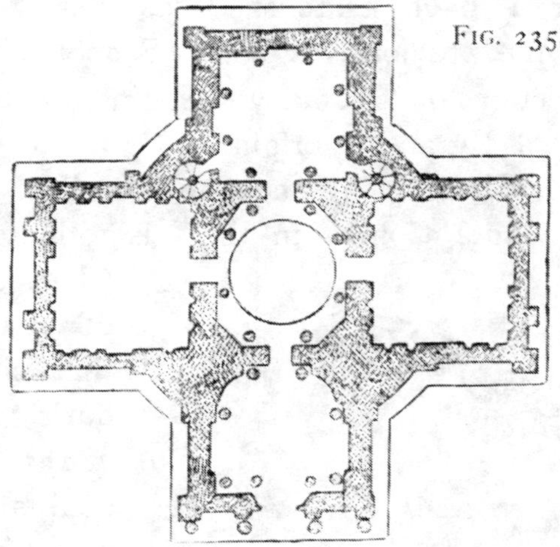

FIG. 235.

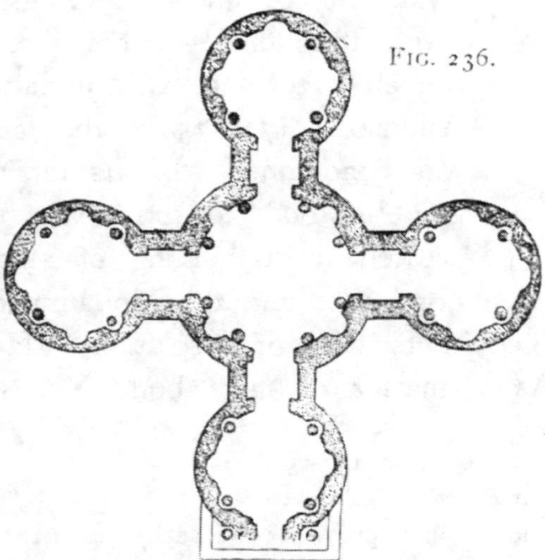

FIG. 236.

FIGS. 234, 235, 236.—Plans of Roman cruciform buildings.
(From MONTANO, *Raccolta*, &c., tavv. 31, 34, 45.)

from Bramantino[1] (Figs. 227, 228, 229, 230, p. 259) and Montano[2] (Figs. 231, 232, 233, 234, 235, 236, 237, pp. 260, 261, 262).

[1] MONGERI, op. cit., tavv. 18, 32, 41, 65.

[2] *Raccolta de tempii, e sepolcri disegnati dall'antico*, tavv. 4, 18, 28, 31, 34, 45; *Scielta de varii tempietti antichi*, tav. 40.

Nor can the likeness which has been pointed out[1] between the church of Bande and the mausoleum of Galla Placidia at Ravenna (about 440) (Fig. 238, p. 263), a new account of which, by the way, has lately appeared,[2] justify the title of Byzantine for the type to which both buildings belong, for I have established, as clearly as it is possible to do, the existence of the previously ignored School of Ravenna, which was responsible for the erection of so many celebrated buildings in that city, hitherto regarded as of Byzantine origin.[3]

There being then no plausible argument for placing the existing church of Santa Comba in the Visigothic period, one might think of the occasion when the body of St. Torquatus, first Bishop of Guadix (about 65),[4] was brought thither from that city. Flórez puts the translation in 777, during the reign of Abd al-Rahman I (756-788).[5] We know, however, that, even though doubts may be thrown on the statement that in 716 Abd al-Aziz, son of Musa, levelled Orense with the ground—'Auriam vero depopulavit usque ad solum'[6]—it being recorded that in 742 the city received with jubilation the troops of Alfonso I (739-756),[7] the fact remains that it was condemned with its territory, in which the church stood, to form part of the desert zone created by the King of Asturias between his dominions and the Mohammedan provinces, and that in 832 it still remained in its state of desolation.[8] Hence the date 777 must be a mistake. As a matter of fact, both Yepes[9] and Morales[10]

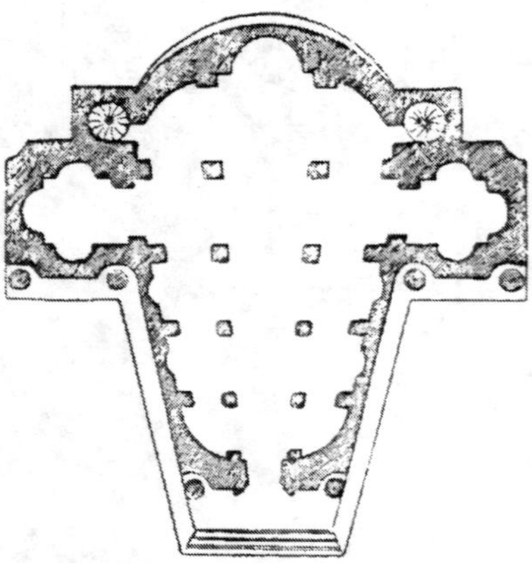

FIG. 237.—Plan of a Roman cruciform building.
(From MONTANO, *Scielta*, &c., tav. 40.)

[1] LAMPÉREZ Y ROMEA, op. cit., vol. i, pp. 153-156.

[2] GHIGI, *Il mausoleo di Galla Placidia in Ravenna.*

[3] RIVOIRA, op. cit. (Loescher), vol. i, pp. 1-125; (Hoepli), pp. 1-125; (Heinemann), vol. i, pp. 1-107.

[4] GAMS, op. cit.

[5] FLÓREZ, op. cit., vol. vii, pp. 27, 28; vol. v, pp. 312-318.

[6] Ibid., vol. xvii, pp. 48, 49.

[7] LAFUENTE, op. cit., vol. ii, p. 153.

[8] DOZY, op. cit., vol. iii, pp. 24-26. FLÓREZ, op. cit., vol. xvii, pp. 48, 49. LAFUENTE, op. cit., vol. ii, p. 153.

[9] *Coronica general de la Orden de San Benito*, vol. v, fol. 24, 25.

[10] *Viaje a los reynos de León, y Galicia, y principado de Asturias*, p. 153.

state that the body of the canonized Bishop of Guadix was carried away to Galicia after the Moslem conquest. In any case the translation of St. Torquatus, whatever may have been its date, caused a change in the title of our church, which now became 'Santa Colomba de San Torquato,'[1] and it may also have led to a restoration of the primitive church. But even granting this, the laying waste of the territory of Orense, and the long and ruinous neglect to which our church, like the other edifices there, was condemned, would demand not a restoration but a rebuilding.

The rudeness and irregularity of the masonry suggest that the rebuilding was done in haste; and this circumstance would be consistent with the date of the gift by Adoarius. The occurrence of the horse-shoe arch would agree with the date of 872, coinciding with the arrival in Galicia of monks from Cordova escaping from the persecution of Abd al-Rahman II and Mohammed II. It must not, however, be put later than the IX century, for though St. Rosendus, or Rudesindus, Bishop of Dumium (before 928-977), in which diocese Santa Comba was situated, was a great builder ('Multa monasteria a fundamentis extruxit, alia reaedificavit, alia correxit et ad primum suum statum restituit'),[2] still, having taken away the body of St. Torquatus, which he transferred (935) to his newly founded church of the Saviour at Celanova, leaving only the coffin at Bande,[3] he is hardly likely to have rebuilt a church which he had robbed of its only treasure. The date was certainly not as late as 1183, when Santa Comba was consecrated,[4] and the masonry and impost cornice of the vaulting added.

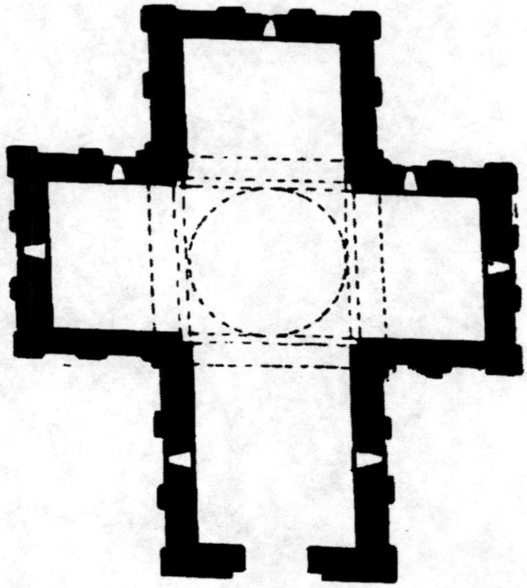

FIG. 238.—Ravenna. Plan of the Mausoleum of Galla Placidia (about 440).

THE CHURCH OF ELCHE.—The remains of this small church, which came

[1] FLÓREZ, op. cit., vol. vii., p. 27.

[2] *Acta Sanctorum*, vol. vi, pp. 102-119.

[3] FLÓREZ, op. cit., vol. vii, pp. 27, 28. YEPES, op. cit., vol. v, fol. 24, 25.

[4] FLÓREZ, op. cit., vol. xvii, p. 99.

to light in 1905 on the site of the ancient Illici, consist of the base of the walls of a rectangular nave, measuring about 11 by 7.50 m. (36 by 24 ft.), with a semicircular apse at the east, elongated so as to form a presbytery. The wall at the east end suggests that the apse was flanked by two chambers, in the Roman fashion first found in the palace of Domitian on the Palatine (about 69-85).[1]

The nave contains a tessellated mosaic pavement with meanders, tendrils, knots, stars, and other forms of ornament, and also three inscriptions in Greek characters.

FIG. 239.—Ravenna. Basilica Ursiana. Fragment of tessellated pavement (370-384).

On the ground, among other things, of these inscriptions; of some of the decorative motives of the mosaic which are related to those of the mosaic pavements of the V and VI centuries at Ravenna; and of the assertion that, between 554 and 624, Illici, together with Carthaginian Spain, Baetica, and Lusitania, was subject to Byzantine rule, the date of the church of Elche is put in the Byzantine period.[2]

I note that the tessellated mosaic pavements of the IV, V, and VI centuries at Ravenna—e.g. the splendid specimens of the Basilica Ursiana (370-384), the design of which has been preserved by Buonamici[3] in a drawing of so much as was visible more than 3 m. (nearly 10 ft.) below the present floor—were the work of Italians, and belonged to a Latin, not a Byzantine tradition (Fig. 239). So much so, that Theodoric the Great (493-526) brought skilled 'marmorarii' from Rome for the works in the basilica of Hercules, as we learn from his letter to the prefect Agapitus.[4] To these artists may be

[1] RIVOIRA, op. cit. (Hoepli), p. 21; (Heinemann), vol. i, p. 22.

[2] PUIG Y CADAFALCH, op. cit., vol. i, pp. 293-295.

[3] *Metropolitana di Ravenna*, pp. xii, xiii; tavv. B, C.

[4] *Monumenta Germaniae historica*; AURELIUS CASSIODORUS, *Variae*, lib. i, epist. vi.

FIG. 242.—Ravenna. Palace of Theodoric. Remains of mosaic pavement (493-526).

FIG. 243.—Rome. Palatine. Fragment of mosaic from the 'Domus Aurea' (65-68).

FIG. 245.—Tarrasa. San Miguel (IX and XII cents.).[1]

[1] Figs. 245, 246, 268, 269, 270, are from photographs by Mas of Barcelona.

ascribed the surviving portions of mosaic from Theodoric's palace (Figs. 240, 241, 242, pp. 256, 265).

This is not difficult to understand, for it was in imperial Rome that the art of mosaic, wedded as it was to architecture, reached its highest development and widest expansion in palaces, mausoleums, basilicas, and baths.[1] In Rome, where the mosaics of the time of Nero (54-68) (Fig. 243, p. 265) and Domitian (81-96) discovered by Boni on the Palatine, not only precede in date, but, considering the rare material used, such as mother of pearl, the variety, vigour, and excellence of design, the grand scale of their compositions, and their marvellous workmanship, surpass the finest specimens of the kind which Ravenna, Istria, and the East can show.

This and many other aspects of the art of Ravenna would become clear if people would read with care, as I have done more than once, the 'Variae' of Cassiodorus, for there is to be found the evidence which forms the basis of my studies on the subject.

Another point to notice is that the church of Elche is probably later than the IV century, or rather than the Basilica Ursiana at Ravenna, on account of its apse at the east end. I may refer to what I said about orientation in my account of the mosque at Damascus.

Considering that the inscriptions in the church of Elche are in Greek and of the late period, the natural conclusion is that it belongs to the VI or VII century, and to the years between 554 and 624.

Before leaving Elche I would point out that elongated semicircular apses were built by the Romans in the imperial age, and before they appeared in the East. An example taken from Montano[2] appears as an illustration in connection with the church which we shall deal with next. Another instance may be found in Fig. 58 (p. 69).

THE CHURCH OF SAN MIGUEL AT TARRASA (Baptistery?).—Of the three ancient churches of Tarrasa the most important and best preserved is that dedicated to St. Michael. We will describe it first.

Its plan is a square of over 12 m. (about 40 ft.), with four recesses having approximately horse-shoe arches at the angles (Fig. 244, p. 268). The interior is divided into nine bays by means of eight columns in the centre and

[1] Associazione artistica fra i Cultori di architettura, 1909; NOGARA, *Mosaici di Roma antica.*

[2] *Raccolta de tempii, e sepolcri disegnati dall' antico,* tav. 33.

as many wall-piers (Fig. 245, p. 266). At the east end projects an apse of horse-shoe form internally, but polygonal externally, after the Ravennate fashion. The entrance was originally at the west end, but this was closed, and a new one opened on the south. The orientation is to the south-east.

The columns of the central square space which carry the cupola are made up, and vary in size and the kind of stone used. Those at the corners are the largest, the intermediate ones being smaller. They stand on rude Attic bases of every sort and height, or on stepped bases and other forms. They are surmounted by alien capitals, two being Composite, or rather a mixture of Corinthian and Composite. The others are Corinthian, and in some cases have had the lower part cut off in order to fit them to the shaft. These mutilated Corinthian capitals, of which there are two, are of good work, and might belong to the II century. The other Corinthian ones belong to the Roman decadence, and appear to be of the V or VI century. They recall in design and execution the VI-century capitals in the old cathedral of Trier (about 560-570).[1] The Composite capitals will be of nearly the same date as the later Corinthian ones, and may have been made for Bishop Irenaeus. The capitals are crowned with abaci of varying height, treated either as plain Ravennate pulvins or with fillets and a shallow cyma. The former were made for their places; the latter are of alien origin. From the abaci spring the round stilted arches which carry the cupola.

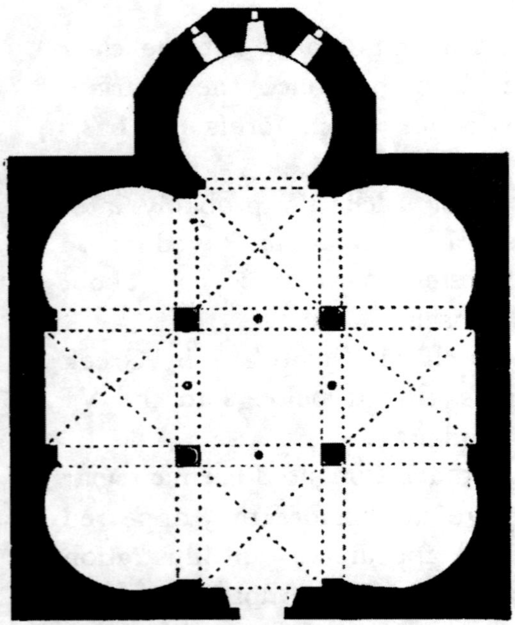

Fig. 244.—Tarrasa. Plan of San Miguel (IX and XII cents.).

The apse is covered by a half dome which tends towards a horse-shoe form at the base, as does the frontal arch. The same is also the case with the heads of the angle recesses. Each of the four bays of the cross has a depressed cross vault, starting from four corbels. Where the vault touches the wall, the arch has a slightly pointed form. The central square passes

[1] Rivoira, op. cit. (Loescher), vol. ii, Fig. 471; (Hoepli), Fig. 550; (Heinemann), vol. ii, Fig. 716.

FIG. 246.—Tarrasa. San Miguel (IX and XII cents.).

FIG. 248.—Ravenna. Baptistery of Neon (V cent.).

into the circle of the cupola by means of four hood-shaped pendentives. The lantern above the cupola is a later addition. The original windows are mere slits splayed inside.

Beneath the sanctuary is a small underground three-lobed chapel, each lobe or recess being of horse-shoe form, covered with a half dome, and lighted by a single loophole splayed inside. The square central space has a roof of flat stone slabs. The wall of the passage leading to it is modern.

On the exterior, the walls are built of small cubes of stone set in mortar, which must have come from some Roman building, and recall the external facing of the old cathedral at Beauvais (987-997). At the top they have evidently been altered, and the projecting angles have been strengthened with large dressed stone blocks brought from ancient buildings. Some fragments of cornice at the summit are composed of Roman tiles (tegulae) arranged in steps (Fig. 246, p. 269).

We do not yet know what the building was intended for. Many have regarded it as a baptistery; and this view was held as long ago as 1819.[1] Recent excavations made in the floor have not solved the problem. In order to do so it would be necessary to extend them to the underground part, and all the space within the walls.

Meanwhile I may note that the dedication to St. Michael recalls that of the circular cemetery church of St. Michael and the Saviour at Fulda (818-822), where also there was from the first a crypt, remodelled in the XI century.[2] It may be that San Miguel at Tarrasa was originally a cemetery church, which later was used for other purposes while it kept its old name.

The dates of San Miguel and of the neighbouring churches of San Pedro and Santa Maria have been put at various periods between the V and the XII centuries.[3] The Visigothic age, however, is the one most generally maintained; and to it, accordingly, we will devote our attention.

[1] *Boletín de la Real Academia de la Historia*, vol. xxxii, pp. 523-527; Riaño, *Iglesias de San Miguel, Santa Maria y San Pedro, de Tarrasa.*

[2] Rivoira, op. cit. (Loescher), vol. ii, pp. 501-506; (Hoepli), pp. 665-669; (Heinemann), vol. ii, pp. 281-285.

[3] Puig y Cadafalch, op. cit., vol. i, pp. 306-340. Lampérez y Romea, op. cit., vol. i, pp. 162-164. *Boletín de la Real Academia de la Historia*, vol. xxxii; Madrazo, *Iglesias de San Miguel, Santa Maria y San Pedro, de Tarrasa*, pp. 523-527. Ibid., vol. xxxiii; Torres Amat, *Egara (Tarrasa) y su monasterio de San Rufo*, pp. 5-30. Ibid.; Fita, *Biblioteca historica de Tarrasa*, pp. 31-79. Michel, *Histoire de l'Art*, vol. i, 2, p. 563; Enlart, *L'architecture Romane.*

It is known that the see of Egara was founded in 450, and that it is not mentioned after 693.[1] It is natural to suppose that the erection of the see was accompanied by the building of a cathedral with its baptistery. This logical inference explains the existence of San Miguel for those who believe it to be a work of the Visigothic period; always excepting the cupola, and the results of a restoration in the Carolingian age. This view is essentially confirmed by the strongly Byzantine character, as they say, of the structure; and also by the assumption that new types of plan and fresh architectural features were imported at that time from the East to the West.

Now these new features and this importation are absolutely imaginary. As a matter of fact, the church of San Miguel contains no supposed Byzantine feature which is not really of Latin origin, and in use in Italy before it was adopted in the East. Let us now establish this, starting with the question of the plan.

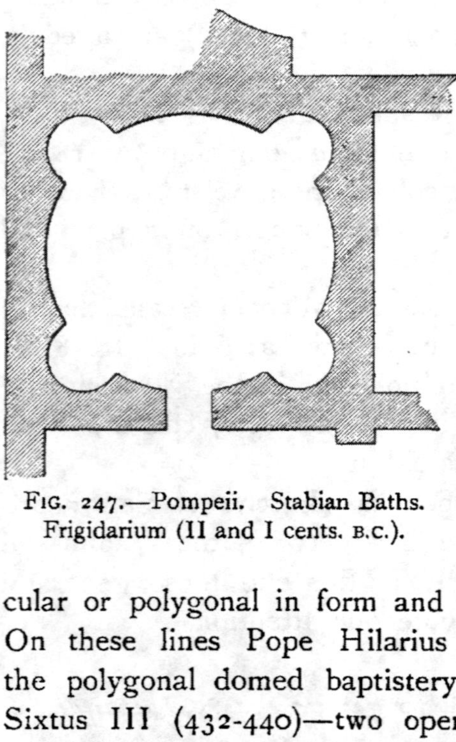

FIG. 247.—Pompeii. Stabian Baths. Frigidarium (II and I cents. B.C.).

The prototype of the plan of the baptistery and of the Roman 'laconicum,' with its recesses to hold basins, is to be found in the frigidarium of the Stabian Baths at Pompeii (Fig. 247). There is no earlier recorded building of similar type. The Greeks were unacquainted with rooms of this form until they learned them from the Romans.[2] This model was copied in the earliest Christian baptisteries, whether circular or polygonal in form and provided with round or rectangular recesses. On these lines Pope Hilarius (461-468) erected three chapels adjoining the polygonal domed baptistery of St. John Lateran at Rome, rebuilt by Sixtus III (432-440)—two opening directly from the walls of the octagon on opposite sides, and known as the chapels of St. John the Baptist and St. John the Evangelist; the third, that of the Cross,[3] being connected with it

[1] RISCO, *España Sagrada*, vol. xlii, pp. 182-184, 196, 197.

[2] *Rivista di Roma*, 1910, fasc. xii and xiii; RIVOIRA, *Origine delle terme dei Romani. Journal of the British and American Archaeological Society of Rome*, vol. iv, pp. 353-360; RIVOIRA, *The Roman Thermae. The Baths of Diocletian.*

[3] DUCHESNE, *Le liber pontificalis*, vol. i, p. 242.

by means of a portico. The original Constantinian baptistery at the Lateran was, perhaps, circular like the old baptistery of St. Sophia at Constantinople, erected under the same emperor (306-337) or Constantius II (337-361).[1] Archbishop Neon (449 or 458-477), again, when he remodelled the baptistery of the cathedral of Ravenna, added four semicircular exedras to the octagon (Figs. 248, 249, pp. 270, 275). That building was erected by local workmen. It influenced the architect of the Arian baptistery, built there in the time of Theodoric the Great (493-526),[2] which originally had four semicircular niches projecting from the octagon. And when St. Sophia at Constantinople was rebuilt by Justinian I between 532 and 537, it was provided with a baptistery —now the tomb of Mustafa I (1617-18, 1622-23)—which had semicircular recesses at the angles, after the Roman pattern.[3] This type of structure, of Latin origin, was not confined to the centuries immediately following the peace given by Constantine to the Christians (313), but was in vogue long afterwards. Thus the baptistery of Agliate (824-860) has two exedras projecting from its nine-sided body,[4] and that of Biella (X century) has four apses projecting from the central square space, producing the form of a quatrefoil.[5]

Again, if we look at San Miguel not as a baptistery, the plan is derived from Pagan Roman or Early Christian Roman models. I give as one illustration out of many the plan of a cruciform structure with circular angle recesses, alternately vaulted and domed, and a central cupola, preserved by Montano[6] (Fig. 250, p. 274). We may also recall the oratory of the Holy Cross erected by Pope Hilarius (461-468) opposite the present door of the Lateran baptistery, destroyed under Urban VIII in 1629, but the plan of which has been preserved by Bramantino[7] (Fig. 251, p. 274) and Sangallo.[8] We know that it was about 11 m. (36 ft.) wide, and that its cupola was made of tubular tiles. I recall, again, the plan of another Roman structure of square form with four round recesses at the angles, preserved by Sangallo (tav. 8).

With regard to the central plan, I have elsewhere shown exhaustively, from the evidence of actual buildings, that circular or polygonal structures with

[1] Rivoira, op. cit. (Heinemann), vol. i, p. 89.

[2] *Mon. Germ. Hist.*, Agnellus or Andreas, *Liber pontificalis*, p. 334.

[3] Rivoira, op. cit. (Heinemann), vol. i, p. 89.

[4] Ibid. (Loescher), vol. i, p. 270; (Hoepli), p 198; (Heinemann), vol. i, p. 165.

[5] Ibid. (Loescher), vol. i, pp. 287-290; (Hoepli), pp. 216-219; (Heinemann), vol. i, pp. 178-180.

[6] *Scielta de varii tempietti antichi*, tav. 29.

[7] Mongeri, op. cit., tav. 30.

[8] Hülsen, op. cit., fol. 30.

a central cupola carried on isolated supports, and vaulted throughout, had their origin in Rome, whence the conception was borrowed by the Eastern architects.[1] And I have returned to the subject in the present volume, when dealing with the Dome of the Rock at Jerusalem.

Another point is that the apse, semicircular internally and polygonal externally, was invented at Ravenna.[2] Later the Byzantines took it over. We have dealt with this subject once more in the account of Walid's mosque at Damascus.

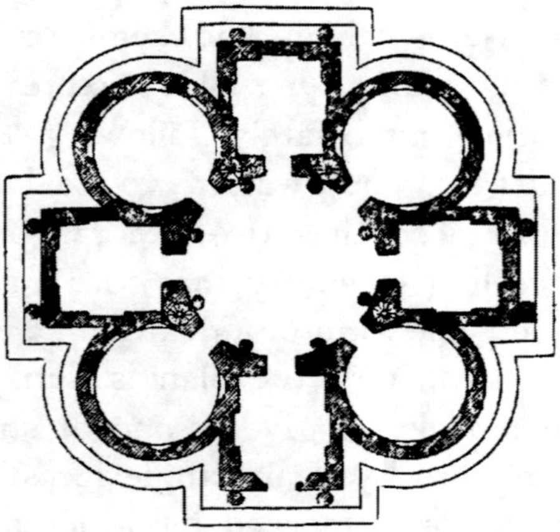

FIG. 250.—Plan of a Roman sepulchral building.
(From MONTANO, *Scielta*, &c., tav. 29.)

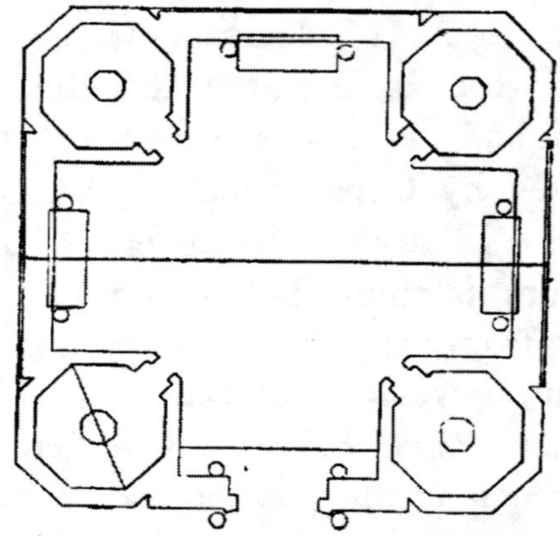

FIG. 251.—Rome. Plan of the Oratory of the Holy Cross at the Lateran (V cent.).
(From MONGERI, *Le rovine*, &c., tav. 30.)

Another invention of Ravenna was the pulvin in the form of an inverted truncated pyramid, as I have demonstrated, while others had an inkling of it.[3] It may, too, have come from Campania, but in any case not from the Byzantines.[4] The Basilica Ursiana at Ravenna and the Basilica Severiana (San Giorgio Maggiore) at Naples (367- about 387) (Fig. 252, p. 276) were furnished with pulvins in the IV century. The subject has been discussed anew in this book under the above-named mosque at Damascus.

[1] RIVOIRA, op. cit. (Loescher), vol. ii, pp. 31-36; (Hoepli), pp. 343-348; (Heinemann), vol. ii, pp. 23-26.

[2] Ibid. (Loescher), vol. i, pp. 26, 27; (Hoepli), pp. 7, 8; (Heinemann), vol. i, pp. 8-10.

[3] ARCHINTI, *Stili nell' Architettura*, vol ii, pp. 93-101.

[4] RIVOIRA, op. cit. (Loescher), vol. i, pp. 11-25; (Hoepli), pp. 8-18; (Heinemann), vol. i, pp. 10-18.

FIG. 249.—Ravenna. Baptistery of Neon (V cent.).

FIG. 252.—Naples. Apse of San Giorgio Maggiore (367- about 387).

FIG. 259.—Rome. Arch of the Neronian Aqueduct on the Caelian (50)

The three-lobed crypt, again, is of Roman origin. The same principle is found in the trefoil type of structure generally, either in its simple form or with the angles emphasized, and with or without buttresses, examples of which occur in Italy from the imperial age onwards.[1] I give illustrations of the plans of some of these, taken from Bramantino[2] (Fig. 253), Montano[3] (Figs. 254, 255, 256, p. 278), Serlio[4] (Fig. 257, p. 281), and Fra Giocondo[5] (Fig. 258, p. 281). We may also mention the two well-known and often discussed 'cellae' of the cemetery of Callistus on the Via Appia Antica near Rome:[6] the cella known as that of St. Soteris, but believed by Wilpert to be the tomb of St. Zephyrinus;[7]

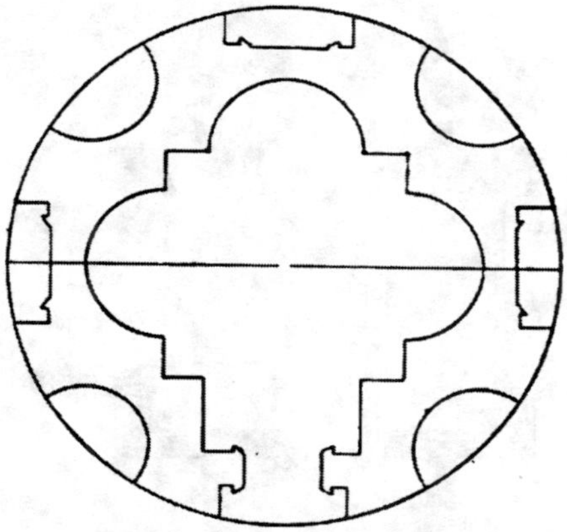

FIG. 253.—Plan of a Roman three-lobed building.
(From MONGERI, *Le rovine*, &c., tav. 21.)

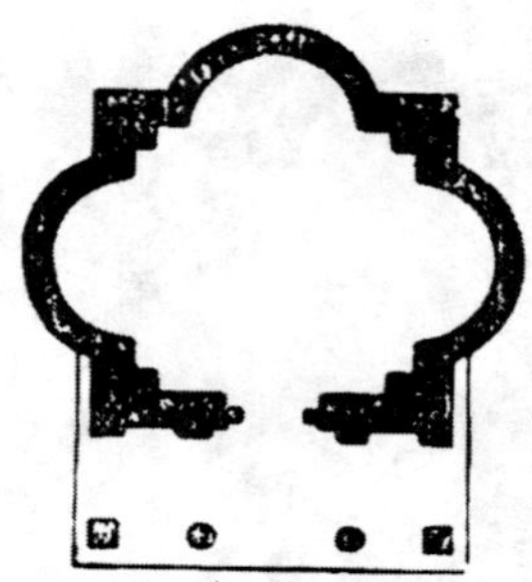

FIG. 254.—Plan of a Roman three-lobed building.
(From MONTANO, *Scielta*, &c., tav. 16.)

and that commonly believed to be dedicated to Saints Xystus and Caecilia, but thought by Marucchi[8] to have been intended to receive the body of the

[1] RIVOIRA, op. cit. (Loescher), vol. i, p. 4; vol. ii, pp. 24, 25, 487, 508, 580, 581; (Hoepli), p. 711; (Heinemann), vol. ii, pp. 276, 316. *Nuova Antologia*, Ap. 16th 1910; RIVOIRA, *Adriano architetto e i monumenti Adrianei.* DE ROSSI, *La Roma sotterranea cristiana*, vol. iii, p. 473.

[2] MONGERI, op. cit., tav. 21.

[3] *Scielta de varii tempietti antichi*, tav. 16; *Raccolta de tempii, e sepolcri disegnati dall'antico*, tavv. 8, 33.

[4] SCAMOZZI, op. cit., fol. 74.

[5] Uffizi Gallery, Florence; Carta 3932, *Catalogo Ferri*, p. 219.

[6] DE ROSSI, *La Roma sotterranea cristiana*, vol. iii, pp. 468-473.

[7] WILPERT, *Die Papstgräber und die Cäciliengruft in der Katakombe des hl. Kallistus*, pp. 91-104.

[8] *Nuovo Bollettino di Archeologia cristiana*, 1908, pp. 157-195; MARUCCHI, *La cella tricora detta di Santa Sotere.*

same Zephyrinus. These cellae, so far as they are original, may date from the III century. Another instance is the chapel of St. Symphorosa on the Via Tiburtina (III century). All these plans may have been derived from the interesting and imposing tri-apsidal structure in the Stadium of Hadrian's Villa at Tivoli,[1] which has been recently excavated.

Next I would remark that with regard to the three-lobed plan, of which we hear so much, in Constantine's churches of the Holy Sepulchre at Jerusalem and the Nativity at Bethlehem, the former never existed, and the latter was

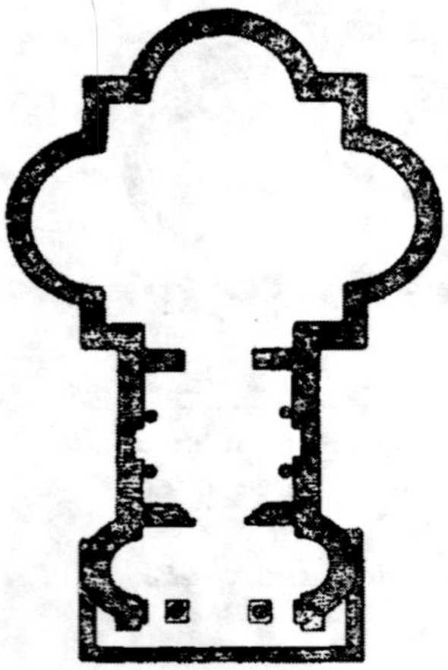

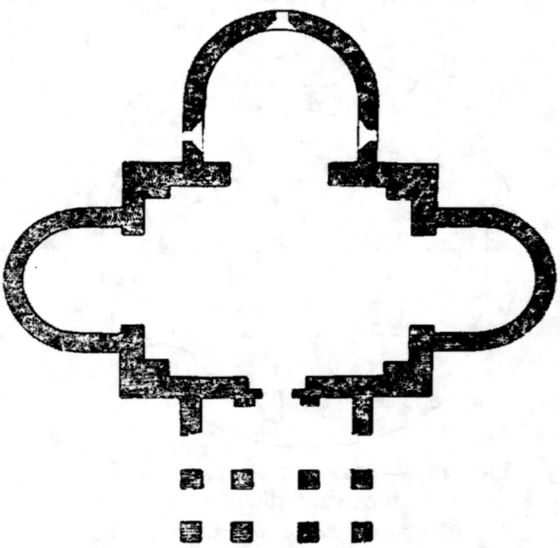

FIGS. 255, 256.—Plans of Roman buildings.
(From MONTANO, *Raccolta*, &c., tavv. 8, 33.)

built by Justinian, as we saw in our account of the al-Aqsa mosque at Jerusalem.

The stilted arches, again, of the central space are not a Byzantine feature. At the Arch of Dolabella and Silanus on the Caelian at Rome the imposing aqueduct of Nero (59) contains arches which are stilted to the extent of more than a metre above the impost cornice (Fig. 259, p. 276).

Lastly, the Romano-Campanian or hood-shaped pendentive was developed in Campania, where it was in use as early as the V century. This discovery of mine we discussed in connection with the Ummayyad mosque at Damascus referred to before.

[1] R. Accademia dei Lincei, *Notizie degli scavi di antichità*, 1906, fasc. 8°; REINA, BARBIERI, *Rilievo altimetrico e planimetrico di Villa Adriana.*

FIG. 260.—Germigny des Prés. Church (801-806).

FIG. 261.—Germigny des Prés. Church (801-806).

It is, therefore, not difficult to see that the principal arguments in favour of the Visigothic date of San Miguel at Tarrasa will not stand the test of facts.

On the other hand, those who put it in a period between the IX and XII centuries either rely on unsafe or unconvincing historical evidence, and produce reasons which, if plausible, have no bearing on the questions of architecture and construction; or have not studied the building on the spot and with the architectural and archaeological equipment which is indispensable; or else, while possessing the latter qualifications, have been led astray by their limited and imperfect acquaintance with the religious buildings of those

FIG. 257.—Ferento. Plan of a Roman three-lobed building. (From SCAMOZZI, *Tutte le opere*, &c., fogl. 74.)

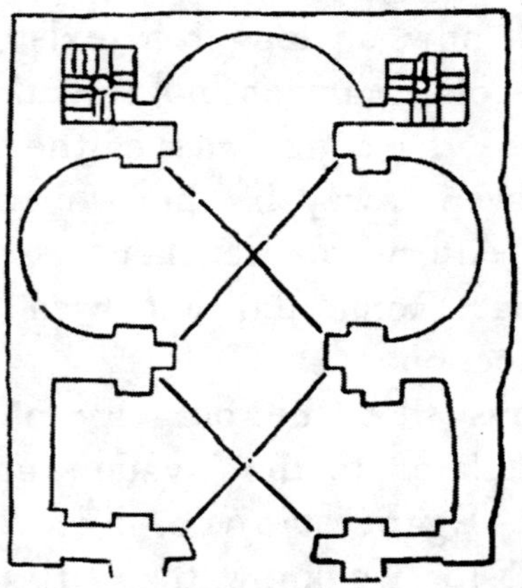

FIG. 258.—Plan of a Roman three-lobed building. (Ascribed to FRA GIOCONDO, in the Uffizi at Florence.)

centuries. Others, again, have taken refuge in the comfortable practice of theorizing.

Such being the case, let us try if possible to extricate the church from the chronological tangle in which we find it involved.

When Nundinarius, Bishop of Barcelona († about 465), divided the diocese in 450, and chose Irenaeus to fill the see of Egara, it is probable that the latter place was provided with sacred buildings befitting the rank to which it had been raised. The first Bishop of Egara seems to have been well suited for his post, and his character was such that Nundinarius on his deathbed pointed him out as his successor. The succession was favourably received by the Catalonian bishops, and also by the clergy and people of Barcelona; but it was opposed by Pope Hilarius, and was not confirmed.[1] It is not clear

[1] RISCO, op. cit., vol. xlii, pp. 182-197.

what happened next. The list of the bishops of Barcelona in Gams[1] shows a gap of fifty years between the death of Nundinarius and the accession of Agricius (516-17); and in this gap, without any indication of date, appears 'Irenaeus intrusus.' Flórez does not help to fill the void.[2]

The date of the death of Irenaeus is not known. All we learn is that his successor in the see of Egara, Nebridius, was present at the Council of Tarragona in 516.[3] However, the fifteen years of his episcopate, from 450 to 465, would be long enough for the erection of a set of sacred buildings, and it is to these years that Riaño[4] ascribes the church of San Miguel and the cathedral, now no longer in existence.

The see of Egara is not mentioned after 693 when the bishop, John, appears among the signatories of the Sixteenth Council of Toledo.[5] It must have been swept away in the whirlwind of the Moslem invasion, never to rise again.[6] Afterwards its name is only mentioned as a thing of the past —a thing that Rome did not wish to see restored—and survived only as a titular distinction.[7]

Risco says that the old city of Egara, being, like Barcelona, poorly fortified, capitulated to the invaders and was allowed to remain.[8] Fita,[9] too, believes that Egara survived, like Saragossa and Pampeluna. This may have been so, for we know that cities which capitulated, though they had to submit to hard terms, such as those inflicted by Tarik on Toledo,[10] were not destroyed, and their churches were left standing. Therefore, Roderic, Archbishop of Toledo, was wrong in saying that 'in tota Hispania non remansit civitas cathedralis, quae non fuerit aut incensa, aut diruta.'[11] Others, on the contrary, think that the place was destroyed and became 'terra rasa,' whence the name Tarrasa instead of Egara.[12] This derivation has been denied,

[1] Op. cit.

[2] Op. cit., vol. xxix, pp. 119-121.

[3] Risco, op. cit., vol. xlii, pp. 182-197.

[4] *Boletín de la Real Academia de la Historia*, vol. xxxii; Riaño, *Iglesias de San Miguel, Santa Maria y San Pedro, de Tarrasa*, pp. 523-527.

[5] Risco, op. cit., vol. xlii, pp. 182-197.

[6] Puig y Cádafalch, op. cit., vol. i, pp. 307-308.

[7] Simonet, *Historia de los Mozárabes de España*, p. 120.

[8] Risco, op. cit., vol. xlii, pp. 197-201.

[9] *Boletín de la Real Academia de la Historia*, vol. xxxiii; *Biblioteca historica de Tarrasa*, pp. 31-79.

[10] Lafuente, op. cit., vol. ii, p. 129.

[11] *Chronicon rerum gestarum in Hispaniis;* Rodericus, *Deploratio Hispaniae*, lib. iii, cap. xxi.

[12] Flórez, op. cit., vol. xxix., App. xi.

and the name explained by the fact that Egara possessed a fortress or castle.[1] Certain it is that in the time of Charles the Bald the former Egara was known as the Castle of Tarrasa.[2]

Whatever may have been the course of events, the churches of Tarrasa, even if not destroyed or injured by the Moslem conquerors (according to Riaño [3] the territory of Egara fell into their hands about 720), certainly remained abandoned, or at least unrepaired, for a considerable length of time. Hence on the recovery of the district by the Franks in 801, when Egara was made dependent on the see of Barcelona,[4] these buildings, by which I mean the old cathedral and its baptistery, supposing that it had a separate one, cannot have been in very good condition after three and a half centuries of existence, and their deficiencies may well have been repaired. Simonet,[5] indeed, says that Egara was restored by Louis the Pious, and changed its name. This statement is supported by the evidence of a record contained in two inscriptions, mentioned by the prior Tapias in 1632, referring to Charles the Great's (768-814) erection of the church of St. Mary upon the ruins of the cathedral of Egara. In confirmation of this the prior cites a Bull of Pope Paschal II (1099-1118) of 1115.[6] There is no reason to accuse Tapias of having confused two Roman inscriptions with those which he quotes, or of having deliberately forged a Papal Bull, especially as he was addressing the reigning pope, Urban VIII (1623-1644).

Fita [7] says that in 856-57 the Moslems, who had once more established themselves in Barcelona through Jewish treachery in 852, laid Egara in ruins, and with the spoils of its church enriched the great mosque of Saragossa. Then Charles the Bald (843-877), having come to terms with Mohammed I, and taken interest in the rebuilding of the cathedral of Barcelona, proceeded to restore the church of St. Mary at Egara. This restoration I believe to

[1] *Boletín de la Real Academia de la Historia*, vol. xxxiii; FITA, *Biblioteca historica de Tarrasa*, pp. 31-79.

[2] RISCO, op. cit., vol. xlii, pp. 197-201.

[3] *Boletín de la Real Academia de la Historia*, vol. xxxii; *Iglesias de San Miguel, Santa Maria y San Pedro, de Tarrasa*, pp. 523-527.

[4] Ibid., vol. xxxiii; TORRES AMAT, *Egara (Tarrasa) y su monasterio de San Rufo*, pp. 5-30. SIMONET, op. cit., p. 288.

[5] Op. cit., p. 288.

[6] *Boletín de la Real Academia de la Historia*, vol. xxxiii, pp. 31-79; FITA, *Biblioteca historica de Tarrasa.*

[7] Ibid.

have been a rebuilding; and it was then that the existing churches of San Pedro, Santa Maria, and San Miguel at Tarrasa were erected.

This would explain the fact that the horse-shoe arch occurs in these churches, for the date of erection would correspond with the exodus of the monks from Cordova in consequence of the notorious persecutions of Abd al-Rahman II (822-852) and Mohammed I (852-886). As we shall see presently, in Asturias the horse-shoe arch in buildings was an importation by these monks. Nothing else can explain its success in another district, and that a Christian one, like Catalonia. The independent Christians of Spain would have had no inclination for an arch of Moslem origin; and it was only when the persecuted Mozarabic clergy carried it with them into Christian territory, that they accepted it.

As a matter of fact, it is only after the IX century and before 1112, when Santa Maria was consecrated, that these three churches are mentioned, either together or separately, in documents of the years 966, 973, 977, 991, 997 (or 995), 1091, 1096, 1101, and 1108.[1] The church of St. Michael the Archangel is expressly mentioned in the document of 973.

Between 977 and 991 came the terrible invasion of Al-Mansur (977-1002), who, after defeating Count Borrell II (954-992), took Barcelona by assault (985), devastated it, set it on fire, and carried away with him to Cordova a multitude of the population, both of the city and of the surrounding district, as slaves.[2] On this occasion the churches of Tarrasa do not appear to have escaped without injury, as we may infer from the account in Riaño[3] of the churches of San Pedro and Santa Maria, which he thought belonged in style to the XI and XII centuries. The fury of the Moslems had wrecked the cathedral of Barcelona to such an extent that it had to be rebuilt, and the new dedication took place in 1058.[4]

Finally, we know that after 1092 Bertran, Bishop of Barcelona (1086-1095), granted the church of Santa Maria to the Augustinian Canons of the monastery

[1] Puig y Cadafalch, op. cit., vol. i, pp. 307, 308. *Boletín de la Real Academia de la Historia*, vol. xxxiii, pp. 5-30; Torres Amat, *Egara (Tarrasa) y su monasterio de San Rufo.* Ibid., vol. xxxiii, pp. 31-79; Fita, *Biblioteca historica de Tarrasa.*

[2] *Boletín de la Real Academia de la Historia*, vol. xxxiii, pp. 31-79; Fita, *Biblioteca historica de Tarrasa. España, sus monumentos y artes*, &c.; Piferrer, Pi Margall, pp. 110-112.

[3] *Boletín de la Real Academia de la Historia*, vol. xxxii, pp. 523-527; *Iglesias de San Miguel, Santa Maria y San Pedro, de Tarrasa.*

[4] Flórez, op. cit., vol. xxix, pp. 228, 229.

of San Rufo;[1] and that in 1112 the church itself was consecrated by Ramon (1108-1115),[2] apparently after a restoration.[3]

The historical evidence and inferences here put together give the two fixed limits of date, from the rebuilding of the ancient churches of Egara down to the restoration and consequent re-dedication of the most important among them, viz. Santa Maria. We shall see presently how and where San Pedro and Santa Maria come in this period. First let us see how the case stands with San Miguel.

The plan is of Latin origin, and one of those revived by Charles the Great in his empire after he had conquered the kingdom of Lombardy (774).[4] It first appeared in Asturias under Ramiro I (842-850) in the church of San Miguel de Lino. The masonry of the outer walls is like that in the churches of San Pedro and Santa Maria close by. The horse-shoe arches point to a date later than the end of the Visigothic kingdom. The columns in the centre suggest a restoration in the course of which ancient capitals and Ravennate pulvins of the V or VI century were adapted, and arches constructed of the high stilted form which was revived after the Renaissance of about the year 1000. The cross vaults in the outer bays, with their pointed wall-arches, evidently belong to the XII century. The cupola with its hood-shaped pendentives points to a date not earlier than the first half of the XI century, and after the Lombard master builders had made them the fashion. As a fact, the oldest example which Catalonia can show is that afforded by the church of San Vicente at Cardona, begun after 1019 and finished in 1040.[5]

We have, therefore, before us a church of the IX century, of which the outer walls, though restored, survive; but of which the interior with its vaulting and central tower was, apparently, reconstructed in the XII century.

Before quitting San Miguel at Tarrasa I may notice the theory of

[1] *Boletin de la Real Academia de la Historia*, vol. xxxiii, pp. 5-30; TORRES AMAT, *Egara (Tarrasa) y su monasterio de San Rufo.*

[2] RISCO, op. cit., vol. xlii, App. x.

[3] *Boletin de la Real Academia de la Historia*, vol. xxxiii, pp. 31-79; FITA, *Biblioteca historica de Tarrasa.*

[4] RIVOIRA, op. cit. (Loescher), vol. i, pp. 209-238; vol. ii, pp. 474-549; (Hoepli), pp. 181-192, 647-694; (Heinemann), vol. i, pp. 151-160; vol. ii, pp. 267-302.

[5] PUIG Y CADAFALCH, op. cit., vol. ii, pp. 166, 167.

Lampérez y Romea about a Spanish origin of the church of Germigny des Prés (801-806) (Figs. 260, 261, 262, pp. 279, 280, 286). Theodulf's famous church was, according to him, inspired by some structure of the type of San Miguel, and Theodulf, being a Spaniard, fetched workmen from his native country to erect it.[1]

Now the Spanish nationality of the celebrated Abbot of Fleury and Bishop of Orleans (788-821) is by some held to be a mere conjecture;[2] and it has also been suspected that his relationship with the Goths of Hesperia (i.e. Spain) which he mentions, is purely metaphorical.[3] On the other hand it has been maintained that he was an Italian. 'Erat Theodulfus natione Italus.'[4] In my view his Italian origin would be confirmed by the fact that he joined Anselm, Archbishop of Milan (814-822), Walfredus, Bishop of Cremona (816-818), and others in the conspiracy which caused Bernard, King of Italy, to lose first his throne (817) and then his life (818) under tragic circumstances.[5]

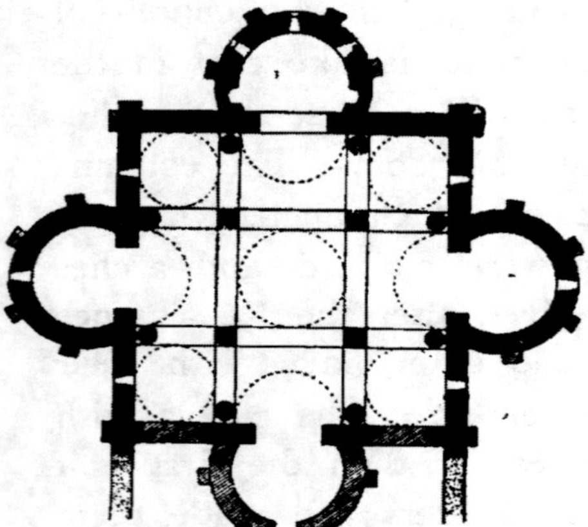

FIG. 262.—Germigny des Prés. Plan of the church (801-806).

As to the church, I have shown elsewhere that its plan is derived from that of San Lorenzo Maggiore at Milan (VI century) (Fig. 263, p. 287), perhaps the work of Julianus Argentarius, the architect of San Vitale at Ravenna (526-547); while its elevation reminds one of the mausoleum of Galla Placidia in the latter city (about 440)[6] (Figs. 264, 265, p. 289), which in its turn was inspired by some Pagan Roman tomb of the type shown in one of Serlio's illustrations[7] here reproduced (Figs. 266, 267, p. 288). In fact, if one thinks

[1] *Revue Hispanique*, 1907, pp. 565-575; LAMPÉREZ Y ROMEA, *Sobre algunas posibles influencias de la arquitectura Cristiano-Española de la edad media en la Francesa.*

[2] *Mon. Germ. hist.*; *Poetae Latini medii aevi*; *Theodulfi Carmina*, vol. i, p. 437.

[3] MIGNE, *Patr. lat.*, vol. cv, col. 187; *Theodulphus Aurelianensis episcopus.*

[4] *Annales Ordinis S. Benedicti*, vol. ii, p. 314.

[5] *Mon. Germ. hist.*, vol. i, p. 204; *Annales Laurissenses et Einhardi.*

[6] RIVOIRA, op. cit. (Loescher), vol. i, pp. 217, 218; (Hoepli), p. 390; (Heinemann), vol. i, p. 55.

[7] SCAMOZZI, op. cit., fol. 63.

of the plan of San Lorenzo without the internal irregular octagon, it is the same, on a different scale, as that of Theodulf's church.

The most important vaulted buildings erected under Charles the Great, either by him directly or with his assistance, were modelled, with variations, on those of the Ravennate-Byzantine style which he had seen at Ravenna. The most celebrated of all, the Palatine Chapel at Aachen (796-804), is substantially a copy of San Vitale at Ravenna.[1]

In my former work I said that the church of Germigny des Prés appears to have been erected by craftsmen brought from Italy, together with French workmen, and that it showed the influence of an Eastern architect.[2] This view I now modify, so far as the architect is concerned. The great number and variety of ancient Roman vaulted and domed structures, which have been preserved for us in drawings, but in the days of Theodulf must have still been standing, make me feel that there was no need to bring in an architect from the East to design the church of Germigny des Prés, seeing that it was so easy to find every sort of plan in Roman monuments. Accordingly, I am of opinion that the man who designed Theodulf's church was an Italian. The horse-shoe arches (perhaps repeated by the same workmen from Germigny des Prés in the campanile of Santa Maria della Cella at Viterbo[3]) must have been part of the original design, and suggested by buildings not far off in the Iberian peninsula, where, thanks to Abd al-Rahman I (756-788), the form had obtained a footing. This, however, is all that can be allowed to Spain, which for churches of the central vaulted type had to resort to Carolingian models.

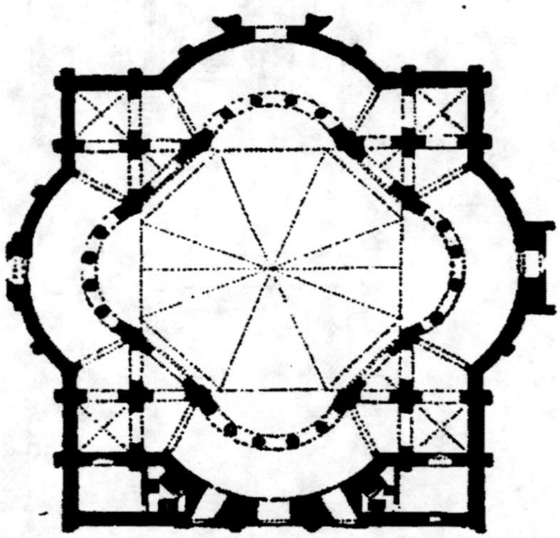

FIG. 263.—Milan. Plan of San Lorenzo Maggiore (VI cent.).

I say the central vaulted type, for, as far back as the VII century,

[1] RIVOIRA, op. cit. (Loescher), vol. ii, pp. 485-487; (Hoepli), pp. 654-658; (Heinemann), vol. ii, pp. 272-276.

[2] Ibid. (Loescher), vol. i, pp. 219-222; (Hoepli), pp. 390-393; (Heinemann), vol. ii, pp. 55-59.

[3] Ibid. (Loescher), vol. i, p. 277; (Hoepli), p. 207; (Heinemann), vol. i, p. 171.

FIGS. 266, 267.—Plan and elevation of a Roman tomb.
(From SCAMOZZI, *Tutte l'opere d'architettura*, &c., fogl. 63.)

Spain possessed an important building in the form of a cross with equal arms, containing colonnades, but not enclosed in a square. I refer to the monastic church of San Román at Hornija, built by King Chindaswinth (642-649) in 646, and of equal-armed cruciform plan. But it no longer retained its original plan when Morales saw it in the XVI century;[1] nor, as a matter of fact, its elevation either. And the only relics of its former splendour were several precious marble columns of Roman origin, and of various kinds and colours, which still adorned the edifice, as is confirmed by Yepes.[2] The work described by Morales as 'obra Gothica' belonged to a restoration of the original church. I may remark by the way that Morales means by 'Gothic work' buildings containing marble columns and the horse-shoe arch. Thus, in describing San Juan Bautista at Baños de Cerrato, he says: 'It is rich with many coloured marbles, after the fashion of the Goths.'[3] Again, in connection with the sanctuary of Santa Maria at Oviedo,[4] he says that it was in the Gothic style, being decorated with marble columns, and still more

[1] *La Coronica general de España*, lib. xii, fol. 137.

[2] YEPES, op. cit., vol. ii, fol. 183-186.

[3] MORALES, *La Coronica general de España*, lib. xii, cap. xxviii.

[4] Ibid., *Viaje a los reynos de León, y Galicia*, &c., pp. 86-92. Ibid., *La Coronica general de España*, lib. xiii, cap. xxxviii.

FIG. 264.—Ravenna. Mausoleum of Galla Placidia (about 440).

FIG. 265.—Ravenna. Mausoleum of Galla Placidia (about 440).

FIG. 268.—Tarrasa. Santa Maria (V, IX, XI, and XII cents.)

because it had horse-shoe arches: 'The three chapels are entirely the work of the Goths, their frontal arches in particular, which bear a strong resemblance to those of San Román de Hornija and of Bamba.'[1]

The monastery of San Román, a couple of leagues from the city of Toro, was destroyed by the Moslems, together with Toro itself and its neighbours, Zamora and Simancas, as well as Dueñas, all of which were rebuilt and repeopled by Alfonso III (866-909). It was on this occasion that the monastery was rebuilt, being shortly after made dependent on the abbey of San Adrián at Tuñón, founded by the same great but unfortunate king.[2]

Hence, if San Román, when Morales saw it before its destruction in the XVIII century to make way for the present church,[3] possessed horse-shoe arches, those arches were not so old as the Visigothic age, and must have been the work of builders coming in all probability from Moslem territory. We should bear in mind that the rebuilding of Zamora was entrusted to architects and workmen brought from Toledo.[4]

The Church of Santa Maria at Tarrasa is of the Latin cross plan, with a horse-shoe apse at the east end covered by a half dome which externally forms a square block (Fig. 268, p. 290). The frontal arch springs from a rude cornice, different from the impost cornice of the arches which carry the cupola. The apse was flanked by two smaller ones, of which there are some remains. Above the crossing rises the cupola, carried on hood-shaped pendentives, and surmounted by a small bell-tower. The arms of the transept are barrel vaulted. The nave, which has a narthex at the west end with a gallery over, has a pointed barrel vault.

On the exterior, the masonry of the apse shows: below the floor line of the church, careless work of the Visigothic period; above, courses of small cubes of stone, like the facing of the external walls of the neighbouring San Miguel, with some admixture of roughly prepared stones and bricks taken from ancient buildings. The outer angles are strengthened by dressed stones of similar origin. The highest part is evidently not in its original state. Some

[1] Morales, *Viaje a los reynos de León, y Galicia*, &c., pp. 86-92.

[2] Yepes, op. cit., vol. ii, fol. 183-186.

[3] *España, sus monumentos y artes*, &c.; Quadrado, *Valladolid, Palencia y Zamora*, pp. 259-263, 535.

[4] Ibid.

fragments of the cornice at the top with stepped Roman tiles (tegulae) recall what we saw at San Miguel. On the other hand, the arms of the transept, the drum of the cupola, and the nave, are built of small cubes of stone, rubble, roughly prepared stones, dressed stones, and broken bricks. The nave walls have been repaired at the top.

The drum of the cupola is ornamented with an arched corbel course interrupted at intervals by lesenas (pilaster strips). The bell-tower above is also decorated with arches, recalling the design of the baptistery of Biella (X century) and its quasi-lantern (XI century).[1] The visible or northern side of the nave is relieved by arched corbel courses grouped in pairs of arches by lesenas. The west front has a stepped arched corbel course, every second or every third arch being carried by a lesena.

The exterior walls betray four principal periods of construction. To the earliest belongs the base of the apse, and this is rightly held to be of the Visigothic age.[2] The apse itself belongs to a second period, viz. the IX century, contemporary with the first period of San Miguel, as is proved by the similarity of the original masonry in either case. To a third belong the transept and the nave; and here we have the rebuilding which necessitated the re-consecration of 1112. The IX-century church had not the arched corbel courses of the present one, for this form of decoration did not appear in Catalonia before the close of the IX century. With a fourth period are connected the cupola and bell-tower. The way in which the former is supported, and the masonry of both, point to a different date from that of the rest of the church, and this may be put in the years following 1112. The domical cross vaults must be ascribed to the rebuilding in the XI-XII centuries. The pointed barrel vault of the nave is to be attributed to an alteration made after the year above-mentioned, the effects of which, I think, may also be seen in the exterior of the north wall.

The lessons to be derived from the architectural decoration and the vaulting of Santa Maria at Tarrasa bring to mind the churches of San Pablo del Campo and San Pedro de las Puellas at Barcelona.

The Church of San Pablo del Campo at Barcelona is first mentioned

[1] Rivoira, op. cit. (Loescher), vol. i, pp. 287-290; (Hoepli), pp. 216-219; (Heinemann), vol. i, pp. 178, 179.

[2] Puig y Cadafalch, op. cit., vol. ii, p. 259.

FIG. 269.—Barcelona. San Pablo del Campo. West front (IX, X, and XII cents.).

FIG. 270.—Barcelona. San Pablo del Campo (IX, X, and XII cents.).

when Count Wilfrid II (898-912)[1] was buried there—not Wilfrid I, 'the Hairy' (874-898), the heroic founder of Catalonian independence, as Zurita states.[2] We may therefore conjecture that Wilfrid II was the founder of the church. There has been much dispute about the date of his burial; but the year is 912, as has been proved by De Bofarull y Mascaró.[3]

It was certainly injured by Al-Mansur in 985, but we do not know whether it was repaired by Borrell II (954-992), together with the other buildings of Barcelona which had been ravaged and profaned by the Moslems, or else left abandoned. It was ultimately rebuilt by Guitart and his wife Rollanda in 1117[4] (Figs. 269, 270, pp. 293, 294).

Puig y Cadafalch's[5] account is as follows. San Pablo was in existence in 977, and the inscription on the lintel of the west door takes it back to the last third of the X century. The names of Bernardus and Raimunda which occur in the inscription seem to be those of the donors of the doorway. Another inscription inserted in a wall inside the church proves that the monastery was in existence at the beginning of that century. Al-Mansur partly destroyed the monastery, and the monks abandoned it. It was rebuilt by Guitart and Rollanda in 1117.

The church has the usual orientation and the form of a Latin cross, the western limb being longer than the eastern. It terminates in an elongated apse, flanked by minor apses, all three covered by half domes. Over the crossing rises a cupola supported by hood-shaped pendentives, which is octagonal in its lower part and nearly circular in the upper. The rest of the church has barrel vaulting.

Two distinct kinds of masonry appear on the exterior; one consisting of courses of roughly cut stones, the other of coursed stones carefully dressed and set. They correspond to the foundation and to the restoration of 1117 respectively. The masonry of the cupola suggests an alteration of a later date than that year.

[1] The chronology of the Counts of Barcelona is taken from De Bofarull y Mascaró, *Los Condes de Barcelona vindicados, y cronologia y genealogia de los Reyes de España; Tabla cronologica.*

[2] *Anales de la Corona de Aragon*, vol. i, fol. 12, 13.

[3] De Bofarull y Mascaró, op. cit., vol. i, pp. 47-63.

[4] Yepes, op. cit., vol. iv, fol. 362. Diago, *Historia de los victoriosissimos antiguos Condes de Barcelona*, fol. 73, 83. *España sus monumentos y artes*, &c.; Piferrer, Pi Margall, *Cataluña*, vol. i, pp. 218-225.

[5] Op. cit., vol. ii, pp. 138-144.

The doorway in the west front is unquestionably of the XII century. This is shown by the stonework exactly like that of the restoration of 1117; by its advanced form; by the spurs at the base of the shafts, a feature which did not come into existence till the end of the X century.[1] The presence of the inscription given by Puig y Cadafalch, and assigned on epigraphical grounds to the X century, must be explained by the fact that the lintel on which it is engraved had been used over again. The round window at the top of the gable is obviously an insertion later than Guitart's restoration.

The decoration of the principal apse with an arched corbel course broken by lesenas, warns us that this feature, created at Ravenna though Roman inspiration,[2] and not in the East, as is still so often stated in defiance of the evidence, while it did not cross the Alps till after the epoch of about the year 1000,[3] had reached the shores of Catalonia a century earlier, where, previous to the close of the X century, the walls of churches appear to have been unrelieved by any ornament.[4] It has every appearance of having been brought thither by the Lombard master builders, who have left so many traces of their presence in Spain.[5] San Pablo, the oldest part of which appears to go back to the last years of the IX or the first of the X century, seems to provide the earliest instance of the feature in Catalonia. And the domical vaulting in the church shows that the pointed barrel vault of Santa Maria at Tarrasa is later than 1112.

The Church of San Pedro de las Puellas at Barcelona.—Its history is as follows. Louis the Pious, during his siege of Barcelona in 801, erected in his fortified camp a small church dedicated to St. Saturninus. After the capture of the city he founded a Benedictine monastery in his camp, under the invocation of St. Peter. In 945 Wilara, Bishop of Barcelona (937-957), consecrated the church of St. Peter in the presence of Count Suniario (912-954) and his family; and on this occasion it was enriched with new and large endowments.

Six years after Al-Mansur's devastation of Barcelona (985) the monks returned to the monastery, which had been sacked and burned, nothing but the walls being left, and set to work to restore, or rather rebuild it, for the operations,

[1] Rivoira, op. cit. (Loescher), vol. i, p. 291; (Hoepli), pp. 220, 221; (Heinemann), vol. i, p. 181.

[2] Ibid. (Hoepli), pp. 36, 37; (Heinemann), vol. i. pp. 36, 37.

[3] Ibid. (Loescher), vol. ii, pp. 49, 55, 56, 389, 575; (Hoepli), pp. 355, 356, 361, 579, 707; (Heinemann), vol. ii, pp. 32, 36, 214, 312.

[4] Puig y Cadafalch, op. cit., vol. ii, pp. 91, 92.

[5] Ibid., vol. ii, p. 78.

which must have been extensive, were still going on in 1010. As the record of the first consecration had been lost, a re-consecration took place in 1147.[1]

This story is confirmed by the existing church. It has a transverse chapel, with rude unraised cross vaulting formed of undressed stone and rubble and supported by angle piers, one of which has been tampered with. The untouched piers have abaci carved with scrolls, interlacing which sometimes is studded, palmettes with interlacing springing from the base. The work is of mediocre design, and all in shallow relief without undercutting. One abacus has a barbarous human face. Vaulting, carving, everything in the building, suggests a date earlier than that of San Pedro; and whether it is a chapel, or the narthex of the original church (as Puig y Cadafalch thinks), it is certainly older than the church to which it is attached, and may be regarded as work of the time of Louis the Pious, and forming part of his chapel of St. Saturninus.

When I saw San Pedro it was in course of being stripped and restored after the fire of 1909. The plan is that of a cross with only three arms more or less preserved. In the interior the salient angles are provided with two columns each surmounted, in the cases where they survive, by Pre-Lombardic cubical capitals carved with leaves packed into shells, of fanciful form and rude treatment, the backs ribbed—recalling the capitals of the ancient ciborium in the church at San Giorgio in Valpolicella (712-740),[2] and generally the ancient continuous capitals in SS. Felice e Fortunato near Vicenza (985);[3]—with roses of rude form like wheels, and birds taking the place of the flower on the abacus; with a curious figure of a serpent, a chain, &c. These capitals, which one would say were of Lombardic workmanship, are surmounted by abaci moulded like a cornice (Figs. 271, 272, p. 299). The bases, which are also rude, stand on plinths, and have a torus, in some cases with a fillet, in others with a shallow cyma. From these columns spring the arches which carry the drum of the cupola.

The walls, where original, are of coursed stone with fairly good masonry. In the arms of the cross, where the original barrel vaults survive, the latter are constructed with dressed stones of various sizes. The crossing is covered

[1] Diago, op. cit., fol. 50, 51, 74, 75, 83. Yepes, op. cit., vol. iii, fol. 345-348. De Bofarull y Mascaró, op. cit., vol. i, pp. 56, 57. *España, sus monumentos y artes*, &c.; Piferrer, Pi Margall, *Cataluña*, vol. i, pp. 216-218. Puig y Cadafalch, op. cit., vol. ii, pp. 54, 55, 88, 94, 113-120.

[2] Rivoira, op. cit. (Loescher), vol. i, Fig. 251; (Hoepli), Fig. 154; (Heinemann), vol. i, Fig. 190.

[3] Ibid. (Loescher), vol. i, pp. 290-292; (Hoepli), pp. 219-221; (Heinemann), vol. i, pp. 180-182.

by a cupola of elliptical form as it rises from an oblong. Later it was surmounted by a bell-tower. The pendentives are hood-shaped, composed of materials different from those in the ancient parts of the church, and not older than the XII century.

All that is left of the original church of San Pedro belongs to one time, with the exception of the cupola. Hence it must have been rebuilt after the devastation of 985. This explains the fact noted by Puig y Cadafalch that the masonry in the ancient part of the church is superior to that of most of the buildings of the first half of the X century in the district. The capitals belong precisely to the close of that century.

From our examination of this church we may infer that the cupola carried on hood-shaped pendentives had not yet made its appearance in the capital of Catalonia when the epoch of about the year 1000 was reached.

The Church of San Pedro at Tarrasa has the form of a Latin cross with a three-lobed apse, the side lobes having the shape of a trapezium inscribed in a horse-shoe arch. The three members are covered by two half domes and a central domical vault carried at the angles by two niches supporting vertical pieces of wall, which gradually merge in the circle of the vault. The pavement is of rough tessellated work, with a design of circles and squares enclosing crosses. The transept is covered in the middle part by a barrel vault, while the two arms or chapels have ramping half-barrel vaults. But it is not the original transept, of which there are only traces. The nave, which has pointed barrel vaulting, has been rebuilt. The portal on the south side, which has retreating concentric arches unbroken by any impost, suggests a date later than the XI century. Puig y Cadafalch[1] puts it at the end of the XII or the beginning of the next century.

On the exterior, the apse, the oldest and most interesting part, has a facing of small stone cubes in courses, exactly like that in the neighbouring churches of San Miguel and Santa Maria. The two re-entrant angles between the lobes are strengthened by triangular buttresses. At the present time the apse is kept up by heavy rectangular buttresses which, if they are a necessity, are also a disfigurement (Fig. 273, p. 299).

This brief statement shows that the church was built at the same time as San Miguel and Santa Maria, viz. at the end of the IX century. The

[1] Op. cit., vol. i, p. 318.

FIG. 271.—Barcelona. San Pedro de las Puellas. Capital (X cent.).

FIG. 272.—Barcelona. San Pedro de las Puellas. Capital (X cent.).

FIG. 273.—Tarrasa. San Pedro (IX, and XII or XIII cents.).

Fig. 274.—Toledo. El Cristo de la Luz (Visigothic period and X, XI-XII, and XV cents.).

view which I take is confirmed by the sort of reredos to the altar formed by two tiers of arches, which has lately been discovered in the central lobe of the apse. I do not find this feature of decorative blank arcading high up in the interior of the principal apse of a church before the date of Theodulf's church at Germigny des Prés (801-806).

THE CHURCH OF EL CRISTO DE LA LUZ AT TOLEDO.—I examined this building during the investigations made in 1910, and therefore under excellent conditions for fairly intimate study. It consists of two parts: the older, supposed to belong to the time of Athanagild (554-567), who made Toledo the capital of the Gothic kingdom in Spain;[1] the other, an addition made by Archbishop Bernard (1086-1124) after the recovery of Toledo (1085), and remodelled in the XV century by Cardinal Mendoza. Our attention will be devoted to the former.

It forms a square block, orientated to the south-west and north-east, measuring internally about 6.60 by 6 m. (21 ft. 8 in. by 19¾ ft.), and divided into nine bays by means of four marble columns of ancient origin, unequal in height and diameter (Fig. 274, p. 300).

Three of the capitals are original; the fourth is due to restoration. Of the former, one, rude alike in form, design, and execution, is encircled by arches framing leaves or plants, above which is a cable moulding surmounted by an abacus, out of the angles of which four projections are cut, the flower being represented by some kind of plant or other object. The second is of Corinthian type, and adorned with leaves of water plants. The third has been damaged, but is of the same type and has similar leaves to the last. The lower range of leaves, however, has been cut off in order to make the capital fit the shaft.

From the isolated columns and wall-piers spring longitudinal, transverse, and wall-arches, all of horse-shoe form. The bays which surround the centre are of two stories, the upper being lighted by cusped openings in the outer and inner walls; and the vaults which cover them have intersecting bands recalling those at Cordova.

Above the central bay rises a drum which passes from the square to the internal octagon by the aid of four small vaults at the angles. It is closed above by a banded or ribbed vault.

[1] PUIG Y CADAFALCH, op. cit., vol. i, pp. 347, 348.

On the south side may be noticed in the upper story a blank arcade with one horse-shoe arch and two intersecting trefoil arches.

The exterior of the north wall is decorated in its upper stage by a range of blank horse-shoe arches framed by three-lobed arches (Fig. 275, p. 303). The western face is treated with intersecting arches (Fig. 276, p. 304).

The original structure of the outer walls, which is about 50 cm. (1 ft. 7½ in.) thick, is composed of courses of stone alternating with bands of fragmentary brick, and is pierced by small rectangular windows and loopholes. On the eastern side, where the XI and XV century addition begins, traces are preserved of two early round arches which have been altered later and converted into the horse-shoe form. This original structure of the wall is very important, for on the strength of it we may form an approximate conjecture about the date of the building.

In origin it was, perhaps, merely a cella, with unrelieved walls both within and without, and a roof. The plaster which covers the walls rising above the columns within, and also the half wall-piers, prevented me from verifying the truth of this conjecture. The rudeness of the masonry, and the use of ancient bricks, point to a period later than the Hispano-Roman; in other words, to the Visigothic age.

After the capitulation of Toledo, due, it was said, to a conspiracy of the Jews against the Visigoths[1]—a reversal of their former opposition to the Prophet and his doctrines at Medina[2]—and the establishment of Moslem rule by Tarik (711 or 712), the chapel was divided by columns, covered with a ceiling, and turned into a mosque, one late Roman capital being used, two being made on purpose, viz. that with the arcade and the unmutilated one with plain leaves, while the fourth is a modern copy. In 980 it was restored by the Moorish architect, Musa ibn Ali, as is stated by the inscription on the front.[3] It was then that the building was completely remodelled, nothing being left of the previous structure except the outer walls and the isolated columns. Inside, the walls were lined with arches, while the exterior was covered with a brick facing in order to strengthen the building and enable it to receive vaulting. The three doors on the north were also made.

[1] *The Cambridge Medieval History*, vol. ii, pp. 180, 181; ALTAMIRA Y CREVEA, *Spain under the Visigoths*.

[2] Ibid., vol. ii, pp. 314-321; BEVAN, *Mahomet and Islām*.

[3] LAMPÉREZ Y ROMEA, op. cit., vol. i, pp. 177-179.

FIG. 275.—Toledo. El Cristo de la Luz from the north-east (Visigothic period and X, XI–XII, and XV cents.).

FIG. 276.—Toledo. El Cristo de la Luz. Details of decoration of the front (X cent.).

FIG. 278.—Toledo. Puerta Visagra (IX cent.).

FIG. 277.—Toledo. Puerta Visagra (IX cent.).

FIG. 279.—Saragossa. Castle of Aljaferia. Arch in the Mosque (XI cent.).

FIG. 280.—Cordova. The Great Mosque. Entrance to the Mihrab (961-976).

FIG. 281.—Granada. The Alhambra (XIII and XIV cents.).

FIG. 282.—Seville. The Alcazár (XIV cent.).

FIG. 283.

FIG. 284.

FIG. 286.

FIG. 285.

FIGS. 283, 284, 285, 286.—Madrid. National Archaeological Museum. Capitals (756-1031).

FIG. 287.—Toledo. Puerta del Sol (XIII or XIV cent.).

Fig. 288.—Monreale. Cathedral (1174).

FIG. 289.—Palermo. Cathedral (1185).

FIG. 291.—Amalfi. Camposanto or 'Paradiso' of the Cathedral (XIII cent.).

Fig. 290.—Durham Cathedral. South aisle looking east (1093-1133).

FIG. 292.—Amalfi. Camposanto or 'Paradiso' of the Cathedral. Supports with inscription (XIII cent.).

FIG. 293.—Toledo. Santa Eulalia (559).

The view here taken is confirmed by the inscription referred to, which states that the mosque was rebuilt and restored in its upper part.

The Cristo de la Luz has a number of lessons to impart. They are as follows:—

(1) The two semicircular arches of the original structure, revealed by the recent operations, show that the horse-shoe arch was not in use at Toledo in Visigothic and early Mohammedan times. The form does not seem to have gained a footing quickly in Toledo or to have been in regular use after 711. Thus in the ancient Puerta Visagra, lately reopened, which I had an opportunity of studying during its restoration, the horse-shoe arch, whether of round or pointed form, is not used exclusively, and the semicircular arch also occurs (Figs. 277, 278, pp. 304, 305). The gate is dated in the IX century, but it must be later than the years 814-15 or 872-73, 879, for the pointed horse-shoe arch was used for the first time in construction, outside Asia Minor, at one of those dates, in the Nilometer at Roda and the mosque of Tulun at Cairo.

(2) The intersecting blank arcading used as an architectural decoration for a wall is the earliest instance of ascertained date that I have met with. I may take this opportunity to correct what I have said elsewhere about its application, under a different form, in the cathedral of Durham, which was rebuilt in 1093.[1]

Its origin is to be sought in the triple vestibule of the mihrab of Hakam II (961-976) in the mosque of Cordova. An instance of earlier date, or else contemporary with that at Toledo, would be afforded by the exquisite mosque of the castle of Aljaferia at Saragossa, if it could be proved to possess an antiquity which in my opinion does not belong to it. The view has been held that it was built in the IX century, but Puig y Cadafalch[2] puts its date in the X, and Saladin[3] in the XI century. Anyone who compares the complicated decoration of the arch shown in Fig. 279, p. 306, with the still restrained treatment of the entrance to the mihrab in the mosque of Cordova (Fig. 280, p. 306), will at once see that the art of Aljaferia is in its decadence: an art which descended to the trifling forms of the age of the reconquest, illustrated by the mosque of Cordova, the Alhambra at Granada (XIII and XIV centuries)

[1] Rivoira, op. cit. (Loescher), vol. ii, pp. 444, 469, 470; (Hoepli), pp. 610, 629, 630; (Heinemann), vol. ii, pp. 238, 253, 254.

[2] Op. cit., vol. ii, p. 551.

[3] *Manuel d'Art musulman*, vol. i, p. 218

(Fig. 281, p. 307), and the Alcazár at Seville (XIV century) (Fig. 282, p. 308). And consequently he will be inclined to date the mosque at Saragossa after the epoch of about 1000, and before the year 1118.

The mosque at Saragossa is of square plan, and within has two tiers of blank arcading, partly simple and partly intersecting. The upper story passes from the square to the octagon by means of small angle arches. Originally there was a cupola, traces of which exist above the present ceiling. The arcading on the ground floor still retains some of the marble shafts supporting the arches, with tall Corinthianesque capitals worked with the drill, recalling some of the capitals ascribed to the epoch of the caliphate of Cordova (756-1031), now collected in the National Archaeological Museum at Madrid (Figs. 283, 284, 285, 286, p. 309).

I do not cite the decorative intersecting arcading on the western face of the famous Puerta del Sol (Gate of the Sun) at Toledo (Fig. 287, p. 310), because it is now recognized that it was added in a renovation of the structure, in the so-called 'Mudejar' style (style of the Moorish subjects), after the recovery of the city in 1085.[1] It may have taken place in the XIII or XIV century.[2]

The most extensive and noblest expression of this decorative feature is to be found in Sicily where, to judge by the important monuments which survive, it was first used in the cathedral of Cefalù (begun in 1133),[3] and then in those of Monreale (founded in 1174),[4] where it attained its greatest development (Fig. 288, p. 311), and Palermo (begun in 1185) (Fig. 289, p. 312).[5]

Before this it had been used in a restricted way in Durham cathedral (begun in 1093) (Fig. 290, p. 313), and also in that of Norwich before the year 1119. Hence it is possible that the Normans, after importing it from Spain into England, carried it with them to their new kingdom of Sicily, where, owing to the greater wealth of the country and a finer artistic sense, it assumed the most attractive forms. From Sicily the craftsmen of the Gulf of Salerno brought it to their homes, transforming its purely decorative nature into a form at once constructive and decorative, and producing the characteristic picturesque cloisters with pointed intersecting arcades: of the former Capuchin convent in the old Cistercian monastery, now the Albergo dei Cappuccini outside Amalfi; of the

[1] IBN EL ATHIR (Fagnan), *Annales du Maghreb*, p. 480.

[2] ALTAMIRA Y CREVEA, *Historia de España y de la civilisación española*, vol. i, p. 547.

[3] PIRRO, Sicilia sacra, vol. ii, p. 426.

[4] Ibid., op. cit., vol. i, p. 397.

[5] Ibid., op. cit., vol. i, p. 127.

unnamed abbey, now the Albergo della Luna, in the environs of the same city; and of San Domenico at Salerno, all of them, apparently, belonging to the XIII century. Another instance is the Camposanto or 'Paradiso' of the cathedral at Amalfi, constructed by order of the Archbishop Filippo Augustariccio (1266-1292) between 1266 and 1268 (Figs. 291, 292, pp. 312, 314).[1] This cemetery cloister has lately been ascribed to a certain Guilio de Stefano (1103) on the strength of an inscription carved on a pair of conjoined pulvins belonging to it, which reads: 'Io Giulio de Stefano Napolitano Māmoraro N.D. MCIII.'[2] But the linguistic forms of the inscription, the work of a semi-literate person who expresses 'Anno Domini' by N.D., cannot be earlier than the XIII century. Besides, the forms *Io* and *Giulio* with which it starts, are enough to suggest doubts of its genuineness. As a matter of fact, such forms do not occur in contemporary documents, and are inadmissible according to linguistic criteria. It is not impossible that the C may be an Arabic 6, which De Stefano put in the middle of Roman numerals; and in that case the date will be 1603. Such are the views of Professors P. Kehr, E. Monaci, and R. Lanciani, expressed in answer to inquiries of mine on the subject. For myself, I may add that the year may even be 1703, when there was a restoration of the cathedral of Amalfi; and the author of the inscription may have been one of the marble workers employed thereon—not, however, one of the superior ones, whose names and origins have been preserved.[3]

(3) The capitals lend themselves to various suggestions and observations which modify recent attempts to attribute several kinds of this architectural member to the Visigothic period. These observations and suggestions are intended to call the attention of archaeologists and writers on architectural and artistic antiquities to the subject, for in these attributions it seems to me that a false track has been followed and is still persisted in.

Let us take the two which fit their columns, and were, apparently, carved expressly for the building. They were made either on the erection of the Visigothic edifice—supposing, that is, that the cella was at that time divided into three aisles, which is not my view—or when, after the capitulation of the city, the chapel was turned into a mosque.

In the first case we have before us a product of the Visigothic age; in the second a work modelled after the fashion of that age, it being reasonable to

[1] CAMERA, *Memorie storico-diplomatiche dell' antica città e ducato di Amalfi*, vol. i, pp. 28-30.

[2] BAEDEKER, *Southern Italy and Sicily*, 1912, p. 204.

[3] CAMERA, op. cit., vol. i, pp. 30, 31.

ascribe it to a carver of the time of Roderic (709-711) who passed into the service of his new masters. And what is more, we have to deal with a work executed in the Visigothic capital, where the best craftsmen were likely to be found. The forms of the capitals produced in the centre of Hispano-Gothic life are here seen to be what we should expect in the Visigothic period: on the one hand a barbaric treatment of the decadent Roman Corinthian capital, with leaves of water plants; on the other an extravagant version of the Roman Composite capital. Thus, the Corinthianesque specimens in Santa Eulalia (Fig. 293, p. 314) and San Sebastián (Fig. 294, p. 319) at Toledo, erected in 559 and 602 respectively, and afterwards remodelled as we see them,[1] belong to that period. Again, in San Miguel at Tarrasa, the two rude capitals of Composite derivation, and the unmutilated Corinthian ones which I ascribe to the V or VI century, are usually regarded as Visigothic.

The Visigothic period saw a deterioration of the already degraded work of the Roman decadence. I believe the view to be mistaken that, because the Iberian peninsula produced, from Paulus Orosius, who flourished in the days of Honorius (395-423) and witnessed the transformation of the nation from Roman to Gothic, down to Isidore of Beja (VIII century), who assisted at its transformation from Gothic to Arabic, writers of reputation, among whom the first place was taken by that 'doctor Hispaniae et lumen Ecclesiae,' St. Isidore, Bishop of Seville (599-636), it therefore also gave birth to craftsmen who, in their own sphere, were their equals in capacity. At that period literature and art were not on the same level in the countries dominated by the Barbarians. When the architectural genius of Julianus created San Vitale at Ravenna (526-547) (Fig. 295, p. 323), and Cassiodorus extolled the glories of the new style,[2] neither Cassiodorus himself (†562) nor Boethius (†524) had produced any intellectual equivalent of the lofty conception of Julianus. Julianus, as I have shown elsewhere,[3] was a member of the Ravennate family of the Argentarii which is mentioned in an inscription of the reign of Tiberius Constantinus (578-582), formerly in the church of San Zaccaria, ten miles from Ravenna, but now inserted in the wall of the Sala Lapidaria of the archiepiscopal palace (Fig. 296, p. 319). It has been suggested that his son Antonius—'Antonius filius Juliani Argentarii'—may be referred to in the mutilated inscription recently discovered

[1] Lampérez y Romea, op. cit., vol. i, pp. 210-213.

[2] *Mon. Germ. hist.; Auctores antiquissimi*, vol. xii; *Variae*, lib. vii, form. xv.

[3] Rivoira, op. cit. (Hoepli), pp. 72, 73; (Heinemann), vol. i, pp. 64, 65.

FIG. 294.—Toledo. San Sebastián (602).

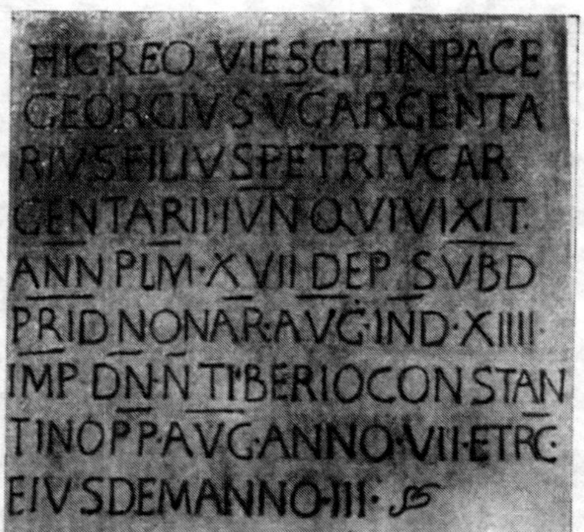

FIG. 296.—Ravenna. Sala Lapidaria in the Archiepiscopal Palace. Epitaph of Georgius Argentarius.

FIG. 297.—Ravenna. San Vitale (526-547).

FIG. 298.—Constantinople. SS. Sergius and Bacchus (527-532).

FIG. 299.—Constantinople. St. Sophia (532-537).

FIG. 300.—Constantinople. St. Sophia (532-537).

near San Vittore at Ravenna, which has been dated in 547 and has had its missing parts completed.[1]

For San Vitale, whatever may be said to the contrary, remains for ever, with its singular, graceful, harmonious form, the first building of central plan, octagonal both within and without, arched and vaulted in every part, which was erected for Christian worship in the first five centuries of our era. If the reader will not make the pilgrimage to Ravenna and Constantinople, as I have done again and again, in order to satisfy himself of the truth of what I say by an actual comparison of San Vitale with its nearly contemporary fellow in the Byzantine world, the church of SS. Sergius and Bacchus (527-532), let him look at Figs. 297 and 298 (pp. 320, 321), and he will have no difficulty in perceiving the heaviness of the latter from an architectural point of view, emphasized as it is by the architrave treatment of the lower story. This heaviness is not confined to SS. Sergius and Bacchus, but is also a feature of Justinian's church of St. Sophia (Figs. 299, 300, p. 322), which I am not alone in thinking heavy and ungraceful.[2] That is due to its original sin of being the offspring of the tepidarium of the Roman Thermae.[3] Its magnificent effect was produced, as it is still produced, by its internal decorations.

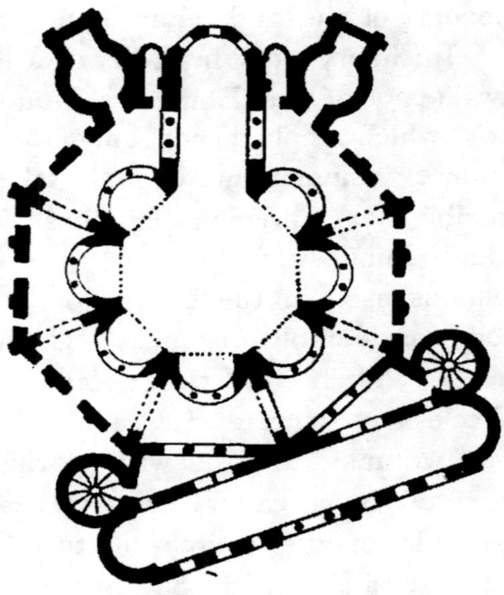

FIG. 295.—Ravenna. San Vitale. Plan (526-547).

Then if we pass from the incomparable San Vitale at Ravenna and the original San Lorenzo at Milan (VI century) to the noble but still inferior art of ornamental carving, we must not suppose that because Corinthianesque and Composite capitals of fair design and execution for that age were made for the crypt of Jouarre (653), therefore results of similar quality, and what is more, of identical style, were produced in Spain, or, for the matter of that, anywhere else. That did not occur in Italy, or in Germany, or in Great Britain; nor

[1] R. Accademia dei Lincei, *Notizie degli scavi di antichità*, 1908, pp. 163-165; MURATORI, *Ravenna: Iscrizione cemeteriale cristiana del secolo VI.*

[2] JACKSON, *Byzantine and Romanesque Architecture*, vol. i, p. 100 (quoting C. R. Cockerell).

[3] RIVOIRA, op. cit. (Loescher), vol. i, pp. 71, 72; (Hoepli), p. 76; (Heinemann), vol. i, p. 66.

did it take place in the Iberian peninsula either. Therefore a number of well-executed capitals, which Spanish writers have ascribed to the Visigothic period, must really have a different set of dates assigned to them. Thus, for instance, the two capitals, one Corinthian and the other Composite, of the portal in the front of San Pablo del Campo at Barcelona, have evidently been made on purpose for the shafts which support them, and are clearly of the same date as the impost cornice above them and the rest of the carving on the front of the church, that is to say, of the year 1117. The capitals produced at Barcelona in the Visigothic age were of a very different character. They had stiff, rude, plain leaves, like the two of Corinthianesque type which form the supports of the high altar in the cathedral.

In Spain, after the Edict of Milan (313), and certainly after the very severe laws (415) of the Emperors Honorius and Theodosius II against Paganism, laws which applied not only to Africa, but to the whole of the Roman Empire,[1] columns and capitals taken from heathen buildings were used, when possible, for Christian churches. The practice still went on in the days of King Chindaswinth (642-649). Yepes[2] states that the numerous marble columns used in the church of San Román at Hornija (646), were brought from considerable distances. Columns of ancient origin were also employed in the church of St. Leocadia at Toledo, built by Sisebut (612-621)—'Ecclesiam sanctae Leocadiae Toleti miro opere fabricavit'[3]—supposing that we may connect with it the portion of a spirally fluted column, surmounted by a capital with leaves of the *Acanthus spinosus*, standing near the side of the church of the Cristo de la Vega occupying the site of St. Leocadia, which had previously been rebuilt by Archbishop John III (1248).[4] In consequence, sculptors had little to do, and their work became poorer and poorer. This explains the rude character of the two capitals above referred to in the cathedral of Barcelona, which was in existence by 540, when a council was held in it.[5]

* * *

We have seen that, with one exception, all the religious buildings in Spain

[1] Haenel, *Codices Gregorianus Hermogenianus Theodosianus*, lib. xvi, tit. x, col. 1623, 1624.

[2] Op. cit., vol. ii, fol. 184.

[3] *Chronicon rerum gestarum in Hispaniis;* Rodericus, *De Sisebuto rege*, lib. ii, cap. xvii. Flórez, op. cit., vol. vi, p. 312.

[4] Mariana, op. cit., p. 308.

[5] Flórez, op. cit., vol. xxix, p. 280.

ascribed to the Visigothic age fail to make good their claims; and that in the one authentic case, the church of Elche, the round arch is used. That arch was also used in the original Cristo de la Luz at Toledo, which has been claimed as Visigothic; and the legend of the systematic use of the horse-shoe arch in these lands at that period is thus discredited.

Let us now try to get rid of this delusion by an examination of the oldest churches in the kingdom of Asturias. For in these, the Christians who had escaped from Moslem fanaticism and tyranny, instead of preserving religiously, as would have been natural, the supposed Visigothic tradition of the horse-shoe arch, maintained, on the contrary, that which had really been the usage in Visigothic times, viz. the round arch. After the rout of Janda (711), followed by the flooding of the Iberian peninsula with Moslem armies, when Toledo had surrendered, and the defeat of Segoyuela, with the supposed death of the last Visigothic king, had taken place (713), the conspirators whose treachery had led to the catastrophe, the great mass of the indifferent and of the cowardly for whom slavery has no terrors, and the evil genius of the time-servers, who in every country and every age have always known how to profit by the work of others without risk to themselves but to their own advantage and the ruin of their fellow-men, all accepted voluntarily the yoke of the invaders whom they had invited, aided, and welcomed.

Those, on the other hand, to whom the enslaving of their country was hateful, and who wanted to preserve their faith uncontaminated and free, after a fruitless struggle with the invaders sought refuge in the mountains of the north of the peninsula, especially in Asturias, where Pelayo (Pelagius) (718-737) raised the standard of independence and started that long crusade which only ended with the capture of Granada in 1491, and whose victories were victories not only for Spain but for Catholicism. May this struggle of the champions of their country and of their creed for ever win the admiration of those who, like me, have realized and appreciated, whether in the records or amid the scenes and in presence of the monuments, that heroic enterprise and its far-reaching consequences.

With all his energies engaged in lowering the pride of the crescent, and in organizing and consolidating the new kingdom of Asturias, the hero of Covadonga (718), whose Roman name suggests that he was not of Gothic race, though he came of a Spanish family,[1] confined himself, so far as churches

[1] Oman, *The Dark Ages; European History*, 476-918, p. 507.

were concerned, to restoration.[1] Morales,[2] however, records the tradition that he was the builder of the now vanished church of St. Eulalia at Velamio in which both he and his wife, Gaudiosa, were buried.[3]

Favila (737-739) erected the church of the Holy Cross near Cangas de Onis,[4] which was rebuilt in 1632. The old church was seen by Morales, who has preserved a brief description of it. It was a hall of fair size, built of hewn stone, the outer facing having been renewed. The interior was whitewashed, and exhibited no decoration to attest the report of its magnificence given by some ancient authorities. In the chancel arch was inserted the dedicatory inscription of Favila, his wife, and their sons. Beneath was a crypt or chapel of the same size as the upper church, access to which was gained through a well.[5]

Alfonso the Catholic (739-756) was a strenuous restorer and builder of churches: 'basilicas plures construxit et instauravit.'[6] But no record of any church built by him has reached us except in the case of the monastery church of St. Peter at Villanueva standing on the banks of the Sella not far from Cangas, which tradition ascribed to him.[7] It has been rebuilt. Nor is there any authority for his erection (740) of the church and monastery of St. Mary at Covadonga,[8] which had been rebuilt when Morales[9] saw it, and was ascribed by him to Alfonso the Chaste, which was the local tradition.

Fruela I (756-768), the founder of Oviedo, where Fromestanus and Maximus had built a monastery with a church dedicated to St. Vincent,[10] appears to have erected the church of the Saviour and the Twelve Apostles, which is believed to have been of basilican plan and modest dimensions, and was provided with a narthex or sepulchral chapel where the unfortunate founder and his wife were buried. The basilica was rebuilt by Alfonso II. He also built on the confines of Galicia the important monastery of Samos, under the

[1] MIGNE, *Patr. lat.*, vol. cxxix, col. 1117; SEBASTIANUS, Salmatiensis episcopus, *Chronicon*.

[2] *La Coronica general de España*, lib. xiii., cap. vi.

[3] MIGNE, *Patr. lat.*, vol. cxxix, col. 1117; SEBASTIANUS, Salmatiensis episcopus, *Chronicon*.

[4] Ibid.

[5] MORALES, *La Coronica general de España*, lib. xiii, cap. ix. Ibid., *Viaje a los reynos de León, y Galicia*, &c., pp. 67-69.

[6] MIGNE, *Patr. lat.*, vol. cxxix, col. 1118; SEBASTIANUS, Salmatiensis episcopus, *Chronicon*.

[7] YEPES, op. cit., vol. iii, fol. 205. MORALES, *La Coronica general de España*, lib. xiii, cap. xv.

[8] RISCO, op. cit., vol. xxxvii, App. iii.

[9] *La Coronica general de España*, lib. xiii, cap. ii.

[10] RISCO, op. cit., vol. xxxvii, App. vi.

invocation of Saints Julian and Basilissa (759), which had been destroyed before the time of the Christian persecution under Abd al-Rahman II (822-852) and Mohammed I (852-886), and was more than once rebuilt.[1]

No building seems to have been erected in the featureless reign of Aurelio (768-774); except, perhaps, the vanished church of St. Martin at Langreo in the territory of Oviedo, in which he was buried.[2] The indolent Silo (774-783) built (774) the monastery of St. John (Santiañes) at Pravia, where he was buried.[3] The church suffered in 1639, in 1836, and in 1868, and all that is left are scanty remains of the nave and outer walls built of stones set in thick layers of mortar. These remains and the literary evidence tell us that it was of very small size; that it had a nave and aisles ending in three rectangular chapels, in which the arches sprang from stone spindle-shaped columns set against the walls; that it had a transept; and that the body of the church was divided by square piers with simple mouldings supporting low and mean round arches, above which was a wooden roof.[4] These facts are of great importance, as they give a clear indication of the poverty of these royal foundations in Asturias, and also, which is the chief point, of the traditional use of the semicircular arch.

It was in his reign that his supposed son, Adelgastro, with his wife, Brunhilda, founded (781) the now vanished monastery of Santa Maria la Real at Obona, twelve leagues from Oviedo.[5] We have no information of any buildings erected by the usurper Mauregato (783-789), or by the good Bermudo (789-791).

Then came the long and glorious reign of Alfonso II the Chaste (791-842). The capital was transferred to Oviedo, and he there carried out the important works recorded by the ancient chronicles and in documents.[6] Among these we may mention the rebuilding of the church of the Saviour, and the erection of the churches of Santa Maria, San Miguel, and San

[1] YEPES, op. cit., vol. iii, fol. 211-234. MORALES, *La Coronica general de España*, lib. xiii, cap. xviii.

[2] MIGNE, *Fatr. lat.*, vol. cxxix, col. 1119; SEBASTIANUS, Salmatiensis episcopus, *Chronicon.*

[3] RISCO, op. cit., vol. xxxvii, App. xv. YEPES, op. cit., vol. iii, fol. 255, 256.

[4] *España, sus monumentos y artes*, &c.; QUADRADO, *Asturias y León*, pp. 61, 62. LAMPÉREZ Y ROMEA, op. cit., vol. i, pp. 281-284.

[5] YEPES, op. cit., vol. iii, fol. 274-277. RISCO, op. cit., vol. xxxvii, App. v.

[6] MIGNE, *Patr. lat.*, vol. cxxix, col. 1120; SEBASTIANUS, Salmatiensis episcopus, *Chronicon.* Ibid., vol. cxxix, col. 1137; *Chronicon Albeldense.* RISCO, op. cit., vol. xxxvii, App. vii, xv. FLÓREZ, op. cit., vol. xvii, p. 286; *Chronicon del monge Silense.*

Tirso, and also of San Julián outside the walls: 'distantem a palatio quasi stadium unum.'[1] I may add that attention has recently been drawn to the churches of Oviedo and its neighbourhood.[2]

The Basilica of the Saviour at Oviedo.—The original structure of Fruela I having been partly ruined by the Moslems, Alfonso the Chaste proceeded to rebuild it with greater splendour, and entrusted the work to the architect Tioda.[3] The consecration took place in 802, and at some time between that year and 812 it became the cathedral.

It was a stone structure: 'templum Sancti Salvatoris cum XII Apostoles ex silice et calce mire fabricavit.'[4] It was orientated as usual, and stood on the site of the present cathedral, rebuilt by the Bishop Gutierre (1377- about 1389), but was smaller both in breadth and length. It had the plan of a basilica, with nave and aisles ending in three square apses, and a transept.[5]

The Church of St. Mary near St. Saviour at Oviedo stood to the north of the cathedral and adjoined it. It was destroyed by the Bishop Tomaso Reluz (1697-1706). The literary sources show that it was an orientated basilica with nave and aisles and a transept, in one arm of which was the principal entrance. At the east end were three rectangular chancels, and at the west was a narthex intended for royal burials: 'Etiam in occidentali parte huius venerandae domus aedem ad recondenda regum adstruxit corpora.'[6] The dimensions were 106 by 52 ft. The greatest height was 63 ft.

The body of the church and the transept had mean wooden roofs. The nave was divided from the aisles by three arches on either side supported by piers. The transept was divided from the nave and aisles by arches, above which rose its central portion. All these arches were semicircular. The structure at the west or narthex, set apart for burials, was low. It was connected with the church by a door; its dimensions were 20 by 12 ft., and it was lighted by a single loophole. Above it was an even lower gallery

[1] Migne, *Patr. lat.*, vol. cxxix, col. 1120; Sebastianus, Salmatiensis episcopus, *Chronicon.*

[2] *The Guardian*, Oct. 6th, 20th, 1909; Hutton, *Some Churches of Northern Spain.*

[3] Risco, op. cit., vol. xxxvii, p. 143.

[4] Migne, *Patr. lat.*, vol. cxxix, col. 1137; *Chronicon Albeldense.*

[5] Morales, *La Coronica general de España*, lib. xiii, cap. xxxii, xxxviii. Selgas, *Monumentos Ovetenses del siglo IX*, pp. 29-46.

[6] Migne, *Patr. lat.*, vol. cxxix, col. 1120; Sebastianus, Salmatiensis episcopus, *Chronicon.*

with a wooden roof. The fronts of the three chapels at the east end were decorated with six marble columns of ancient origin, bigger than the other six which supported the barrel vaults of the chapels.[1] Morales[2] says that the frontal arches of these chapels were rather like those in San Román at Hornija, and in the church of Bamba. At the present day the chancel of San Román has disappeared with the rest of the church. But the three chancels of the church of Bamba, a couple of leagues from Valladolid, still exist, which church was seen by Morales, though even in his time it was not the building erected by Receswinth (649-672),[3] and containing his tomb,[4] but the result of two reconstructions.[5] The arches in this case are of the horse-shoe form. Hence we may infer that the entrance arches of the three eastern chapels in St. Mary at Oviedo were also of that form.

Considering that in Alfonso the Chaste's churches at Oviedo, either still in existence or of which the description has been preserved, the round arch was used exclusively, with the one exception of St. Mary, this anomaly seems inexplicable. And we are obliged to ascribe it, either to an alteration of the east end of the church during the episcopate of Pelagius (1098-†1153), when, among other things, the altar in St. Mary was replaced by one of better design and larger size,[6] or else to a caprice or experiment of Tioda's, the architect of the royal churches, who may, perchance, have heard of the fame of the great mosque of Cordova, or even have seen it himself.

THE CHURCH OF SAN MIGUEL OR CÁMARA SANTA AT OVIEDO was erected to the south of St. Saviour, and was designed with two stories, the upper, reached by stairs ('ubi ascensio fit per gradus'),[7] being set apart for the custody of the relics, while the lower was used as a church under the invocation of St. Leocadia: 'fecit quoque Sanctae Leocadiae Basilicam fornicio opere cumulatam, super quam fieret domus, ubi celsiori loco Arca Sancta a fidelibus adoraretur.'[8] At

1 MORALES, *La Coronica general de España*, lib. xiii., cap. xxxviii. SELGAS, op. cit., pp. 68-88.

2 *Viaje a los reynos de León, y Galicia*, &c., p. 87.

3 YEPES, op. cit., vol. ii, fol. 306.

4 MIGNE, *Patr. lat.*, vol. cxxix, col. 1115; SEBASTIANUS, Salmatiensis episcopus, *Chronicon*.

5 LAMPÉREZ Y ROMEA, op. cit., vol. i, pp. 240, 241. *España, sus monumentos y artes*, &c.; QUADRADO, *Valladolid, Palencia y Zamora*, pp. 263-265.

6 RISCO, op. cit., vol. xxxviii, App. xl, p. 371.

7 Ibid.., vol. xxxvii, App. xv; PELAGIUS, Ovetensis episcopus, *Historia de Arcae Sanctae translatione, deque Sanctorum Reliquiis, quae in ea asservantur*.

8 FLÓREZ, op. cit., vol. xvii, p. 286; *Chronicon del monge Silense*.

the present day the church occupies the angle between the south arm of the cathedral transept and a side of the cloister.

The crypt or church of St. Leocadia, so far as one can see, is a rectangular chamber with walls of rubble. It has a rude semicircular unbroken barrel vault, barely 2.60 m. (8½ ft.) high at the crown. Originally it was lighted by very narrow windows, mere loopholes, splayed internally, in the side walls, and by one large window at the east end. The sanctuary is marked off only by the step in the floor.

The Cámara Santa, as its ancient parts show, consists of a square eastern sanctuary, attached to a rectangular cella (Fig. 301, p. 331). The sanctuary has a low barrel vault. Its frontal arch is carried by two marble columns of Roman origin. A pair of similar columns decorate the east window, which internally has an arch, but externally a square head with a rude brick relieving arch, just like the east window of the crypt below. Their capitals are Corinthianesque, with leaves packed into shells, of rude work, relief being produced by the drill, and recall an angle capital in San Julián de los Prados.

It has been suggested that the cella originally had a wooden roof;[1] and that, in any case, its present appearance is the result of a remodelling of the building which followed the pilgrimage to Oviedo of Alfonso VI, King of Castile and León (1073-1109). In support of this theory, the example of the Panteón de los Reyes at León, ascribed to Ferdinand I (1037-1065) (Fig. 302, p. 332), is adduced.[2] In my opinion, however, the present vault of the nave with its transverse bands has no connection with Alfonso, whose work was limited to making a new and larger relic chest.[3] It is really due to a remodelling of the entire building carried out, it appears to me, in the XIII century, in the course of which the walls were faced with arcading on the exterior, a cornice of figure corbels was added at the top, and the interior of the nave was richly decorated. This decoration consists of three arches—one at the east, one at the west, and the other in the middle—supported by pairs of statues of the Apostles standing on fantastic bases and surmounted by richly carved capitals, above which runs an impost cornice.

The Panteón de los Reyes at León, known as the chapel of Santa Catalina, is not contemporary either with the Benedictine church of San

[1] Selgas, op. cit., p. 65.

[2] Morales, *Viaje a los reynos de León, y Galicia*, &c., pp. 41, 42. Lampérez y Romea, op. cit., vol. i, pp. 316, 317.

[3] Risco, op. cit., vol. xxxviii, p. 84.

FIG. 301.—Oviedo. San Miguel or Cámara Santa (VIII or IX and XIII cents.).

FIG. 303.—León. San Isidoro (XII cent.).

Fig. 302.—León. Panteón de los Reyes or Chapel of Santa Catalina (XII cent.).

Fig. 304.—León. San Isidoro (XII cent.).

FIG. 305.—Oviedo. San Julián de los Prados. East end (VIII or IX cent.).

FIG. 306.—Chapel called the 'Temple of the Clitumnus' near Spoleto (IV cent.

FIG. 307.—Naranco. Santa Maria. North side (IX cent.).

Isidoro built 'de luto et latere' by Alfonso V (999-1027), King of León, or with the second church dating from its reconstruction in stone by Ferdinand I of Castile and León.[1] On the contrary, it is a work of the XII century, and, to be precise, of the reign of Alfonso VII (1126-1157), crowned Emperor of Spain in 1135, who rebuilt San Isidoro, entrusting the work to the master Petrus de Deo (otherwise Pedro de Deum Tamben or Petro Vitamben), and being present at the consecration of the new building, which is recorded in 1149 (Figs. 303, 304, pp. 331, 333).[2]

The following are the conclusions which I formed from an examination during the recent works of restoration in the ancient part of the east end. The Panteón de los Reyes is attached to the western end of Alfonso's church, and its unraised cross-vaulting and, still more, its capitals with their foliage of Pointed character and figures, show that it is of the same date as the church. If the carving at León be compared with the decorative work in the Cámara Santa at Oviedo, it is easy to see that the latter represents a more advanced art, especially the figures of the Apostles, which in some cases are full of expression, have excellent drapery, have lost the rigidity of the figures in San Isidoro, and are certainly later than the time of Alfonso VII: perhaps work of the XIII century, when the chapter-house of the cathedral of Oviedo was erected.

Before leaving San Miguel at Oviedo and the Panteón de los Reyes at León, I would call attention to the spurred bases in the latter. This feature would suffice by itself to date the building, for I have fully demonstrated that these angle spurs, invented in Italy in the X century, did not cross its borders till about the middle of the XI.[3]

THE CHURCH OF SAN TIRSO AT OVIEDO.—The building has suffered so much from alterations that only the general plan has been preserved. It is that of a basilica with nave and aisles divided by rude stone piers set at unequal intervals, from which round arches spring. In the easternmost bay, however, owing to the smaller span, the arch was made sufficiently pointed to

[1] YEPES, op. cit., vol. v, fol. 128-135.

[2] RISCO, op. cit., vol. xxxv, pp. 206, 207, 356. *España, sus monumentos y artes*, &c.; QUADRADO, *Asturias y León*, pp. 481, 482. LAMPÉREZ Y ROMEA, op. cit., vol. i, pp. 460-463.

[3] RIVOIRA, op. cit. (Loescher), vol. i, pp. 236, 251, 291, 292; vol. ii, pp. 83, 201, 395, 485, 569, 635-640, 644; (Hoepli), pp. 188, 220, 221, 274, 385, 582, 584, 596, 747-749; (Heinemann), vol. i, pp. 158, 181, 221; vol. ii, pp. 51, 100, 216, 225, 272, 306, 310, 321, 322, 340, 341, 343.

raise its crown to the same height as the others.[1] This irregularity is not surprising, for—and the point has not been noticed by anyone else—as far back as Imperial Roman times barrel vaults were given a pointed form, when, in order to make the height of rooms of varying size uniform, it was necessary to raise the crown of the vault in some of them. This is illustrated by the substructures of the villa known as 'Centroni' (III century) on the Via Latina near Rome, and by various chambers in the House of Tiberius on the Palatine.

There is no satisfactory explanation of the 'many angles' which the building is said to have presented: 'Basilicam quoque sancti Tirsi miro aedificio cum multis angulis fundamentavit.'[2]

In the rectangular sanctuary the triplet round-arched window is preserved. With its barbarous bases, rough brick arches, and capitals with rude packed leaves, it gives an idea of the better style of building and carving in the time of Alfonso the Chaste; for we know that in San Tirso, which was the Chapel Royal ('basilicam in honorem S. Martyris Tyrsi prope palatium condidit'),[3] the architect Tioda had displayed all the magnificence he knew: 'basilicam in memoriam S. Tyrsi condidit, cuius operis pulchritudinem plus praesens potest mirari quam eruditus scriba laudare.'[4]

The Church of San Julián de los Prados (Santullano) outside Oviedo has come down to us almost intact. The plan, published for the first time in 1904,[5] was a cruciform church, with nave and aisles, three rectangular eastern chapels, and a narthex in three divisions.

Within, the two-storied sanctuary has its sides and end embellished with blank arches springing from marble wall-columns and piers. The columns at the end stand on a continuous plinth; the others are partly buried by the raised pavement. The rude bases which are visible are Attic. The capitals, some of which are surmounted by an abacus, are Corinthianesque, having cauliculi and rude leaves with stiff turnover points, all in shallow carving. Here and there the drill has been used to give relief. They are inferior to those belonging to the east window in San Tirso.

[1] Selgas, op. cit., pp. 89-94.

[2] Migne, *Patr. lat.*, vol. cxxix, col. 1137, *Chronicon Albeldense.*

[3] Risco, op. cit., vol. xxxvii, App. xv.

[4] Migne, *Patr. lat.*, vol. cxxix, col. 1120; Sebastianus, Salmatiensis episcopus, *Chronicon.*

[5] Redondo, *Iglesias primitivas de Asturias*, pp. 35-44.

The two marble shafts forming part of the frontal piers of the sanctuary arch have geometrical decoration of pavement design, with compartments containing circles, rosettes, leaves, and plants, carved in shallow relief. The capitals have, among other things, leaves meant for those of the *Acanthus spinosus*, here and there treated with the drill.

The sanctuary and its side chapels all have semicircular barrel vaulting. The transept was designed with extended arms, each arm being represented by a chapel, of which only the northern survives. The nave is separated from the aisles by three arches on either side, supported by square piers. Originally both the body of the church and the transept had wooden roofs. The existing vaulting is an alteration. The tripartite vestibule also had a wooden roof originally.

The walls are built of roughly hewn stone; and dressed stones of various sizes, set horizontally, reinforce the exterior angles and the buttresses. The outside wall of the sanctuary and its chapels is strengthened by six buttresses. It contains five original windows of rectangular form, with brick relieving arches leaving a shallow recess. One window still has its original stone lattice. Below the gable is a three-light window, the middle division being higher than the sides. The dividing colonnettes have Corinthianesque capitals (Fig. 305, p. 334). The surviving north transept chapel also contains original windows with relieving arches.

The roofs were carried by large projecting brackets. The walls of the aisles have buttresses corresponding to the transverse arches of the transept and to the bays of the interior. The arches throughout are of semicircular form.

We may notice in this church, as in all those built by Alfonso II, the chancels of square form, and not semicircular in the Roman fashion. This form, which has been described as 'Visigothic and Asturian,' while others call it 'Celtic,' 'Irish,' 'Scotch,' or 'Saxon,' was really introduced by the Romans in imperial times. An instance is to be seen in Hadrian's villa at Tivoli, where the palace (125-135) contains a basilica with nave and aisles and a rectangular apse.[1] I think that it was adopted by Tioda because it was easy and simple to construct, and did not require materials specially prepared; but, above all, owing to want of experience in the difficult art of dome construction. Dome vaulting was, in fact, for a long time avoided in Asturias.

[1] R. Accademia dei Lincei, *Notizie degli Scavi*, 1906, fasc. 8; Reina, Barbieri, *Rilievo planimetrico e altimetrico di Villa Adriana*.

Ramiro I (842-850) rebuilt the church of Santa Maria at Naranco, and erected that of San Miguel at Lino on the slope of the ridge known as the Sierra de Naranco near Oviedo.

THE CHURCH OF SANTA MARIA AT NARANCO.—The name of the builder of the existing church is given by Sebastian, Bishop of Salamanca (880): 'Interea supradictus rex ecclesiam condidit in memoriam S. Mariae in latere montis Nurantii, distante ab Oveto duorum millia passuum, mirae pulchritudinis, perfectique decoris; et ut alia decoris eius taceam, cum pluribus centris forniceis sit concamerata, sola calce et lapide constructa, cui si aliquis aedificium consimilare voluerit, in Hispania non inveniet.'[1] This is confirmed by the much-discussed inscription on a fragmentary votive stone of 848 set in the 'mensa' of the altar in the church, and published by Canella y Secades,[2] which refers to Ramiro's reconstruction of it.

The church consists of two rectangular halls standing east and west, one above the other, each being prolonged at either end by two small rectangular bays. The lower church or crypt, which has an altar just below that in the presbytery above, is covered with low semicircular barrel vaulting springing from a plinth. The central portion is strengthened by transverse arches. The vaulting is constructed of roughly prepared stones, and the arches of dressed stone. There was an entrance at the west end, and two porches at the sides, only the northern of which survives. These were carried up so as to form two porches on the upper story, reminding one of the well-known chapel called the Temple of the Clitumnus near Spoleto (IV century) (Fig. 306, p. 334).[3] The porch on the south was reached by two flights of steps, which were seen by Morales.[4] The church is entered through the remaining north porch, approached by modern flights of steps (Fig. 307, p. 334), which has a barrel vault crossed by two arches corresponding to buttresses outside. Its three outer arches spring from columns bearing rude Corinthianesque capitals with leaves packed into shells, and others of cylindrical form decked with palm leaves of elementary design. The door which opens into the nave is later.

The nave or central rectangular space is not quite 4.20 m. (13 ft. 10 in.)

[1] MIGNE, *Patr. lat.*, vol. cxxix, col. 1122; *Chronicon.*

[2] CANELLA Y SECADES in *España, sus monumentos y artes*, &c.; QUADRADO, *Asturias y León*, p. 118.

[3] RIVOIRA, op. cit. (Heinemann), vol. ii, pp. 131, 132.

[4] *La Coronica general de España*, lib. xiii, cap. liii.

FIG. 308.—Naranco. Santa Maria. Nave and sanctuary (IX cent.).

FIG 309.—Naranco. Santa Maria. Western end (IX cent.).

FIG. 310.—Naranco. Santa Maria. Medallion in the nave (IX cent.).

FIG. 311.—Buddh Gaya. Carved post from the railing of a sacred enclosure (about II cent. B.C.).

wide, and its walls are lined with a continuous arcade, which is blank at the sides and open at the ends—an idea derived from San Julián de los Prados at Oviedo. It is covered by a barrel vault with transverse ribs carried by rude corbels (Fig. 308, p. 339). The annexes at either end also have the transverse arch and blank arcading round the walls. The one at the east formed the sanctuary, while the western one is thought to have been the choir (Fig. 309, p. 339).

The arches spring from clusters of twisted columns, piers with similar clusters attached to both faces, and single shafts. The capitals of the clustered supports are Ravennate pulvins with the corners cut off so as to form triangles, and are carved with triangles formed of cables, human figures, pairs of lions facing one another or the reverse. The capitals of the single shafts are Corinthianesque with leaves packed into shells, recalling those in San Julián de los Prados. The bases, consisting of a roll either plain or in the form of a cable, stand on a plinth.

The spandrel spaces between the arches are decorated with medallions either isolated or attached to bands suspended from the corbels which support the transverse arches of the vault. These medallions and bands are carved with scrolls, lions, crosses, arches framing figures of men (a sort of telamon supporting what looks like a squared stone), and armed horsemen (Fig. 310, p. 340). They remind one of the curious stone posts bearing medallions belonging to railings round sacred trees, pillars, stupas, and temples in India, e.g. those at Bharhut and Buddh Gaya (Figs. 311, 312, pp. 340, 343), ascribed to the II and III centuries B.C. respectively,[1] or to a date later than the time of Asoka (272-236 B.C.).[2] The Spanish carvings are in low relief, the scroll work and cables fairly well executed; but the lions, which seem to be copies from a single pattern, are flat and of poor design and execution. The men and horses are frightful caricatures.

The external facing of the walls is of irregularly coursed stone, roughly hewn; and at intervals corresponding to the transverse arches within occur buttresses measuring 50 by 30 cm. (1 ft. 7½ in. by 11½ in.), with shallow fluting. High up may be seen traces of windows with moulded arches springing from small Corinthianesque capitals; and below are windows with their round heads and jambs also moulded. In the western gable is a three-light window divided by shafts with capitals of leaves packed into shells and moulded arches. The original arches throughout the church are round.

[1] FERGUSSON, *History of Indian and Eastern Architecture*, p. 85.

[2] VINCENT A. SMITH, *A History of Fine Art in India and Ceylon*, pp. 67-73.

Such is Santa Maria—a truly singular structure. Its form led the monk of Silos (XII century) to believe that it had been built by Ramiro as a palace for himself, which was afterwards converted into a church.[1] The dedicatory inscription mentioned above is fatal to this story. And its novelty both in construction and decoration was at the time so surprising in Spain, that Sebastian of Salamanca believed it to be beyond the reach of imitation.

It is not difficult to understand Sebastian's wonder when we reflect that the internal decoration of the church has no parallel, so far as I know, in any other church of that century; and that it was constructed of masonry throughout, whereas, as late as the reign of Alfonso the Chaste, churches had still in part wooden roofs. Vaulting was, perhaps, adopted by Ramiro I in consequence of the raids of the Normans, who had landed at Corunna in 843 and been defeated by him there.[2] It was well known that these terrible corsairs, who were far more destructive than the Moslems, burned every church which fell into their hands. The reasons were all the more convincing as Santa Maria de Naranco did not stand in a walled town. And so it was that the church, together with San Miguel de Lino, led the way in vault construction in the Asturias. In those lands the art of vault construction was little practised, and its statical principles barely known. The fact is brought home to us if we remember that in Santa Maria, with barrel vaults of such moderate span and walls quite 90 cm. (nearly 3 ft.) thick, the architect did not feel that his work was safe until he had strengthened the walls, at the points where the transverse arches occurred, by solid buttresses.

The Church of San Miguel at Lino was built by Ramiro I,[3] and it is mentioned in two documents of Ordoño I and Alfonso III.[4] Though it has lost a part, it is possible from what is left, with the help of facts mentioned by Morales,[5] to form an idea of what it was like originally. It consisted of a square block divided into eight bays, of which a central and larger one, flanked by two smaller ones on either side, rose into the cupola; while at the west end were three bays in two stories. A chancel projected at the

[1] Flórez, op. cit., vol. xvii, p. 290; *Chronicon.*

[2] Lafuente, op. cit., vol. ii, p. 248.

[3] Migne, *Patr. lat.*, vol. cxxix, col. 1138; *Chronicon Albeldense.* Flórez, op. cit., vol. xvii, pp. 289, 290; *Chronicon del monge Silense.*

[4] Risco, op. cit., vol. xxxvii, App. x, xi.

[5] *La Coronica general de España*, lib. xiii, cap. liii.

FIG. 312.—Buddh Gaya. Carved post from the railing of a sacred enclosure (about II cent. B.C.).

FIG. 313.—Lino. San Miguel. Details from one of the jambs of the door (IX cent.)

FIG. 314.—Lino. San Miguel. Abacus and carving on arch (IX cent.).

FIG 315.—Lino. San Miguel. Base of column (IX cent.).

east end. The surviving parts are the three western bays, and half of the central bay with two out of the four lateral ones.

The three western bays, which are only about 9 m. (28 ft. 9 in.) in breadth on the outside, consist of a vestibule with two lateral annexes containing the stairs to the upper floor. The vestibule is entered by a wide arched door, the jambs of which are carved with figure subjects framed by bands of imbricated leaves varied with rosettes, pine cones, and cable borders. The figure representations consist of panels containing three human figures, separated by another with the curious scene of a man taking a somersault between a gaoler who whips him and a lion preparing to devour him. The whole is carved in very low and flat relief; and the figures are very elementary (Fig. 313, p. 343). The jambs are surmounted by an impost cornice formed of a waved band bordered by a pair of cables and fillets. These carvings have been thought to show the style of the XII century,[1] but the figure carving in the north-west of the Iberian peninsula was, at that date, of another character, as may be seen by that in San Isidoro and the Panteón de los Reyes at León.

The staircases on either side of the vestibule lead to a gallery with a chamber on either side. Originally the stairs went on up to the bell-tower, as we learn from Morales. This bell-tower must have been formed by continuing upwards the wall of the middle section of the west front.

The two bays which flank the central one, and also those at the west end, including the staircases, are barrel vaulted. The arches in the interior are supported by marble columns carrying pulvin-shaped capitals hollowed out at the lower corners and ornamented with scrolls, roses, vine stems, &c. Others have monstrous abaci of rectangular shape decorated with cables arranged in herring-bone fashion, framing a waved band (Fig. 314, p. 344). The bases have extraordinary decoration of arches made of cables, with human heads and figures, and winged creatures (Fig. 315, p. 344). Other ornamented capitals and bases from the church are to be seen in the Museum of Asturian Antiquities at Oviedo. The arches are carved with vine stems, roses, and whorls.

The outer face of the walls, where original, is of rubble, with squared blocks at the angles. They are strengthened by buttresses also of squared stone, carefully cut, and slightly fluted (Fig. 316, p. 347).

[1] MICHEL, op. cit., vol. i 2, p. 560; ENLART, *L'architecture Romane.*

The windows have arched heads and stone transennae. A round opening filled by a pierced rosette should be noticed.

San Miguel de Lino is evidently the work of the same architect and the same carvers as those of Santa Maria de Naranco; but in Santa Maria the architectural and artistic decoration is the most important feature, whereas in San Miguel the construction takes the first place. Both exhibit the same heaviness in the interior, the same lavish use of slightly fluted buttresses, the same elementary character of the figure sculpture.

Its form seems to be inspired by Theodulf's church at Germigny des Prés. Accordingly I believe it to be the earliest dated example of this type in Asturias and the neighbouring districts.

While we are unable to mention any church founded by Ordoño I (850-866), an event of importance for us which took place in his reign may be noticed, and that is the cruel persecution of the Christians of Cordova, begun by the Emir Abd al-Rahman II (822-852), and continued by Mohammed II (852-886). To escape from this the 'half-Arabic' monks of Cordova—that is to say the Mozárabes or Christians who had become vassals of Islam [1]—sought refuge in Asturias and the neighbouring districts; and in this way the horse-shoe arch was introduced there. One of the earliest instances would be found in the monastery of St. Julián at Samos, rebuilt by these monks in 862, if it had not been reconstructed in 922.[2]

Any shortcomings of Ordoño in this respect were fully made up by his son, Alfonso III the Great (866-909), whose reign saw the erection, either by himself or by others, of numerous buildings, especially in the interest of the Benedictine Order, of which he was the shield and stay.[3] Among them may be mentioned the cathedral of Santiago de Compostela, the royal monastery of San Benito at Sahagún, San Adrián at Tuñón, and San Salvador at Val de Dios.

The famous sanctuary of Compostella was a reconstruction (899), in hewn and cemented stone with marble columns, of the modest church raised by Alfonso II: 'ex lapidibus ex luto opere, parvam.'[4] Destroyed by Al-

[1] SIMONET, op. cit., Introduction.

[2] YEPES, op. cit., vol. iii, fol. 217.

[3] SANDOVAL, SAMPIRUS episcopus Astoricensis, *Historia*, p. 57. YEPES, op. cit., vol. iv, fol. 163. RISCO, op. cit., vol. xxxvii, pp. 217-219.

[4] SANDOVAL, SAMPIRUS episcopus Astoricensis, *Historia*, p. 57. FERREIRO, op. cit., vol. ii, pp. 27-60, 183-201.

FIG. 316.—Lino. San Miguel (IX cent.).

FIG. 319.—Val de Dios. San Salvador (IX cent.).

FIG. 317.—Santiago de Compostela. Cathedral.

FIG. 318.—Santiago de Compostela. Cathedral.

FIG. 320.—Lena. Santa Cristina (X cent.).

FIG. 321.—Lena. Santa Cristina (X cent.).

Mansur and then restored, it was rebuilt between 1074 and 1705 by the architect Bernard in the Lombardic style (Figs. 317, 318, pp. 348, 349).

The church of the celebrated monastery of Sahagún, dedicated to SS. Facundus and Primitivus, which had been built in 874 by the abbot Alfonso and his monks from Cordova in place of an older parochial chapel, was destroyed by the Moors in 883. Rebuilt by Alfonso III in 905, it was again destroyed in 988 by Al-Mansur, but was re-edified by order of Alfonso V (999-1027).[1]

San Adrián at Tuñón, a couple of leagues from Trubia, endowed by Alfonso III in 891,[2] was rebuilt and reconsecrated in 1108. There remains

THE CHURCH OF SAN SALVADOR AT VAL DE DIOS, a league from Villaviciosa, which was consecrated in 892.[3] It is a small basilica with a two-storied western narthex containing three divisions, a nave and aisles separated by piers crowned by heavy mouldings, and three rectangular chancels at the east end, the central one having two floors. Barrel vaulting is used throughout, and all the arches are round. Except at the west end, the buttresses outside do not correspond to the piers within. To the south side is attached a porch, the walls of which are not bonded into that of the church, the masonry being different and superior. When it was added, the buttresses were transformed into half wall-piers. The discovery of the consecration stone of 892 does not prove, as has been thought, that the porch is contemporary with the church. Risco[4] had already noticed elements in the structure of later date than the foundation. In fact, apart from the porch, other alterations are apparent, for instance in the western gable (Fig. 319, p. 347).

Some writers put the church of Santa Cristina at Lena also in the IX century (Figs. 320, 321, p. 350). It is true that its masonry recalls that of San Salvador at Val de Dios, while the twisted columns and pulvin-shaped figured capitals remind one of those in Santa Maria at Naranco. But, on the other hand, the stilted round arches, and the horse-shoe arches in the transennae point to a later date which may well be that of the abbot Flaginus mentioned in the inscription on the three carved stones in the presbytery of the church,

[1] YEPES, op. cit., vol. iii, fol. 167-177. RISCO, op. cit., vol. xxxiv, pp. 130, 131, 308, 330-333. *Boletín de la R. Academia de la Historia*, vol. xxxi, pp. 466-515; FITA, *San Miguel de Escalada Inscripciones y documentos*. ESCALONA, *Historia del R. Monasterio de Sahagún*, pp. 11-53.

[2] RISCO, op. cit., vol. xxxvii, pp. 217-219.

[3] Ibid.

[4] Ibid.

that is to say the years immediately following 905. These views have been already put forward by other writers.

Thus we have reached the end of the glorious reign of Alfonso III without finding in Asturias any except the semicircular form of arch. The only exceptions are the three horse-shoe arches in Santa Maria at Oviedo, which, perhaps, were later than the original structure. The earliest dated church in this district with horse-shoe arches is San Salvador at Priesca in the territory of Villaviciosa, consecrated in 920 as we learn from the inscription preserved in the church. Here the nave arches springing from square piers with rude impost cornices are of slightly horse-shoe form.

In the dominions of the Kings of Asturias, the oldest authentic instance is to be found in

THE CHURCH OF SAN MIGUEL AT ESCALADA in the province of León, as rebuilt by the abbot Alfonso—the refugee with other monks from Cordova in the time of Alfonso III—between 913 and 914. Risco [1] gives the text of the consecration stone, which he had seen. The building must surely have suffered when Al-Mansur in 988 destroyed León and devastated everything that he came across. It must also have been restored under Alfonso V, who brought back the inhabitants of León. It is clear that it was in good condition when a portico was added on the south in 1050 by the abbot Sabarico (1047-1059).[2]

The church has a nave and aisles, an armless transept, and at the east end three apses of horse-shoe plan internally, taken out of the end wall (Figs. 322, 323, p. 353). The nave is separated from the aisles by marble columns taken from ancient buildings, with late Roman and Visigothic capitals, and also some made expressly for their places (Fig. 324, p. 354), such as the Corinthianesque examples in the arcade which divides the transept from the body of the church. The band of carving above this arcade is obviously later work.

All the arches are of horse-shoe form. The side bays of the transept and the apses have cross vaults. The other parts of the church have timber roofs. The capitals of the portico, though having a certain affinity with the

[1] Op. cit., vol. xxxv, pp. 310-312.

[2] *España, sus monumentos y artes*, &c.; QUADRADO, *Asturias y León*, p. 550. *Boletín de la R. Academia de la Historia*, vol. xxxi, pp. 466-515; FITA, *San Miguel de Escalada. Inscripciones y documentos.*

FIG. 322.—Escalada. San Miguel (X and XI cents.).

FIG. 323.—Escalada. San Miguel (X and XI cents.).

FIG. 324.—Escalada. San Miguel. Capital (X cent.).

FIG. 325.—Escalada. San Miguel. Part of the portico (XI cent.).

Corinthianesque specimens made for the church, are really more advanced in style, and betray another hand and date (Fig. 325, p. 354).

The building with a tower connected with the western porch shows a different style of masonry from that of the church and its porch.

* * *

By way of completing the task which we undertook in the second part of this book, we will give a short account of the most famous Moslem religious building in Spain.

THE GREAT MOSQUE OF CORDOVA.—On the surrender of Cordova, the Christians were allowed to keep only the cathedral dedicated to St. Vincent, which was still in their possession in 747. Soon after, however, they were obliged to give up half of it to the Moslems; and at length, in 784, Abd al-Rahman I (756-788), finding this half insufficient for their worship (a wooden gallery had already been erected, with a roof so low as to inconvenience the faithful), wished to acquire the other half. Its owners at first refused his offers, but afterwards consented on the payment of a large sum of money, and on condition of being allowed to build a new church for their exclusive use.

It was then that Abd al-Rahman took in hand the demolition (785) of the church, and laid the foundations (786) of the congregational mosque of Cordova, personally supervising the work in order that it might be hurried on as quickly as possible. But he did not live to see its completion, and it was finished by his son, Hisham I (788-796), who also built the minaret, not, however, before 793, for in that year, on his return from Septimania, he set aside the fifth part of the rich booty taken in war for the express purpose of completing the mosque.

Having become too small for the Moslem population of Cordova, Abd al-Rahman II (822-852) enlarged and embellished it. His successor, Mohammed I (852-886), completed the decorations. Mundzir (886-888) repaired the cracks which had appeared in the walls, and improved the fabric. Abd al-Rahman III (912-961), the first Caliph of Cordova, rebuilt the minaret and the front of the mosque, and made the floor even. Hakam II (961-976) again enlarged the existing buildings. In this he was followed by Al-Mansur (977-1002), the terrible prime minister of the weak Hisham II (976-1009, 1010-1013). In this state it remained till the recovery of the city (1236) by Ferdinand III (1217-1252), after which it was dedicated to the Virgin of the Assumption, and became the cathedral (1238). This new character given to the building, which had been the largest and most splendid in the Moslem world, was the beginning of the alterations from which it has suffered, reaching their culmination in the XVI century.[1]

When erecting his mosque at Cordova, Abd al-Rahman I, the wise grandson of the Ummayyad caliph, Hisham (724-743), had before his mind a far-famed work of a caliph of his own family—the mosque of Damascus. And he was guided in what he did by the changes and the plans which Walid had been the first to adopt at Damascus.

On taking possession of the basilica of San Vicente (said to be of the VI century, and, apparently, a Roman temple converted into a church), he built a new outer wall strengthened with massive turret buttresses, within which he erected longitudinally, north and south, ten rows of columns forming eleven aisles opening on to the court in front, the central one which led to the mihrab being wider than the others. The columns were designed to carry horse-shoe arches, and also a second tier of semicircular arches with the object of raising the roof as high as possible. This upper story had a flat ceiling.

The columns, of Roman origin and different kinds of marble, and varying in height and diameter, were taken from ancient buildings. It is impossible to say how many, if any, belonged to the previous church. The capitals, surmounted by abaci of every sort, were also of ancient origin. They were of Corinthian, Corinthianesque, and Composite pattern, in some cases not fitting their columns; and their design and execution show that they range between the I and the VII century (Frontispiece). One of Composite type is surmounted by a broken pulvin of the Visigothic period closely related to two others in the main entrance to the mosque—the Gate of Palms—which

[1] DOZY, op. cit., vol. ii, pp. 36, 48, 49. *España, sus monumentos y artes*, &c.; MADRAZO, *Cordova*, pp. 49-107, 119, 195-216, 224-235, 258-428. ADZĀRI (Fagnan), *Histoire de l'Afrique et de l'Espagne intitulée Al-Bayano' l-Mogrib*, vol. ii, pp. 92, 109, 137, 156, 160, 253, 254, 377-387, 392, 393, 398, 413, 477-479. DE GAYANGOS, *The History of the Mohammedan Dynasties in Spain*, vol. i, pp. 217-231. EDRISI, *Géographie*, vol. ii, p. 58. LAFUENTE, op. cit., vol. ii, p. 190.

FIG. 326.—Cordova. Mosque (VIII-XI cents.).

Fig. 327.

Fig. 328.

Fig. 329.

Fig. 330.

Figs. 327, 328, 329, 330.—Madrid. National Archaeological Museum. Capitals ascribed to the period of the Caliphate of Cordova (756-1031).

FIG. 331.—Cordova. Mosque. Vestibule of the Mihrab of Hakam II. (961-976).

Fig. 332.—Cordova. Mosque. Cupola of the Mihrab of Hakam II. (961-976).

FIG. 333.—Cordova. Mosque. Vestibule of the Mihrab of Hakam II. Cupola (961-976).

FIG. 334.—Cordova. Mosque. Chapel of Villaviciosa (961-976).

bear erased crosses. A few examples of simple Composite, neither Roman nor Visigothic, are the result of restoration or rearrangement.

These capitals have nothing in common with the Composite and Corinthian ones made expressly for the enlargement of the building by Abd al-Rahman II, Hakam II, and Al-Mansur. One has only to look at the numerous simple Composite capitals in the colonnades erected by Abd al-Rahman II, and especially in those of Hakam II and Al-Mansur, in order to assure oneself of the fact. They are of clumsy form, with meagre, plain turn-over leaves, the tall bell being finished off with an echinus or with leaves (Fig. 326, p. 357). Or else give a glance at the Corinthianesque and Composite specimens with carved leaves in the mihrab of Hakam II and the cupola of the vestibule in front of it, and also at those in the cupola of the two vestibules flanking the one in front of the mihrab. As examples of Composite capitals of the Moslem period I illustrate here some of those collected in the National Archaeological Museum at Madrid (Figs. 327, 328, 329, 330, p. 358).

Whether, in preparing for his mosque, Abd al-Rahman I preserved much or little of the old walls, it is impossible to tell, as the east side and the back wall were demolished by Abd al-Rahman II and Al-Mansur respectively; while the front was rebuilt by the Caliph Abd al-Rahman III, as is recorded by the well-known inscription on the door into the principal nave (the Puerta de las Palmas), and by historians.[1] Certain, however, it is that the surviving western side shows that the wall and the buttresses were built at the same time, which was, undoubtedly, not in the Visigothic period, as has been suggested,[2] for it is incredible that the façade of a church should be strengthened in such a manner at that period.

It has been maintained, on the word of Arabic writers, that the founder did not make much change in the appearance of the Christian building, and that the mosque was erected within the year 786;[3] an idea not in accordance either with the possibilities of construction, or historical facts. On the death of Abd al-Rahman I in 788, the operations which he had contemplated were unfinished;[4] and in the two years or more of work, pushed on as we know it was, they cannot have gone further than the erection of the mosque proper.

[1] Adzari, op. cit., vol. ii, p. 381.

[2] *Cultura Española*, 1906, pp. 785-811; Gómez-Moreno, *Excursión*, &c.

[3] Adzari, op. cit., vol. ii, pp. 378, 379. *Cultura Española*, 1906, pp. 785-811; Gómez-Moreno, *Excursión*, &c.

[4] Adzari, op. cit., vol. ii, p. 109.

And we cannot even imagine that this happened, if we consider that the five years required for Hisham's completion of the building are too much for merely constructing the cloistered court and the minaret on the north side of the mosque. The period of eight years (from 786 to 793) is the same as that which the mosque of Damascus, the source of inspiration for that at Cordova, demanded from Walid for the full expansion of its beauty (706-714).

The enlargement of Abd al-Rahman II was on the south, as far as the qibla.[1] On this occasion the end wall and mihrab of the original mosque disappeared. Marble columns of alien origin were used, and also others made on purpose. Some of the capitals also were ancient—Composite, Corinthian, and Corinthianesque, ranging from the I to the VII century—while others were carved expressly. The latter belong to the simple Composite type mentioned above. Here too the upper arches are round and the lower ones of horse-shoe form.

Abd al-Rahman III, besides reconstructing the front of the mosque, rebuilt (945-46) Hisham's minaret, which was only 40 cubits high, and had been overthrown in the earthquake of 880. The new one was a square tower, some say 72 and some over 100 cubits in height, ascended by a double staircase. It was embellished with mosaics, and encircled by a double tier of arches. At the top was a kiosk crowned by three balls of gold and silver between two flowers, the whole surmounted by a golden pomegranate.[2]

Hakam II's addition was also on the south, and was the last made in that direction, as the slope towards the Guadalquivir prevented any further extension. The arcades have both round and horse-shoe arches, and most of the capitals are of the simple Composite type, and made for their places. The marble shafts are partly ancient, partly made expressly for the building. There was no lack of ancient marble columns, for Abd al-Rahman III in 1013 made use of such which had been brought from Africa, for the works at al-Zahra.[3]

One of the features of Hakam's work is the striking group of structures connected with the mihrab (Fig. 331, p. 359). The mihrab is a chapel of octagonal form internally, covered by a monolith marble cupola of shell design (Fig. 332,

[1] Adzari, op. cit., vol. ii, p. 137.

[2] De Gayangos, op. cit., vol. i, pp. 217-231. Edrisi, *Géographie*, vol. ii, pp. 62, 63. Adzari, op. cit., vol. ii, pp. 381.

[3] Adzari, op. cit., vol. ii, pp. 381, 382.

p. 360), and flanked by two small chapels. It is approached through a central space or vestibule which has intersecting multifoil arches—trefoil and multifoil arches have their source in India (see below, p. 366)—and horse-shoe arches. The intersection was necessitated by the considerable height at which the arches are set, being boldly raised on a series of small columns. This vestibule is covered by a cupola crossed by outstanding ribs springing from shafts, and forming intersecting arches. This design was suggested by the simple arches which decorate the interior of Ibrahim II's (874-902) cupola at Kairawan. In Hakam's cupola recesses, derivatives of the Romano-Campanian pendentive, are taken out of the angles, and serve to transform the square base into an octagon. Each has a frontal overhanging cusped arch (Fig. 333, p. 361). This principal vestibule is flanked by two smaller ones, corresponding to the chapels on either side of the mihrab, which have cupolas of the same pattern as the central one, but simpler. The result is a sanctuary consisting of nave and aisles ending in chapels. In the eastern aisle formerly stood the minbar, which Edrisi says had no equal in the world.[1]

For the execution of the mosaics in this sanctuary the Emperor of Constantinople, by request, sent a mosaic worker, and a present of 320 quintals of tesserae.[2] This proves that if Spain produced builders and artists worthy of the praises lavished on them by Ibn Khaldun,[3] for mosaics she still depended on foreigners; and those foreigners were not Copts.

From this vestibule was derived the suggestion for the so-called Chapel of Villaviciosa, restored in 1892, with its multifoil arches, whether simple or intersecting (Fig. 334, p. 362), and its cupola crossed by visible ribs arranged so as to form a geometrical pattern, the intervening spaces being filled with shells, stars, and other forms of ornament (Fig. 335, p. 367). The analogies between this chapel and Hakam II's tripartite structure suggest that it belongs to the reign of that caliph; while its position leads one to think that it occupies the site of Abd al-Rahman II's mihrab, which was destroyed by Hakam.[4] Its purpose, however, is unknown. Lampérez y Romea suggested to me that its object may have been to give light to the mosque.

The latest enlargement of the mosque, that by Al-Mansur, was on the eastern side, there being no room on the west, where the caliph's palace

[1] *Géographie*, vol. ii, p. 61.

[2] Adzari, op. cit., vol. ii, p. 392.

[3] *Prolégomènes historiques*, vol. ii, pp. 361, 362.

[4] Adzari, op. cit., vol. ii, p. 393.

stood.[1] It took the form of seven new rows of arches, the mosque now containing nineteen aisles, and forming a rectangle of over 115 by 130 m. (378 by 428 ft.) square.[2]

In this part of the huge edifice the columns are again, in many cases, of ancient origin. The capitals, however, of the simple Composite type, were all made for the building. The horse-shoe arch is used without exception in the colonnades.

None of the ancient mosques built as such, which I have studied, compared with that of Cordova produce anything like the same impression of unlimited space, due to the unusual number of its rows of columns, and of majestic dignity.

The side walls of the mosque are extremely interesting, owing to the openings and arches which they contain (Figs. 336, 337, 338, 339, pp. 368, 369). On the east side the pointed horse-shoe arch may be noticed: the earliest example which I have found in the Iberian peninsula.

The remodelled cloisters of the court in front of the mosque are not in their original state, as is shown by the Composite capitals with plain turn-over leaves, made expressly to fit the Roman columns brought from elsewhere. These capitals are evidently of the IX or X century (Fig. 340, p. 370).

Three important and singular features, at once constructive and decorative, are to be noticed in the mosque of Cordova, viz. the multifoil arch, intersecting arches used in construction, and the visible intersecting ribs of the cupola.

The multifoil arch has its origin in the trefoil arch first used in Gandhâra as an ornamental form for the walls and domes of 'viharas,' i.e. monasteries or houses of idols, and 'stupas' or shrines to preserve relics or the memory of sacred events. This was before 600; and later it was used in construction in Kashmir, but not before the VII century. An early and remarkable instance is afforded by the temple of Martand (724-760).[3]

It has been imagined that the trefoil arch made its appearance, earlier than the instances in Gandhâra and at Mathurâ, in Magadha in Northern India.[4]

[1] ADZARI, op. cit., vol. ii, pp. 477-479.

[2] *Museo Español de Antigüedades*, vol. ix, pp. 287-316; AMADOR DE LOS RIOS Y VILLALTA, *La mezquita-aljama de Córdoba.*

[3] *Atti del Congresso internazionale di Scienze storiche* (Rome, 1-9 April 1903), vol. vii; PULLÉ, *Riflessi indiani nell' arte romaica*, pp. 112-114. FOUCHER, *L'Art gréco-bouddhique du Gandhâra*, pp. 125-132, 139-145. VINCENT A. SMITH, op. cit., pp. 45-48.

[4] HAVELL, *Indian Architecture*, pp. 79-84.

FIG. 335.—Cordova. Mosque. Chapel of Villaviciosa. Cupola (961-976).

FIG. 336.—Cordova. Mosque (VIII-XI cents.).

FIG. 337.—Cordova. Mosque (VIII-XI cents.).

FIG. 338.—Cordova. Mosque (VIII-XI cents.).

FIG. 339.—Cordova. Mosque. A doorway.

FIG. 340.—Cordova. Mosque. Arcade and court.

It has also been asserted that the multifoil arch was known in India from early Buddhist times, as seen, for example, in the larger niches of a pavilion adjoining the temple of Vitthalaswâmi in Southern India.[1]

As early as the IX century it is found used constructively in Mesopotamia, for the mosque of Samarra (847-861) contains examples in the inside of the windows of the south wall. In the same century it occurs as a decorative feature in the dome erected by Ibrahim II (874-902) in the great mosque of Kairawan. But it is in the mosque of Cordova, and the part due to Hakam, that it appears for the first time used systematically in construction. And it is there, too, that it is first used systematically in intersection as described above.

For the subject of intersecting arches I may refer to what I said in my account of the Cristo de la Luz at Toledo.

With regard to the cupola with visible intersecting ribs, I have never found one earlier than the time of Hakam II. I have explained elsewhere[2] the Roman origin of visible ribs, which were afterwards applied, with the same object though in a more developed form, to cross vaults and cupolas.

* * *

The task which I undertook to perform is completed. After so many years of study, research, and the toil and sometimes risks of travel, I lay down the pen with which I have told the story of the origin and development of the chief elements which formed the basis of the great styles of religious architecture in the Later Empire and the Early Middle Ages, both in the West and in the Near East. I leave it to others to continue the study, so that more light may be thrown on a noble theme.

[1] Havell, *Indian Architecture*, pp. 182, 183.

[2] Rivoira, op. cit. (Hoepli), pp. 94, 95, 307; (Heinemann), vol. i, pp. 82, 83, 248.

INDEX OF PLACES

The first numbers generally give the most important references to a subject

GENERAL INDEX

The greater part of the photographs used for the illustrations in this volume were taken expressly for the work. Those relating to Armenia were taken by Padre Gabriele Nahapetian (Mechitarist of Venice), with a view to the study of Armenian architecture, and he has allowed me to make use of them. These do not include the few (not previously published) relating to Aghthamar, which are due to the archaeologist, Ervand Lalaiantz. For a small number of others I am indebted to Prof. R. Altamira y Crevea, Dr. S. Aurigemma, Comm. G. Boni, Miss Bulwer, Prof. C. Enlart, Prof. M. Gómez-Moreno, Mr. H. Johnson, Mr. P. Hart, Sig. L. Mauri, Sacerdote G. Mesini, Dr. G. Mugnaini, Dr. L. Muñiz-Miranda, Dr. R. Paribeni, Prof. V. Spinazzola, and the late Mr. F. F. Tuckett. The illustrations relating to India are derived from photographs belonging to the India Office, by permission of H.M. Secretary of State for India, or from others lent by Prof. Pullé. Lastly, Señor J. Lacoste of Madrid has allowed me to make use of soms of his Spanish photographs. To all the above-named I offer my best thanks.

Published by

Facsimile Publisher
Ashok Vihar, Delhi-110052 (India)
Website: www.facsimilepublisher.com

Distributed by

Gyan Books Pvt. Ltd.
5, Ansari Road, Daryaganj, New Delhi-110002 (India)
E-mail: books@gyanbooks.com, Website: www.gyanbooks.com

2 222000 014001

INTERIOR OF THE MOSQUE AT CORDOVA